We'Moon 2022
Gaia Rhythms for Womyn

Cataclysm Portends © Jakki Moore 2014

The Magical Dark

41st Edition of We'Moon
published by
Mother Tongue Ink

WE'MOON 2022: GAIA RHYTHMS FOR WOMYN
SPIRAL, STURDY PAPERBACK BINDING, UNBOUND & SPANISH EDITIONS
© MOTHER TONGUE INK 2021

Mother Tongue Ink
Estacada, OR 97023
All Correspondence:
P.O. Box 187, Wolf Creek, OR 97497
www.wemoon.ws

We'Moon Founder: Musawa, *Special Editor:* Bethroot Gwynn
We'Moonagers: Sue Burns, Barb Dickinson *Graphic Design:* Sequoia Watterson
We'Moon Creatrix/Editorial Team: Bethroot Gwynn, Sequoia Watterson, Sue
Burns, Leah Markman, Barb Dickinson *Production Coordinator:* Barb Dickinson
Production Assistant & Retail Sales: Leah Markman *Proofing:* EagleHawk,
Sandra Pastorius, Kathryn Henderson, Becky Bee, Amber Torrey
Promotion: Leah Markman, Sue Burns, Susie Schmidt, Barb Dickinson
Accounts Manager: Sue Burns *Order Fulfillment:* Susie Schmidt, Dana Page

<u>Astrological Data</u> graciously provided by Rique Pottenger.

This eco-audit applies to all We'Moon 2022 *products:*

Hansol Paper Environmental Benefits Statement:

We'Moon 2022 is printed on Hansol paper using 60%
recycled content: 50% pre-consumer waste, 50% post-
consumer waste, with Solvent-free Soy and Vegetable Based
inks with VOC levels below 1%.
By using recycled fibers instead of virgin fibers, we saved:
115 fully grown trees
45,947 gallons of water
32 million BTUs of energy
2,709 pounds of solid waste
8,107 pounds of greenhouse gasses

As a moon calendar, this book
is reusable: every 19 years the moon
completes a metonic cycle, returning
to the same phase, sign and degree of
the zodiac.

We'Moon is
printed in South Korea
by Sung In Printing
America on recycled
paper using low VOC
soy-based inks.

Order directly from Mother Tongue Ink
For more information see p. 235.
Retail: 877-693-6666 or 541-956-6052 Wholesale: 503-288-3588

We'Moon 2022 Datebooks: • $21.95
Spiral ISBN: 978-1-942775-31-7
Sturdy Paperback ISBN: 978-1-942775-32-4
Unbound ISBN: 978-1-942775-33-1
Spanish Edition ISBN: 978-1-942775-34-8
In the Spirit of We'Moon • $26.95
Paperback ISBN: 978-1-890931-75-9
Preacher Woman for the Goddess • $16
Paperback ISBN: 978-1-942775-12-6

The Last Wild Witch • $9.95
Paperback ISBN: 978-1-890931-94-0
Other *We'Moon 2022* **Products:**
We'Moon on the Wall • $16.95
ISBN: 978-1-942775-35-5
Greeting Cards (6-Pack) • $11.95
ISBN: 978-1-942775-36-2
Organic Cotton Totes • $13 & $15
Cover Poster (11" x 17") • $10

2022

JANUARY
S	M	T	W	T	F	S
						1
2	3	4	5	6	7	8
9	10	11	12	13	14	15
16	17	18	19	20	21	22
23	24	25	26	27	28	29
30	31					

FEBRUARY
S	M	T	W	T	F	S
		1	2	3	4	5
6	7	8	9	10	11	12
13	14	15	16	17	18	19
20	21	22	23	24	25	26
27	28					

MARCH
S	M	T	W	T	F	S
		1	2	3	4	5
6	7	8	9	10	11	12
13	14	15	16	17	18	19
20	21	22	23	24	25	26
27	28	29	30	31		

APRIL
S	M	T	W	T	F	S
					1	2
3	4	5	6	7	8	9
10	11	12	13	14	15	16
17	18	19	20	21	22	23
24	25	26	27	28	29	30

MAY
S	M	T	W	T	F	S
1	2	3	4	5	6	7
8	9	10	11	12	13	14
15	16	17	18	19	20	21
22	23	24	25	26	27	28
29	30	31				

JUNE
S	M	T	W	T	F	S
			1	2	3	4
5	6	7	8	9	10	11
12	13	14	15	16	17	18
19	20	21	22	23	24	25
26	27	28	29	30		

JULY
S	M	T	W	T	F	S
					1	2
3	4	5	6	7	8	9
10	11	12	13	14	15	16
17	18	19	20	21	22	23
24	25	26	27	28	29	30
31						

AUGUST
S	M	T	W	T	F	S
	1	2	3	4	5	6
7	8	9	10	11	12	13
14	15	16	17	18	19	20
21	22	23	24	25	26	27
28	29	30	31			

SEPTEMBER
S	M	T	W	T	F	S
				1	2	3
4	5	6	7	8	9	10
11	12	13	14	15	16	17
18	19	20	21	22	23	21
25	26	27	28	29	30	

OCTOBER
S	M	T	W	T	F	S
						1
2	3	4	5	6	7	8
9	10	11	12	13	14	15
16	17	18	19	20	21	22
23	24	25	26	27	28	29
30	31					

NOVEMBER
S	M	T	W	T	F	S
		1	2	3	4	5
6	7	8	9	10	11	12
13	14	15	16	17	18	19
20	21	22	23	24	25	26
27	28	29	30			

DECEMBER
S	M	T	W	T	F	S
				1	2	3
4	5	6	7	8	9	10
11	12	13	14	15	16	17
18	19	20	21	22	23	24
25	26	27	28	29	30	31

© Wilma L. Hoffman 2019

● = NEW MOON, PST/PDT

○ = FULL MOON, PST/PDT

Cover Notes

Venus Rising © Marnie Recker 2020

Mother moon pulls the tides and Venus pulls the heartstrings. The sacred power of the feminine, of birth, unconditional love and the protective spirit is called to witness the Great Turning. From the depths of the dark mystery, we remember who we are. Embodying wisdom and compassion, these wings promise to take us further than we've ever gone before.

Freedom and Responsibility © Sophia Rosenberg 2020

Freedom and Responsibility was created during a thirteen week meditation in the spring of 2020 when the Covid lockdown began. Using only black and white, I made a series of prints focussing on polarities; exploring the tension, volatility, and creative energy between the poles. The work forms part of an upcoming lunar oracle crafted in collaboration with Jennifer Brant.

Dedication

Every year we donate a portion of our proceeds to an organization doing good work that resonates with our theme. This year, we are partnering with The New Orleans Women & Children's Shelter (NOWCS) to help amplify the light that they bring into the lives of the families they serve.

NOWCS was born out of a very dark time: the chaos and loss following Hurricane Katrina. They formed around the acute needs for food, shelter and security, specifically to help vulnerable women and children.

In the wake of the Covid-19 pandemic, the people hit hardest by health issues and economic distress are those who were in vulnerable

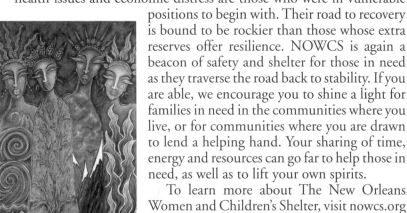

positions to begin with. Their road to recovery is bound to be rockier than those whose extra reserves offer resilience. NOWCS is again a beacon of safety and shelter for those in need as they traverse the road back to stability. If you are able, we encourage you to shine a light for families in need in the communities where you live, or for communities where you are drawn to lend a helping hand. Your sharing of time, energy and resources can go far to help those in need, as well as to lift your own spirits.

To learn more about The New Orleans Women and Children's Shelter, visit nowcs.org

Barbara Dickinson © Mother Tongue Ink 2021

Earth, Air, Fire, Water ◻ *Suzanne Grace Michell 2019*

TABLE OF CONTENTS

INTRODUCTION

MOON CALENDAR: THE MAGICAL DARK

APPENDIX

WE'MOON 2022 FEATURE WRITERS:

We'Moon Wisdom: Musawa; **Astrologers**: Maeanna Welti; Heather Roan Robbins; Sandra Pastorius; Gretchen Lawlor; Susan Levitt; Mellisa Kae Mason, Mooncat!; Beate Metz; **Introduction to the Theme**: Bethroot Gwynn, **Holy Days**: Debra Hall; **Lunar Phase Card**: Susan Baylies; **Herbs**: Karen L. Culpepper; **Tarot**: Leah Markman.

What Is *We'Moon*? A Handbook in Natural Cycles

We'Moon: Gaia Rhythms for Womyn is more than an appointment book: it's a way of life! We'Moon is a lunar calendar, a handbook in natural rhythms, and a collaboration of international womyn's cultures. Art and writing by wemoon from many lands give a glimpse of the great diversity and uniqueness of a world we create in our own images. We'Moon is about womyn's spirituality (spirit-reality). We share how we live our truths, what inspires us, and our connection with the whole Earth and all our relations.

Wemoon means "we of the moon." The Moon, whose cycles run in our blood, is the original womyn's calendar. We use the word "wemoon" to define ourselves by our primary relation to the cosmic flow, instead of defining ourselves in relation to men (as in woman or female). We'Moon is sacred space in which to explore and celebrate the diversity of she-ness on Earth. We come from many different ways of life. As wemoon, we share a common mother root. We'Moon is created by, for and about womyn: in our image.

We'Moon celebrates the practice of honoring the Earth/Moon/Sun as our inner circle of kin in the Universe. The Moon's phases reflect her dance with Sun and Earth, her closest relatives in the sky. Together these three heavenly bodies weave the web of light and dark into our lives. Astrology measures the cycle by relating the Sun, Moon and all other planets in our universe through the backdrop of star signs (the zodiac), helping us to tell time in the larger cycles of the universe. The holy days draw us into the larger solar cycle as the moon phases wash over our daily lives.

We'Moon is dedicated to amplifying the images and voices of wemoon from many perspectives and cultures. We invite all women to share their work with respect for both cultural integrity and creative inspiration. We are fully aware that we live in a racist patriarchal society. Its influences have permeated every aspect of society, including the very liberation movements committed to ending oppression. Feminism is no exception—historically and presently dominated by white women's priorities and experiences. We seek to counter these influences in our work. We'Moon does not support or condone cultural appropriation (taking what belongs to others) or cultural fascism (controlling artistic expression). We do not knowingly publish oppressive content of any kind. Most of us in our staff group are lesbian or queer—we live outside the norm. At the same time, we are mostly womyn who benefit from white privilege. We seek to make We'Moon a safe and welcoming place for all wimmin, especially for women of color (WOC) and others marginalized by the mainstream. We are eager to publish more words and images depicting people of color created by WOC. We encourage more WOC to submit their creative work to We'Moon for greater inclusion and visibility (see p. 236).

Musawa © Mother Tongue Ink 2019

HOW TO USE THIS BOOK
Useful Information about We'Moon

Refer to the **Table of Contents** to find more detailed resources, including: World Time Zones, Planetary and Asteroid Ephemeris, Signs and Symbols, Year at a Glance, and Month at a Glance Calendars.

Time Zones are in Pacific Standard/Daylight Time with the adjustment for GMT and EDT given at the bottom of each datebook page.

The **names and day of the week and months** are in English with four additional language translations: Bengali, Spanish, Irish and Croation.

Moon Theme Pages mark the beginning of each moon cycle with a two-page spread near the new moon. Each page includes the dates of that Moon's new and full moon and solar ingress.

Susan Baylies' **Lunar Phase Card** features the moon phases for the entire year on pp. 228–229

There is a two-page **Holy Day** spread for all equinoxes, solstices and cross quarter days, from a Northern Hemisphere perspective. These include writings by a different feature writer each year.

Astro Overview gives a synopsis of astral occurrences throughout the year from one of our featured astrologers, Heather Roan Robins, on pp. 8–10.

Read the **Astrological Prediction** for your particular sign on the pages shown on the right —>

Astrological Overview: 2022

2022 is a year of gestation and release, echoing the dark before a New Moon. It is not a year for flash and boom but for real reorganization and real liberation. 2022 begins with Pluto in Capricorn, Uranus in Taurus, and Saturn halfway through its own traditional sign of Aquarius, and this earthy, saturnine line-up prioritizes stabilizing systemic shifts rather than quick change. It's time to investigate assumptions, rebuild foundations of houses, review and renew our social contracts.

Pluto now spends its last full year in Capricorn before it enters Aquarius for the next few decades and births a fresh chapter. America experiences its first Pluto return, Pluto comes back to where it was in the country's birth chart in February, June, and December and asks the same formative questions about power and purpose now as when the country was born.

Planets often get more intense and summarize their work just before they leave a sign, a chapter review. As Pluto finishes in Capricorn it asks all of us to look at the power dynamics in our home and society and contemplate our source of power in our personal relationships, our ecological orientation, and in our political action. We need to explore how we can move from the decades of Pluto in Capricorn, which leaned into the old ways and elders on a good day and challenged us with power hierarchies and abuse of power on a bad day—into the upcoming decades of Pluto in Aquarius and its gift and challenge of collective power.

The next question that burns throughout this year is about the nature of

La Luna Doula ¤ *S. I. Zimmerman 2016*

truth—political, personal, spiritual truth—as Neptune continues its delicious and problematic tour of its own sign of Pisces from 5/2011–1/2026, magnified this spring by a Jupiter/Neptune conjunction in April, echoing in orb all year long.

Neptune in Pisces has encouraged us to renew our connection to magic, to spirits and our spiritual connection to the organic world. It helps us honor the sacredness of water. It encourages our intuition, helps us soften old limitations, see beyond concrete reality, experience psychic connection to one another and to the trees, and experience emotions outside of the box. But once we let go of the box, this Neptune can leave the psyche untethered and open our culture up to craziness, sending many down the rabbit holes of conspiracy theories or lost in their own hopes and fears.

As we open our intuition and dissolve old constructs, it becomes essential that we learn to sift between what we want, what we are afraid of, and our honest and accurate intuition, because they operate on the same plane. We can do powerful magic, but strong emotions and anxiety can distort our intuition. As Jupiter conjuncts Neptune this year, it can bring to a head any ongoing negative-Neptune problems like alcoholism, collective fears, passivity, and flooding ecosystems. We have to choose to stay grounded in the process in order to use this Neptune wisely; feed our soul and our imagination, vision the future, but also rigorously check our facts and add action to our dreams.

As the year begins, Uranus turns direct after several months retrograde, on January 18, which can both stir chaos but help us remember our priorities. Both Venus and Mars enter Aquarius March 5 and conjunct for several weeks, cranking up the emotions and encouraging a loving development of our community, our Sangha or circle. We feel the restlessness of the spring revolution around the spring Equinox as Mercury conjuncts expansive Jupiter while Mars squares Uranus March 22, and can direct this towards a better future rather than just against an old paradigm. Act rather than react; reinvent the paradigm.

Jupiter activates this whole year and asks what liberates us, not just the personal us, but what liberates humankind. Jupiter is several times larger than all the other planets put together. On a good day Jupiter brings us freedom and helps us create spaciousness. It can also be the planet of disempowering enabling unless we ask what would really help—and listen carefully to the answer.

Throughout 2022 Jupiter bunny hops from Pisces—where it can liberate the soul through compassion, creativity, and empathy—into Aries on May 10—where it liberates through action and radical reinvention—back into Pisces Oct 27, then to Aries again on Dec 20.

A partial solar eclipse/new Moon in Taurus April 30 helps us make this a fertile time to plant our dreams. On the Total lunar eclipse May 15, the Sun and Moon square Saturn and can prune back that which is overgrown and asks us to check the foundations of our work, the structures of our organizations.

Retrograde season asks us to review our work, go back and strengthen what we've done, fix what needs fixing, deepen rather than push forward. Mercury retrogrades January 14–February 3, May 10–June 4, September 9–October 2. The main retrograde season kicks in June 4 as Saturn retrogrades, joined by Neptune on June 28, Chiron July 19, Jupiter July 28, Uranus August 24. Forward motion picks up as Pluto turns direct October 8, Saturn October 22, Jupiter November 23, and finally Neptune turns direct December 3.

Those eclipses echo again in the fall with a Scorpio solar eclipse October 25 and lunar eclipse, conjunct change-inducing Uranus on November 8, also square Saturn, which asks us to check the structures of our organizations and make the changes necessary so authority is used in the best way possible, both personally and politically. We need to search for hope, for progressive action and the dream of liberation as Jupiter ends the year in Aries Dec 20, and approaches Chiron.

Heather Roan Robbins © Mother Tongue Ink 2021

6 Moons *© KT InfiniteArt 2018*

ASTROLOGICAL YEAR AT A GLANCE
INTRODUCTION

Rebirth Earth
© Helena Arturaleza 2017

This year is a year of deepening into the realities of the changes that we have been calling in. Change is a cycle of many processes. In stages we name, release, tear down, review, envision, sow, grow, build. No one part of the process is quite like any other, and all are needed. Since 2008, when Pluto entered Capricorn, we have been digging out the foundation of many toxic structures and systems that have seemed unchangeably set and stable. Pluto leaves Capricorn for the first time in 2023, making 2022 a year of delving into the final stages of our work with this transit. This is the year we check the corners, dig out the deepest roots, take stock of all we've learned about ourselves, and let our sense of meaning, reality and purpose be forever changed, not just temporarily challenged. This is how we heal and build in this magical dark.

With Saturn in Aquarius and Uranus still in Taurus, this year calls forward the work and influence of the fixed signs. Both Saturn and Uranus will be squared many times throughout the year by faster moving planets, and will twice square each other. Fixed signs make things real. In between the instigation of the cardinal signs and the flexibility of the mutable signs, the fixed signs look at how things last, how they play out in real lived experience. This is the part of the change cycle in which we apply everything we have fought for and dreamed about into daily life at every scale—in which we affirm this new paradigm as an enduring reality. This time is about stamina, nurturance and follow-through. We will be both challenged and supported as we look at what it takes to build a new foundation, grow new roots. Our attention, collectively and individually, will be called and recalled to thoroughness, innovation and livability. 2022 will ask us how we can dream and build big, radical visions into reality and live beautifully, comfortably, simply and well, in alignment with the generosity of the Earth.

Maeanna Welti © Mother Tongue Ink 2021

To learn more about astrological influences for your sign,
find your Sun and Rising signs in the pages noted to the right.

11

Moon & Sun □ *Liz Darling 2016*

FOCUS FOR **2022**

As Jupiter and Neptune conjunct in Pisces, exact in April, echoing throughout 2022, they challenge us to use our sensitivity, vision, and imagination to open a visionary portal, while at the same time staying grounded enough to not get lost, to stay present and use this vision wisely.

Aries: You're a natural leader but this year, lead by introspective example. A portal can open within your psyche, in the dream world, and behind the scenes. Some new level of self-honesty can take you on a journey which improves your mind-body connection. Next year be ready to step into leadership.

Taurus: Be a healing influence on the people around you, on your community groups, collectives and circles, help them have a vision for how to work better together. Using your steadiness and pragmatic loving within your community this year can bring new freedom to your spiritual life in 2023.

Gemini: Sort your intuition carefully; practice healthy psychic hygiene. True intuition can take you closer to your life purpose and help you channel healthy personal authority. Magic, logic, and fact checking need to weave together to inspire your work and unfold your path. From this growth you can create fresh collaborations in 2023.

Cancer: 2022 beckons you out of your comfort zone to explore the larger world to travel, learn, or investigate your sense of global citizenship. Manifest your spiritual beliefs within worldly action. Be willing to learn by unusual means and help all of us envision a better life; this can create interesting work developments in 2023.

Leo: You may draw in real magical moments this year; listen for guidance from spirits, the earth beneath and crystals within. Just remember that because a spirit is non-corporeal, doesn't necessarily mean it is wise; always think for yourself. With an open mind, open heart, and clean boundaries you prepare for new exploration in 2023.

Virgo: Intuitively sort through new opportunities for collaboration, alliance, and partnerships. Negotiate for your needs fairly and enthusiastically rather than have to take it all in or block it all. Practice sensitive and dynamic engagement with forthright boundaries; grow intimacy and collaboration this year and take it even deeper in 2023.

Libra: Balance; what brings you health, what improves your working situation, what helps your mind and body work together. Explore a special connection with animals. Become sensitively aware of your health. Treat yourself like you would be like to be treated in relationship, and open to healthier companionship in 2023.

Scorpio: This could be a wildly inspired creative year—open to your muse, dance with the spirits, tap into the deeper resources within. Be careful to stay present in relationships; see what is actually occurring and not just what you long for or fear. This new creative burst can lead to positive outcomes for health and work next year.

Sagittarius: Changes flow in your home life. This is a place to call in the ancestors, guides and guardians to help chosen and biological family flow into a good shape. Come to know each other with deeper acceptance and accountability; drop old baggage and create room within. This new spaciousness forms room for creative work in 2023.

Capricorn: Your words have extra power in 2022; be a force for thoughtful truth. Help people examine assumptions, question their fears, and search for clear answers and a new vision. Put your own imagination to a good, creative use and keep it out of trouble. The truth you find this year will help rebuild foundations next year.

Aquarius: You've had interesting lessons around the material world recently, 2022 challenges you to revision your approach to matter. Let go of limiting beliefs and magical thinking; vision a way you, and your community, can move forward with both security and visionary practicality. Next year you'll be called to collaborate.

Pisces: Engage opportunities to help others deal with their sensitivity without getting lost in their anxieties. People may project onto you their hopes and fears, so be grounded in who you are, authentic in what you project. Your focus is to be sensitive, yet centered, and ready to take the vision into action next year.

Heather Roan Robbins © Mother Tongue Ink 2021

ECLIPSES: 2022

Solar and Lunar Eclipses occur when the Earth, Sun and Moon align at the Moon's nodal axis, usually four times a year, during New and Full Moons, respectively. The South (past) and North (future) Nodes symbolize our evolutionary path. Eclipses catalyze destiny's calling. Use eclipse degrees in your birth chart to identify potential release points.

April 30: Partial Solar Eclipse at 10° Taurus serves us up the will we need to leave behind our blunders and blocked energies. When the light re-emerges, we may bring forward our deeper awareness and understand the healing lessons at work.

May 15: Total Lunar Eclipse at 25° Scorpio may obscure the obvious and keep us at bay until the emerging light brings us face to face with our insecurities, ready for release. Cut the ties that bind, and make meaningful recovery.

October 25: Partial Solar Eclipse at 2° Scorpio allows close questioning so that we can deepen our understandings of underlying motivations and ego investments. Beckon the light's return, and let surfacing secrets free up inner space.

November 8: Total Lunar Eclipse at 15° Taurus holds us under the sway of the mysterious dark. We are understandably absorbed by our inner reaches that both entice and repel us. When the veil lifts, imagine the breakthroughs that let love prevail.

MERCURY RETROGRADE: 2022

Mercury, planetary muse and mentor of our mental and communicative lives, appears to reverse its course three or four times a year. We may experience less stress during these periods by taking the time to pause and go back over familiar territory and give second thoughts to dropped projects or miscommunications. Breakdowns can help us attend to the safety of mechanics and mobility. It's time to "recall the now" of the past and deal with underlying issues. Leave matters that lock in future commitments until Mercury goes direct.

Mercury has three retrograde periods this year in air signs:

January 14–February 3: While Mercury is retrograde in Aquarius then goes direct in Capricorn, we are challenged to take our ideas, and bring them into the realm of the concrete. As we release the puzzles of the past, our intentions gain ground and grow.

May 10–June 3: As Mercury appears to reverse course in Gemini, use this inwardly mobile period to find agreement among your inner selves. Apply penetrating attention to harvest the insights ripe for expression. When Mercury goes direct in Taurus, play as you go.

September 9–October 2: During this Libra period raise the unexpressed issues that are important to you, and then make the attitudinal shifts for reconciliations when Mercury directs in Virgo. Use your intuitive edge to meet needs.

Sandra Pastorius © Mother Tongue Ink 2021

SKY MAP 2022

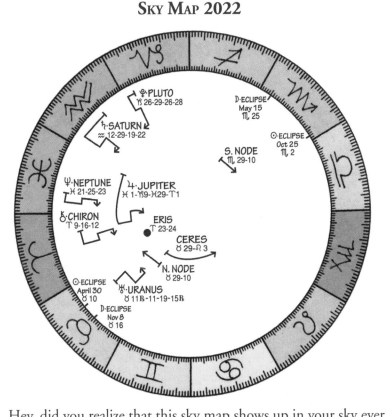

Hey, did you realize that this sky map shows up in your sky every day and night of your year? Even if you can't see them—and most of the planets in this particular sky map are not visible—you can experience these powerful forces, catalysts, teachers and guides.

Any student of astrology (and we're all forever learning) must take time to look up from the charts and books on a regular basis. Get outside; be with your sky.

To begin—locate the "Belt of the Zodiac" (the path all the planets tread in your sky overhead) by finding where the Sun or Moon rises in the east and sets in the west at your location. This varies slightly from place to place and from season to season. There are apps and maps to help you locate local planetary risings and settings. The Sun and Moon always move along this narrow predictable path or belt.

Go out around sunrise or sunset to let the Moon or Sun amplify your experience. And to do so on an equinox or solstice . . . aah, more potent, your calibration to this sky-university!

Blessings on your stellar journey, Gretchen.

Gretchen Lawlor © Mother Tongue Ink 2021

15

DIVINING THE DARK

"There is work to be done in the dark before dawn"*

The Sun and Moon are in a cycle of relationship, a dance of periodic change. This celestial phenomenon offers us a dynamic mandala for exploring and growing in our own phases of life. We may view and use the Lunation or Moon Phase Cycle as our personal Teaching Wheel and Divining Guide.

As the Moon's visible light waxes, matures and then wanes every 29.5 days, we can become consciously entranced and entrained to its magical rhythms. A Lunar Divining practice helps us attune with our sacred self, cultivate our inner witness, and call in the wisdom of the Moon's ebb and flow of unfolding light and dark.

Begin Divining in the Balsamic, darkening phase, which is three days before the emerging New Moon. When we experience the culminating Dark phase of any cycle, we relinquish aspects of the known and reside for awhile in the remains of the past cycle. In this liminal space, pressed between the pages of what was and what will come, we begin reckoning with impermanence, allowing reconciliation in our hearts and doing the work of self-redemption. Like imaginal cells waiting to become butterfly wings one day, we are held in suspension, dwelling in possibility.

In the New Moon Phase when the arc of light begins to increase we may engage with the initiatory energy of the next Moon cycle. During the transition into the waxing light, reflect on the insights from the previous cycle. Illuminated by the wisdom of the dark, we may glimpse ways to re-orient ourselves. It is time to ready ourselves to re-imagine and re-enchant life again.

Divining with your holy voice.

Welcome each of the Moon phases with a meditation to attune with your intuitive nature. Let the prompts offered here follow the inclinations of your spirit. Practice the art of divining to bring a sense of harmonious connection to your self and your world. Go ahead . . . conjure angels, pack your wings and divine the light of your heart's potential!

* Shine On *song by May Erlewine*

Moon-Seed Creations
Chants/ songs/ poems/ prayers
Create your own chants, songs, poems and prayers by combining the words and phrases offered here as prompts, in addition to your own. Use repetition and varied tones, sing out, improvise, hum, cast your spell! (Consult calendar for dates).

Waxing Phases:
Dark/New Moon—Introspection, intuition, initiation, wishes, surrender, shadows, release, open, conjure, project, promise, feel free. *Kore*

Crescent Moon—First light, rise up, smile on me, stepping out, impulse, mobilize, give, hasten, hope, reach, begin it. *Artemis*

First Quarter Moon—Activate, urgency, building, risk, commit, free up, plunge, independent, expressive, promise. *Diana*

Gibbous Moon—Clarity, carefully, perseverance, ask how, perfection, design, progressive, devotion, swell, reach, renew, change. *Vesta*

Waning Phases:
Full Moon—Give thanks, share prayer, awaken, reflections, inspire, shine, bountiful, feel, play, gift, dream, magic, passion, love. *Aphrodite*

Disseminating Moon—Spread, messenger, believe, creativity, express, seek praise, understand, wander, spin, courage. *Quan Yin*

Last Quarter Moon—Crucial turning, time crossing, forgive, release, ask why, insight, re-orient, make ready, sweep, reveal. *Hecate*

Balsamic/Dark Moon—Listen, trust, muse, fate, sensitively, memories, absorb, shape shifter, wisdom, ebb, descent, revelation. *Persephone*

Full Moon Example:

I awaken and give thanks,
I awaken and give thanks
Oh Aphrodite,
in love share my prayer.
Behold my dream, I rise and shine.

Sandra Pastorius © Mother Tongue Ink 2021

A Ritual for the Magical Dark

I am calling in the mighty baobab tree whose roots appear exposed, reaching towards our futures and galaxies beyond. Our worlds have been turned upside down. Our black mirrors reveal our truths: the ways in which we perform our lives and reflect back the illusions, distortion and fracturing within ourselves. How did we move so far away from our wholeness?

Gather around for a healing recalibration that centers remembrance. Bring your healing salves and follow the scent of rosemary under the dark moon. Let us converge in the sacred meadow of periwinkle, a plancestor of endurance and resilience, marking the graves of descendants of captured Africans.

Join the circle of compassionate truth. Let us breathe together, sync our hearts and share our liberatory intentions. May we be in right relationship with The Oneness, our bloodlines, ourselves and each other. Let us lay down our trauma identities, collective sensitivities and not continue to wield our wounds as weapons. In this circle of safety, let us name and reveal our uniquely perfect scars, share the gifts of our words and the wisdom of our experiences. Apply healing salve to the places on our bodies that call for tenderness and healing.

Allow your body to sink deep into the Earth. Call in the nourishment and protection of a triphala and schisandra concoction. Allow the triphala to dislodge the things that no longer serve your highest good. Let thoughtforms, memories and traumas release. Let Mother Earth, the container and witness, compost these learnings. Allow schisandra to meet you where you are and fill the tender spaces with exactly what you need in this moment.

When you are ready, uproot yourself and give thanks to the Earth. Move gently and take time to integrate and rest. Nourish yourself with the collective gumbo of endurance, discovery, deep connection, alignment and courage. Celebrate with a tea of nettles, tulsi and lemon balm to nourish, fortify and lift the spirit. Let us bring our full awareness to our interconnectedness and to the sacredness of all our relations. May our time together center being, evolving, loving, healing and thriving.

The Earth Tree
© *Robin Lea Quinlivan 2006*

Karen L. Culpepper © Mother Tongue Ink 2021

The Year of the Tiger: 2022

The Year of the Tiger begins on the new Moon of January 31st. Chinese New Year begins on the second new Moon after Winter Solstice. Tiger brings a year of power, passion, and daring. Now is the time to pounce, take a risk, and start new endeavors. Bravery,

We Even Share Tears © Helen Seay Art 2020

leadership, and bold actions are rewarded on a grand scale. In global politics, forceful Tiger tends not to compromise, and can result in heated conflicts with neither side wanting to back down.

There are five Taoist elements—Fire, Earth, Metal, Water, and Wood. 2022 is a Water Tiger or Black Tiger year, the most sensitive Tiger, making this the year to act on gut instinct and trust your intuition. Under the influence of shamanic Water Tiger, follow the lunar signs in your We'Moon, and contact spirit guides and ancestors as you seek freedom and blaze new paths. Next year, Water Rabbit 2023 will be the time for gentle diplomacy, but not now.

Wemoon born in Tiger years (1902, 1914, 1926, 1938, 1950, 1962, 1974, 1986, 1998, 2010, 2022) are exciting, independent, and charismatic. They rarely allow anyone to tell them what to do, or how to do it, because they possess a regal quality. Tiger is a power animal in the Chinese zodiac, so Tiger wemoon manage power and are strong decisive leaders. Regardless of the obstacles in her path, mighty Tigress will pursue goals, leaping over any blocks she encounters. Determined Tiger wemoon can achieve heights that seem improbable, impossible even. Beneath her magnificent coat of fur, though, the Tigress is a pussy cat, especially in relationships. She is highly sentimental, surprisingly delicate emotionally, and can be easily hurt by others although she may not show it.

Tiger is a powerful ally and animal totem for protection in the spirit realm because Tiger protects the Dead, can assist in banishments, and scares off ghosts, thieves, and fires. Tiger correlates to the free-thinking, non-conformist western Air sign Aquarius, and is most compatible with the Horse, Dog, Pig, and another Tiger. Energy for dynamic change is strongest in spring, and calmest in winter, when it's best to slow down and rest. The element Water rules the kidneys and bladder in Chinese medicine, so take some time to attend to these parts of your body in the cooler months.

Susan Levitt © Mother Tongue Ink 2021

Timing is Everything

Did you know you've got a built-in strategic planner in your astrological chart? One that shows you the best time to tend to specific issues in your life, from work to relationships, creativity, health, finances, home and family.

To create this strategic planner, you need to know your rising sign. From this it's easy to find your dates for your own month-by-month map to the year ahead. You'll be happier, thriving with less effort when you time your efforts to your own astrology. There truly is a best month in your year for: significant travel (your **Explore Horizons** month); a best month to **Play, Create and Shine**; a month optimal for a new work technique or to quit a bad habit (in **Organize, Improve, Heal**).

You interested? Here's how to set up your strategic planner using your astrology chart, the Manifestation Map below, and your We'Moon datebook for the current year:

A. Looking at your astrological birth chart, find your **Rising Sign**, on the left-hand horizontal line of your chart. (You can get an image of your birth chart free and fast from astrology charting sites like astrodienst.com.)

B. Using your We'Moon datebook, find the date the Sun enters your **Rising Sign**, and write that date in the circle at the end of the left-hand horizontal line of the Manifestation Map. For example, if you have Libra rising, in 2022 the sun enters Libra on September 22. For Cancer rising, you will be writing June 21 in that left horizon circle, for Pisces rising, Feb 18, and so on.

C. Moving in a counterclockwise direction around the wheel, repeat this process using your We'Moon to find the date the Sun enters the next sign. Write the date in each circle.

D. The key words found in these sections of your Manifestation wheel will alert you to the most important themes, issues and opportunities to show up in that month, where you can be most effective, satisfied and successful.

For Example:

• You have an optimal month to **Choose Priorities and Goals** most likely to succeed. There's a best month to **Tie Up** old business that will **Make Space** for your new priorities to manifest in the year ahead. Then you'll feel ready during your month to **Be Courageous, Instigate and Assert**.

• The month at the bottom of your wheel will alert you to conditions in your **Family, Home and Foundations** needing attention now to steady your base of operations for the rest of the year.

• The **Complete Goals** month is the best time to bring a project to a head, put on a show or publish your book.

• You'll have fresh insights into your significant relationships during the **Form, Review and Renew Relationships** month. Many meet important people in this month; think back to see if it's been true at this time in past years.

There's some real peace to be found in this tool as you realize that some efforts are favorable now, and others can be scheduled for a more timely, potent moment. Each year's map will only differ by a day or two; this is a lifetime strategic planner! This powerful annual timing tool can bring ease to your efforts by keeping you in the cosmic flow. As sung by so many musicians, including The Byrds, Judy Collins and Nina Simone, inspired by Ecclesiastes, it is true: "To everything there is a season, a time for every purpose under heaven."

Gretchen Lawlor © Mother Tongue Ink 2021
if you need help or more information, including an expanded guide to activities, contact me:
light@whidbey.com

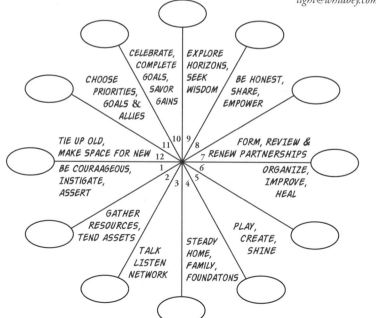

After the Storm
© *Sandy Bot-Miller 2015*

INTRODUCTION TO THE HOLY DAYS

Organizing our lives around the seasons and cycles and honouring the Holy Days is not a luxury extra, it is a radical necessity. The Earth urgently needs all of humanity to slow down and come back into intimate affiliation and rhythm with her. The global climate crisis cannot be solved by external fixes, three day working weeks, artificial intelligence or new technologies. Solutions need to be led by the Earth on her own terms.

The holy days are our soul's watering holes where we ritually recalibrate ourselves, express our full palette of colours, our innate wholeness, delight and reverence through self-styled ceremonies and celebrations. They infuse our energy with joy and sublime gratitude, make our chosen actions more potent. They are how we open the weave, bring in all the tender ways of the sacred, give unbroken ancestral connection back to ourselves.

Half of the Earth's quest for regenerative healing takes place in dormancy and darkness. She needs our fallow time with the land and trees as much as she needs our activism. Dark holy days are where we restore our depth, "see" the most far-reaching solutions especially during our bodies' times of heightened consciousness which include menstrual bleeding, giving birth, menopause, elder age and dying.

On the holy days themselves we leave our homes as if on paws, on the wing for a feast of noticing what herbs want our attention, what Goddess, what advice the ancestors want to give us through which bird, animal, stone, tree. Inside each holy day and at the hub of the mandala they form, is the temple of the ineffable feminine. Here in the fecund unknown we scan the WorldSoul for something to help the burning world—a personification of source consciousness that only heals because it is rooted real in our most ancient provenance when hearth, art and religion were one, homes temples and temples homes—shining in the very fabric of the magical dark—Black Terra Mother.

Debra Hall © Mother Tongue Ink 2021

THE WHEEL OF THE YEAR: HOLY DAYS

The seasonal cycle of the year is created by the Earth's annual orbit around the Sun. Solstices are the extreme points as Earth's axis tilts toward or away from the sun—when days and nights are longest or shortest. On equinoxes, days and nights are equal in all parts of the world. Four cross-quarter days roughly mark the midpoints in between solstices and equinoxes. We commemorate these natural turning points in the Earth's cycle. Seasonal celebrations of most cultures cluster around these same natural turning points:

February 2, Imbolc/Mid-Winter: celebration, prophecy, purification, initiation—Candlemas (Christian), New Year (Tibetan, Chinese, Iroquois), Tu Bi-Shevat (Jewish). Goddess Festivals: Brighid, (Celtic), Yemanja (Brazilian).

March 20, Equinox/Spring: rebirth, fertility, eggs—Passover (Jewish), Easter (Christian). Goddess Festivals: Eostare, Ostara, Oestre (German), Astarte (Semite), Persephone (Greek), Flora (Roman), Norooz/New Years Day (Ancient Middle East).

May 1, Beltane/Mid-Spring: planting, fertility, sexuality—May Day (Euro-American), Walpurgisnacht/Valborg (German and Scandinavian), Root Festival (Yakima), Ching Ming (Chinese), Whitsuntide (Dutch). Goddess Festivals: Aphrodite (Greek), Venus (Roman), Lada (Slavic).

June 21, Solstice/Summer: sun, fire festivals—Niman Kachina (Hopi), Tirgan (Ancient Middle East). Goddess Festivals: Isis (Egyptian), Litha (N. African), Yellow Corn Mother (Taino), Ishtar (Babylonian), Hestia (Greek), Sunna (Norse).

August 2, Lammas/Mid-Summer: first harvest, breaking bread, abundance—Green Corn Ceremony (Creek), Sundance (Lakota). Goddess Festivals: Corn Mother (Hopi), Amaterasu (Japanese), Hatshepsut's Day (Egyptian), Ziva (Ukraine), Habondia (Celtic).

September 22, Equinox/Fall: gather and store, ripeness—Mabon (Euro-American), Mehregan (Ancient Middle East), Sukkoth (Jewish). Goddess Festivals: Tari Pennu (Bengali), Old Woman Who Never Dies (Mandan), Chicomecoatl (Aztec), Black Bean Mother (Taino), Epona (Roman), Demeter (Greek).

October 31, Samhain/Mid-Fall: underworld journey, ancestor spirits—Hallowmas/Halloween (Euro-American), All Souls Day (Christian). Goddess Festivals: Baba Yaga (Russia), Inanna (Sumer), Hecate (Greek).

December 21, Solstice/Winter: returning of the light—Kwanzaa (African-American), Soyal (Hopi), Jul (Scandinavian), Cassave/Dreaming (Taino), Chanukah (Jewish), Christmas (Christian), Festival of Hummingbirds (Quecha), Shabeh Yalda/Birth Night (Ancient Middle East). Goddess Festivals: Freya (Norse), Lucia (Italy, Sweden), Sarasvati (India).

* Note: Traditional pagan Celtic / Northern European, Jewish and Muslim holy days start earlier than the customary Native / North American ones—they are seen to begin in the embryonic dark phase: e.g., at sunset, the night before the holy day—and the seasons are seen to start on the Cross Quarter days before the Solstices and Equinoxes. In North America, these cardinal points on the wheel of the year are seen to initiate the beginning of each season.

© *Mother Tongue Ink 2003 Sources:* The Grandmother of Time *by Z. Budapest, 1989;* Celestially Auspicious Occasions *by Donna Henes, 1996 & Songs of Bleeding by Spider, 1992*

Tarot: Turning Reversals on Their Heads

The candle is lit. Atop an altar cloth, the Tarot deck waits, uncut and full of possibilities. Seeking guidance, you shuffle, cut the cards and pull. As you turn the cards one by one, panic turns to terror: nearly every card is upside-down! Did you take a wrong turn? Is this the tarot spread of nightmares?! For a moment, you want to right them and run from the ominous messages.

Breathe deep. These sometimes-unnerving signs can have deep and comforting meanings. Traditionally, card reversals are ignored and simply turned right side up or read as the exact opposite of the card's upright meanings; they are the shadows of Tarot. Every shadow has been cast by play of light, and shadows hide secrets, mystery and growth. Often when we face our fears and dare to look into the darkness, we find brilliant epiphanies. Reversals can act as keys to unlocking imbalances or blocks in your life. They may highlight underlying issues or bring into focus emotional process, or internal turmoil.

What do you see in this topsy-turvy card? Is the Hanged One now standing upright and calm? Is the bearer of two cups spilling her drinks? These cards offer plenty of freedom and fun for your imagination. Let go of traditional meanings and sink into the imagery.

A reversed card representing a person or archetype encourages you to see this person in a new light; don't assume you know their story. This is a clue to understand and love someone for their struggles and imperfections as well as their lively well-lit attributes. Reversals also give hints about the nature of a situation; an upright card can indicate your outward environment, while the reversed encourages you to look inward for clarity. It's important to note where the card sits within

the spread. Is a reversed card telling you to reimagine your past, or envision a new future from a different perspective?

Reversed tarot cards can be filled with doom and gloom, but darkness isn't always a scary place to be once our eyes adjust. New perspectives await you in this mystery. Once we stop seeking a way out and accept our surroundings, subtle beauty appears in the periphery, like an owl in flight.

Leah Markman © Mother Tongue Ink 2021

Gizmo's Two Queens ¤ *Penn King 2019*

Introduction to We'Moon 2022

2021 marked the completion of We'Moon's pattern of divining each year's theme from the Tarot's 21 Major Arcana cards. With *We'Moon 2022*, we begin a new thematic cycle, using the eight phases of the Moon as touchstones for the datebook theme. First things first: The Dark Moon. Our Creatrix circle gathered in deep winter 2020 to conjure meaning and nuance for this new and challenging We'Moon theme. Darkness. What can we make out in the Dark? In Nothingness. In the Void.

This conjuring took place pre-pandemic. Before the world's population began to be ravaged by a rampant disease. Before the demon of racial injustice was exposed again and again with violence on America's streets. Before the unimaginable: insurrection in the US capitol—the specter of which reverberates fearfully as we write. What future tragedies may explode from the Unknown?

We take a deep breath. We and the contributors to *We'Moon 2022* have steeped ourselves in the Dark for many months—actually and gratefully in *The Magical Dark*! What gifts and blessings may be hiding in the Unknown realms, the mysteries of Darkness? We offer you this book of devotions with gratitude for its magical surprises, including its sharp lessons. We bow before our Dark Teacher and invite you to join us in this sacred journey.

The rods in the outer reaches of our ocular universe are made to detect light. Go into the darkness and allow your eyes to adjust and relax into the vastness of the dark, and you will begin to recognize the glow and twinkle in the periphery around you. Giving over to the Dark Moon theme, our senses begin to pick up a rich and varied world. "Hands reach out to mold the overwhelming night into spark/Ears strain to glimpse tones that might fire/Noses inhale deeply to detect scents of hidden light/Tongues probe the void to discern the taste of a preternatural dawn" (p. 126, Shelley Blooms). Come, explore the treasures that *The Magical Dark* has revealed.

As it turns out, nearly everything is created in Darkness! Seeds germinate underground; embryos mature in the womb's dark; we sleep and dream under cover of darkness; the shadowy aspects of our spirits come out to play in obscurity. "Half of the Earth's quest for regenerative healing takes place in dormancy and darkness" (p. 22, Debra Hall). Here in the darkened pause are the wisdom of seeds who teach us letting-go and right-timing; the dream medicines that heal as we sleep; the Muses who invent art ex nihilo; night creatures who cultivate marvels of the unseen; secrets of the creative In-Between.

We open this edition with honor to the Dark Goddesses—those mysterious and often feared archetypes known for bringing us hard-won lessons, guiding us (sometimes kicking and screaming) back to ourselves through the shadows and through the dark garden gates of death, "grinding time as pestle steers/deep mortar beyond darkest dusk" (p. 41, Kathryn Howd Machan).

As this book of days unfolds, we commit ourselves to earth-rescue: pray away and fight against the oblivion that threatens so many of our creature-friend species and the precious environments they depend on. Ancestor spirits emerge from the curtains of the past, inspiring sacred rituals, insisting on justice for their children's children. The Dark powers both taunt and befriend us, inviting us into the shadows of reckoning with who we are, offering "the great unfurling you must go through/to find your lost and forgotten self" (p. 35, Adriana Attento).

And in this magical but dangerous year, what do the starry skies recommend? Maeanna Welti, our Year at a Glance astrologer writes: "This is the year we check the corners, dig out the deepest roots, take stock of all we've learned about ourselves, and let our sense of meaning, reality and purpose be forever changed, not just temporarily challenged" (p. 11). Forever changed! In this year 2022? In the Darkness of food-challenge, greed-challenge, violence-challenge, climate-challenge, truth-challenge? Yes, in this very Darkness. Magic-full. Vibrant with unseen surprise.

"A million dances in each land/will keep the planet spinning./ Embrace the madness swirling around us/moving through it still" (p. 90, Earthdancer).

With gratitude to the sparkling contributions from all of our 2022 artists and writers. Blessed be.

Barbara Dickinson and Bethroot Gwynn © Mother Tongue Ink 2021

Dark Moon Priestess II ¤ Diana Denslow 1992

O Mother Dark   O Nyx   Goddess of Night Sky
Held tight by your vast emptiness
We invoke your Magic, Daughter of Chaos!
What can you show us in the Heart of Nothing-to-see?
For you, it's the Home of Every Possibility.
Yes, please give us some new possibles:
Hope, Curiosity. Compassion, and Peace, even.
Dare we conjure You for Help?
You have a bad rap, after all,
You and your Sisters Hecate, Kali, Inanna, Morrigan
You and your children Death, Strife, Blame
You ate the Moon again. That seems to be an addiction.
You feast on Change.
Very well: Touch us   Change us   Devour us
To the Bottom The Black Hole Where light goes extinct.

What did you say? Hocus Pocus?!
Don't make light of this, dark humored one
Or Do, Sacred Witch!
Give us Dream. Give us Surprise.
Miracle. Wonder. Renewal. Another Chance.
Your Shadow secrets sing Mystery.
Your Shadow secrets birth Everything.

© Bethroot Gwynn 2020

Footprints in the Dark

She appeared just before New Year's Eve in the Bronx. It was getting dark out. We are trained not to go out after dark. We do it anyway.

The graffiti whispered like the ending to a bedtime story: "Earth is Alive, She is the Mother of the Humans." It was not the usual writing on the wall. It was not beautiful or colorful. It was written in huge, stark white letters. There She was, just outside the parking lot at Target with the Major Deegan to her left, and the #1 train to her right.

My journey to the Dark Goddess, through Durga Maa and Kali, had been underway for years. It began in dreams from lands far from home, and in darkness. I arrived at her feet, like so many before me, bent over in despair. She taught me cycles of descent and ascent. She taught me that my body was the original calendar, my blood the translator of the moon. The darkness became holy and offered sanctuary for seeds of every kind. I learned and listened and bloomed under cover of night.

She has, of late, been circling closer. She is even willing to meet me at Target to tell me the story that She was once known as the "Mother of the Humans" and that She is Alive. It is news I need, news we all need; I smile and take a picture. I want to call Univision, but they only come for the Virgin Mary.

She of a thousand names and faces has never been lost, only hidden and carried in whispers at dusk. In my neighborhood, as a child, some called her Mary, others Maria, others still Yemanya, Oshun, Oya. They lit candles to Santa Barbara, but really all of it was for Her: the unassailable refuge.

I found Her in a dream, then a book, then a journey. She invited me to recognize Her footprints in the dark in graffiti on a wall in the Bronx. I found Her because I gave myself permission to leave my house after dark.

excerpt © Melissa Coss Aquino 2016

I. THE DARK GODDESS

Moon I: January 2–January 31

New Moon in ♑ Capricorn Jan. 2; Full Moon in ♋ Cancer Jan. 17; Sun in ♒ Aquarius Jan.19

Head in the Clouds © *Corinne "Bee Bop" Trujillo 2019*

December 2021
Mí na Nollag

Hail, Hecate!
Creatrix, Destroyer
Mother of womb and tomb
stone and bone, green fire of life.
All hail!
excerpt ▫ *Christine Irving 2015*

ⅅⅅⅅ Dé Luain

♋︎

Monday
20

☽✶♅ 12:16 am
☿△♅ 12:18 pm
☽△♆ 7:00 pm

♂♂♂ Dé Máirt

♋︎
♌︎

Tuesday
21

☽☍♇ 5:10 am
☽☍♀ 6:44 am v/c
☉→♑ 7:59 am
☽→♌ 1:53 pm

Winter Solstice

☉→♑

Sun in ♑ Capricorn 7:59 am PST

☿☿☿ Dé Céadaoin

♌︎

Wednesday
22

☽△♂ 2:24 am
☽☍♄ 11:28 am
☽□♅ 11:50 am

♃♃♃ Dé Ardaoin

♌︎

Thursday
23

☽☍♃ 10:39 pm v/c
♄□♅ 11:17 pm

♀♀♀ Dé Haoine

♌︎
♍︎

Friday
24

☽→♍ 12:24 am
☉△☽ 6:05 am
☽□♂ 3:52 pm
☽△♅ 9:24 pm

ALL ASPECTS IN PACIFIC STANDARD TIME; ADD 3 HOURS FOR EST; ADD 8 HOURS FOR GMT

Hail! Dark Hecate

From Above we come
bearing white banners.
Angels, djinn, daemons
glide down moonbeams
dusted in starlight,
draped in sequined scarves.
Celestial voices raised,
we sing silver notes of praise.

Mexico: Between Sunlight & Shadow
© Betty LaDuke 1996

From Below we come
bearing black banners,
four-leggeds of myth and fable.
Spirts of ayahuasca, divas of the garden, nymphs, dryads,
Gaia's first-born sing ebony notes of praise.

From Earth we come bearing red banners,
Earth walkers, our path unfurls steadily before us.
Our short impassioned lives flare like candles
against your dark mystery,
willingly we seek you, singing crimson notes of praise.

Approaching your crossroad, even the bravest
hides her eyes in awe. Terror washes over us.
Joy tumbles in its wake, notes meld, song rises.

excerpt ¤ Christine Irving 2015

ᚻᚻᚻ Dé Sathairn

♍

Saturday
25

♂△♄ 2:37 am
♀☌♇ 4:02 am
☽△♅ 12:08 pm
☽♂♆ 3:07 pm

⊙⊙⊙ Dé Domhnaigh

♍
♎

Sunday
26

☽△♀ 12:12 am
☽△♇ 12:39 am v/c
☽→♎ 8:24 am
☿⚹☽ 1:29 pm
⊙□☽ 6:24 pm

Waning Half Moon in ♎ Libra 6:24 pm PST

MOON 0

31

Dec. '21–Jan. '22
diciembre / enero

Invocation (Return to Power)
Turn all lies to stone
and we will smash them at your feet,
as we rise under your shield,
goddesses of our own making.
excerpt © Megan Welti 2018

─────── ☽☽☽ lunes ───────

Monday
27

☽✶♂ 2:07 am
☽△♄ 4:55 am

─────── ♂♂♂ martes ───────

Tuesday
28

☽□♅ 12:56 am
☽□♀ 4:19 am
☽□♇ 6:06 am
☽△♃ 1:10 pm v/c
☽→♏ 1:16 pm
♂⊼♅ 5:04 pm
♃→♓ 8:09 pm

─────── ☿☿☿ miércoles ───────

Wednesday
29

☿♂♀ 2:27 am
☉✶☽ 2:42 am
☽☍♅ 7:51 am
☽□♄ 8:58 am
☉□♅ 3:53 pm
♂✶♄ 4:22 pm
☽△♆ 11:51 pm

─────── ♃♃♃ jueves ───────

Thursday
30

☿♂♇ 1:53 am
☽✶♀ 5:18 am
☽✶♇ 8:27 am
☽✶♅ 9:10 am v/c
☽→♐ 3:08 pm
☽□♃ 3:42 pm

─────── ♀♀♀ viernes ───────

Friday
31

☽✶♄ 10:15 am
☽♂♂ 12:01 pm

─────────────────────

ALL ASPECTS IN PACIFIC STANDARD TIME; ADD 3 HOURS FOR EST; ADD 8 HOURS FOR GMT

Ave Medusa, Goddess of the Harrowing Future
© *Jeanne K. Raines 2015*

 ♌♌♌ sábado

♐
♑

Saturday
1

January

☽□♇   12:16 am v/c
☉△♅   1:50 am
☽→♑   3:02 pm
☽PrG   3:08 pm
☽✶♃   4:13 pm
♄→♒   11:09 pm

───── ☉☉☉ domingo ─────

♑

Sunday
2

☽△♅   8:19 am
☉♂☽   10:33 am
☽✶♇   11:52 pm

New Moon in ♑ Capricorn 10:33 am PST

MOON I   33

January

sijeÄanj

♑
♒

Monday
3

☽☌♀ 1:59 am
☽☌♇ 8:20 am v/c
☽→♒ 2:44 pm
☽☌♅ 6:37 pm

**Black Madonna
with Dove of Peace**

© Sue Ellen Parkinson 2017

♒

Tuesday
4

☽□♅ 8:25 am
☽☌♄ 10:44 am
☽⚹♂ 4:45 pm v/c

♒
♓

Wednesday
5

♀⚹♆ 8:03 am
☽→♓ 4:16 pm
☽☌♃ 6:57 pm

♓

Thursday
6

☽⚹♅ 11:04 am
☉⚹☽ 9:41 pm
☽□♂ 10:55 pm

♓
♈

Friday
7

☽⚹♀ 2:41 am
☽☌♆ 4:40 am
☽⚹♇ 2:23 pm v/c
☽→♈ 9:26 pm

ALL ASPECTS IN PACIFIC STANDARD TIME; ADD 3 HOURS FOR EST; ADD 8 HOURS FOR GMT

Black Madonna

You know who she is.
And somewhere, deep inside,
you know she's rising up from within you.
She is the sacred, the holy, Black Madonna.

As Madonna, she is Mother,
a symbol for the great and pregnant Void,
the nothingness from which all form arises.
She represents all that is dark,
the mysterious, the unknown,
and the great unfurling you must go through
to find your lost and forgotten self.
She represents the darkness of winter,
the black night,
Death, and the Unknown.

As she rises up from within you, give her your attention.
She is there to teach and heal.
She will encourage you to create
and use the creative-sexual energy of the cosmos.
She will say, "*You can heal yourself.*"
She will bring with her the long-awaited opportunity
to see and accept the part you keep pushing away.
Above all, she will point the way for you
to finally see the world as a living, breathing Whole.

© Adriana Attento 2009

──────── ♄♄♄ subota ────────

♈ Saturday
♉

♀PrH	1:22 am
☽⚹♅	11:37 am
☉♂♀	4:47 pm
☽⚹♄	9:26 pm

──────── ☉☉☉ nedjelja ────────

♈ Sunday
9

☽□♀	8:01 am
☽△♂	9:58 am
☉□☽	10:11 am
☿⚹♇	6:06 pm
☽□♇	11:23 pm v/c

Waxing Half Moon in ♈ Aries 10:11 am PST

January
Poush

Kali Ma—
The Dark Mother

© Jo Jayson 2015

────────── ☽☽☽ sombar ──────────

♈

♉

Monday
10

☽→♉ 6:47 am
☽⚹♃ 11:48 am
☉⚹♆ 7:28 pm

────────── ♂♂♂ mongolbar ──────────

♉

Tuesday
11

☽□♅ 1:38 am
☽♂♅ 4:21 am
☽□♄ 8:53 am
♂□♆ 1:43 pm
☽△♀ 4:34 pm

────────── ☿☿☿ budhbar ──────────

♉
♊

Wednesday
12

☽⚹♆ 12:38 am
☉△☽ 3:19 am
☽△♇ 11:39 am v/c
☽→♊ 7:08 pm

────────── ♃♃♃ brihospotibar ──────────

♊

Thursday
13

☽□♃ 1:24 am
☽△♅ 4:10 pm
☽△♄ 10:26 pm

────────── ♀♀♀ sukrobar ──────────

♊

Friday
14

☽ApG 1:25 am
☿R   3:41 am
☽□♆   1:50 pm
☽☍♂   6:21 pm v/c

────────────────────────────────

ALL ASPECTS IN PACIFIC STANDARD TIME; ADD 3 HOURS FOR EST; ADD 8 HOURS FOR GMT

Kali Speaks

The Goddess Kali wakes me in the night
Get up, she says. Get up!
You hear girl? Get up!
The heat is on
There is no choice
Time to fall to rise   Time to eat rage
Ingest burdens   Turn liquid meal to fire
Listen to me girl
My heat's brittle   My earth's dry
Listen now   Rise
I am the storm on your shoulder
No more petty lies
Eat your rage   Make it salt   Make it brine
Eat your murdering hatred
Turn blood to light
See your frustration
Turn that coiling spike into amber wine   Into change
Feel fear? Don't care   Feel revenge? Out of time   Feel lost?
Child's play
Time's a death rattle
The world an upturned hourglass   Shatter it
Take flinging arrows in cupped hands
Swallow them   Digest them
Do what I say and you can save the world you love

◻ Dianne Adel 2020

––––––– ♄♄♄ sonibar –––––––

♊
♋   ◖   Saturday
15

☽→♋   8:10 am
☽△♃   3:31 pm

––––––– ☉☉☉ robibar –––––––

♋   ◗   Sunday
16

☽⚹♅   5:58 am
☉♂♇   6:51 am
☽☍♀ 12:50 pm

January
Mí Eanair

━━━ ꙷꙷꙷ Dé Luain ━━━━━━━━━━━━━━━━━━━━━━

♋
♌

Monday
17

☽△♆ 2:19 am
☽☍♇ 1:08 pm
☉☍☽ 3:48 pm v/c
☽→♌ 8:03 pm

━━━ ♂♂♂ Dé Máirt ━━━━━━━━━━━ Full Moon in ♋ Cancer 3:48 pm PST

♌

Tuesday
18

☿⚹♄ 2:03 am
♅D 7:26 am
☽☍☿ 12:39 pm
☽□♅ 5:11 pm
♇ApH 6:29 pm
☽☍♄ 11:18 pm

━━━ ☿☿☿ Dé Céadaoin ━━━━━━━━━━━━━━━━━━━━━━

♌

Wednesday
19

☉→♒ 6:39 pm

☉ → ♒

━━━ ♃♃♃ Dé Ardaoin ━━━━━━━━━ Sun in ♒ Aquarius 6:39 pm PST

♌
♍

Thursday
20

☽△♂ 12:15 am v/c
☽→♍ 6:02 am
☽☍♃ 2:58 pm

━━━ ♀♀♀ Dé Haoine ━━━━━━━━━━━━━━━━━━━━━━

♍

Friday
21

☽△♅ 2:28 am
☽△♀ 5:19 am
☽☍♆ 9:43 pm

2022 Year at a Glance for ♒ Aquarius (Jan. 19–Feb. 18)

This is a big year for you. Saturn is moving through Aquarius, helping you manifest all the unique gifts of who you are. The year starts and finishes with squares between Saturn and Uranus, energizing desire to evolve. No one does individuation like Aquarius. But this year will challenge you to zoom in, instead of out. Constantly contextualizing and referencing the bigger pattern, which you love to do, will likely not yield the best results. The more situated you get in your skin, the more room you will have to grow. The more you live in your body, the more you slow down. You will need to sort through what you perceive to be contradictions and tensions between being comfortable and being the visionary oddball that you are. Many of those supposed contradictions are part of a problematic inheritance. This is a time for you to discover that you can connect to your broad visions of humanity in very personal ways indeed, ways that will have you feeling deeply—emotionally and physically. The summer gives you a chance to both soften into compassion and enter the deep seas of your own beauty, and to expose some cherished illusions (inflated, deprecating, or both) you may have about your own worth. Call yourself back into your body. Experience and explore the emotions this work brings up. Ecosystem wisdom says that the work you do at the center of yourself will indeed serve the whole.

Maeanna Welti © Mother Tongue Ink 2021

Inseparable Union *© Ashley Foreman 2015*

♄♄♄ Dé Sathairn

♍
♎

Saturday
22

☽△♇ 7:53 am
☽□♂ 11:46 am v/c
☽→♎ 2:02 pm
☉△☽ 7:42 pm
☽△☿ 8:47 pm

☉☉☉ Dé Domhnaigh

♎

Sunday
23

☉☌☿ 2:28 am
☽□♀ 11:21 am
☽△♄ 4:26 pm

January
enero

――――))) lunes ――――

Monday
24

♂→♈ 4:53 am
☿PrH 11:50 am
)□♇ 2:10 pm v/c
)→♏ 7:57 pm
)⚹♂ 8:48 pm
)□☿ 9:51 pm

―――― ♂♂♂ martes ――――

Tuesday
25

☉□) 5:41 am
)△♃ 6:01 am
)☍♅ 2:52 pm
)⚹♀ 3:41 pm
☿→♈ 7:05 pm
)□♄ 9:42 pm

Waning Half Moon in ♏ Scorpio 5:41 am PST

―――― ☿☿☿ miércoles ――――

Wednesday
26

)△♆ 8:47 am
)⚹♇ 6:09 pm
)⚹♅ 9:28 pm v/c
)→♐ 11:34 pm

―――― ♃♃♃ jueves ――――

Thursday
27

)□♃ 10:02 am
☉⚹) 12:47 pm

―――― ♀♀♀ viernes ――――

Friday
28

)⚹♄ 12:39 am
)□♆ 10:59 am v/c
☉⚹♏ 6:57 pm
☿♂♇ 8:15 pm

―――――――――

ALL ASPECTS IN PACIFIC STANDARD TIME; ADD 3 HOURS FOR EST; ADD 8 HOURS FOR GMT

Baba Yaga Greets Me Walking

in her forest hut
on chicken legs,
the odor
of fresh garlic pouring
from her soup pot
through green air.
I'm lost;
she sees me wandering
and offers down
a whiskered grin
I can't refuse,
her stern-paned window
open to dark morning cold. I know
her eyes are danger's doors, her ancient
cowl drips filthy blue, she reads her spells
by candlelight held in a gargoyle's hands.
Yet all my bones call out her name:
I taste October on my tongue
and understand I'll ride with her
grinding time as pestle steers
deep mortar beyond darkest dusk.

© Katharyn Howd Machan 2014

Transition
© Janet Newton 2020

♐
♑

Saturday
29

♀D	12:46 am	☽△♅	6:47 pm
☽→♑	1:09 am	☽♂♀	7:08 pm
☽♂♂	7:10 am	☽PrG	11:04 pm
☽⚹♃	12:03 pm		

⊙⊙⊙ domingo

♑

Sunday
30

⊙□♅	11:32 am
☽⚹Ψ	11:47 am
☽♂♅	6:26 pm
☽♂♇	8:44 pm v/c

Mysterious Dark

How good is your night vision in times like these?
Can you train yourself to see in the dark?
Light can sometimes be blinding
Keeping all those shadows in hiding
What can you call in, when you are in the dark?

Owl sees straight through, the total truth
Bringing messages in the dark
In dreams and meditation
Keen insights emerge

Dreams teach us how to live
They warn us about dangers and give us foresight
Dreams heal us and allow us to process
They keep moving us, even when we are in the mud

Enter the dark void of emptiness

How do we carry the emptiness, as women
without needing to fill it?
Return to the dissolved self
Deep rest and surrender
Gestation in becoming
To be a clear vessel of life
Emptiness contains all you ever need
Emptiness is intimacy with life
Emptiness holds space for everything

¤ Sophia Faria 2020

II. DREAMSCAPE

Moon II: January 31–March 2

New Moon in ♒ Aquarius Jan. 31; Full Moon in ♌ Leo Feb. 16; Sun in ♓ Pisces Feb. 18

Dreaming of a Better World
© *Janet Newton 2020*

January / February
sijEčanj / veljača

♑
♒ ## Monday
31

Lunar Imbolc

☽→♒ 1:42 am
☽□♅ 7:25 pm
☉☌☽ 9:46 pm

New Moon in ♒ Aquarius 9:46 pm PST

♒ ## Tuesday
1

February

☽☌♄ 3:01 am v/c

♒
♓ ## Wednesday
2

Imbolc / Candlemas

☽→♓ 2:59 am
☽✳︎♂ 2:33 pm
☽☌♃ 3:57 pm
☽✳︎♅ 9:30 pm
☽✳︎♀ 10:35 pm

♓ ## Thursday
3

☽☌♆ 3:54 pm
☿D 8:13 pm
☽✳︎♅ 8:55 pm

♓
♈ ## Friday
4

☽✳︎♇ 1:41 am v/c
♄ApH 5:08 am
♂✳︎♃ 5:37 am
☽→♈ 6:56 am
☉☌♄ 11:05 am
☽□♂ 10:27 pm

ALL ASPECTS IN PACIFIC STANDARD TIME; ADD 3 HOURS FOR EST; ADD 8 HOURS FOR GMT

Imbolc

Fragile stirrings at the threshold of spring. The great snaking energy of life has hibernated, shed a skin; its strike-ready kinetic energy is slowly uncoiling.

We leave our caves for early signs of growth, a clear sighting of the crescent moon, first spring flowers spiking last year's leaves, new colours to live by as we turn towards fresh beginnings.

Forge and anvil, grove and well, we invoke Brighid of the bright knowledge, triple Goddess of midwifery, smithcraft and healing to help us stay grounded and find our balance between savouring and protecting the Earth.

Holy fire, sacred hearth, keeping a perpetual flame on gentle burn, we "see" her holding a wild swan onto her heart, lorica, not armour but prayer to keep her open to the flow of creative grace as we wait for our next thread of molten imagination to ignite.

Our visions gather heady momentum as we hammer them in copper, fire them in heats that could raze the roof off, pound them on the rocks of our foremothers' hopes for the land and children.

Debra Hall
© *Mother Tongue Ink*
2021

Generation to Generation
© *Barb Levine 2018*

The Lullaby

Enter the night
as solemnly as a diver,
leaving behind
daylight's manic song.

Sink, sink
stripped and solitary

your ears muffled and vague,
your eyes uncomprehending,
the purchaseless dark
yielding beneath your touch.

Time has no allegiance here:
unhooked, it drifts
and changes course.

You, too, drift
brined in quiet.

Child, it has to be this way:
all hope of home released
like a dying
stream of bubbles.
Fists softening, opening.
Mind and memory
succumbing.

When cockcrow
blazes your eyes awake
you will barely even notice
how you know
that the stillness
is its own melody:
horizonless,
suffusing you
like breath
as you kick hard
and swim up toward morning.

Moonrise © *Jenny Hahn 2018*

Star Water © *Tamara Phillips 2019*

♈ Saturday
5

☽□♀ 4:56 am
☽⚹♄ 12:22 pm
☉⚹☽ 2:17 pm

♈ Sunday
♉ 6

☽□♉ 4:42 am
♂□♅ 4:57 am
☽□♇ 9:21 am v/c
☽→♉ 2:52 pm

February
Magh

© K.A.K. Lecky 2018

Moth Moon

─── ☽☽☽ sombar ───

♉ Monday
7

☽⚹♃ 7:58 am
☽△♂ 11:12 am
☽☌♅ 12:22 pm
☽△♀ 4:00 pm
☽□♄ 11:01 pm

─── ♂♂♂ mongolbar ───

♉ Tuesday
♉

☉□☽ 5:50 am
♂△♅ 6:57 am
☽⚹♆ 9:40 am
☽△♉ 5:48 pm
☽△♇ 8:48 pm v/c

Waxing Half Moon in ♉ Taurus 5:50 am PST

─── ☿☿☿ budhbar ───

♉
♊ Wednesday
9

☽→♊ 2:27 am
☽□♃ 9:28 pm

─── ♃♃♃ brihospotibar ───

♊ Thursday
10

☽△♄ 12:20 pm
☽ApG 6:31 pm
☽□♆ 10:43 pm

─── ♀♀♀ sukrobar ───

♊
♋ Friday
11

☉△☽ 12:22 am v/c
☿☌♇ 6:04 am
☽→♋ 3:27 pm

In Between Time, or Void of Course

Waking up, in that moment,
coming from the dream world,
the real world,
to this one,
before rolling over,
before feet touch the floor,
the feel of other places
still swimming around me,
I am in between time.

Sometimes lost,
sometimes found,
leaping from one world
to another,
carrying in my rucksack
more secrets
in the hidden pouch inside,
waiting
for just the right moment to
empty them onto the page.

excerpt ¤ Elise Stuart 2018

Destination: Now © *Autumn Skye 2009*

ካካካ sonibar

♋ ☽ **Saturday**
12

☽△♃ 11:34 am
☽⚹♅ 1:49 pm
☽☍♂ 8:21 pm
☽☍♀ 9:45 pm

--- ☉☉☉ robibar ---

♋ ☽ **Sunday**
13

☽△♆ 11:15 am
☽☍♇ 10:07 pm

February
Mí Feabhra

♋
♌

Monday
14

☽☍♉ 2:27 am v/c
☽→♌ 3:17 am
☿→♒ 1:54 pm

Memories © Amanda Sage 2006

♌

Tuesday
15

☽□♅ 12:56 am
☽☍♄ 12:38 pm

♌
♍

Wednesday
16

♀♂♂ 6:29 am
☉☍☽ 8:56 am v/c
☽→♍ 12:42 pm

Full Moon in ♌ Leo 8:56 am PST

♍

Thursday
17

☽☍♃ 9:26 am
☽△♅ 9:33 am
♃✶♅ 4:13 pm
☽△♀ 9:47 pm
☽△♂ 10:13 pm

♍
♎

Friday
18

☽☍♆ 5:22 am
☉→♓ 8:43 am
☽△♇ 3:19 pm v/c
☽→♎ 7:51 pm

☉→♓

Sun in ♓ Pisces 8:43 am PST

ALL ASPECTS IN PACIFIC STANDARD TIME; ADD 3 HOURS FOR EST; ADD 8 HOURS FOR GMT

2022 Year at a Glance for ♓ Pisces (Feb. 18–March 20)

This year has you exploring what supports connection. It's in your nature to seek union, and delight in its permutations. But connection needs special care, no matter how built for it you are. Over the last few years, you have likely been having a tour of how your wounding and the trauma built into every facet of the dominant culture affect your ability to be in community freely and fully. Without ways to support healing, without structures for creating healthy boundaries, in a culture that doesn't believe in consent, connection can happen, but does not nourish or flourish. For you to get what you actually need from your enormous capacity to connect, it is important for you to focus on being spiritually diligent and resourced. This year will reveal the consequences of neglect in this area. If you have intentions about tending your body but don't follow through, you will hit walls. If you talk a good game about joyful embodiment, but don't fight to be comfortable in your own skin, you will find it harder to connect to the golden flow of source. What you have previously been able to do just by softening and reaching outward is less likely to be available without consistent, structured support of your ability to turn inward. This year is an exploration of what is real and what is possible. In order to explore these things, we have to confront the ways we confuse ourselves. Your body is a reliable compass.

Maeanna Welti © Mother Tongue Ink 2021

Higher Self *© Vasalisa 2018*

───────── ♄♄♄ Dé Sathairn ─────────

♎

Saturday
19

☽△♅   4:18 am

───────── ☉☉☉ Dé Domhnaigh ─────────

♎

Sunday
20

☽△♄   3:46 am
☽□♀   6:33 am
☽□♂   7:25 am
☽□♇   9:02 pm v/c

February
febrero

Stride © *Mary Ancilla Martinez 2017*

───── ☽☽☽ lunes ─────

♎︎
♏︎

Monday
21

☽→♏︎ 1:19 am
☉△☽ 6:28 am
☽□♉ 2:27 pm
☽☍♅ 9:10 pm
☽△♃ 10:45 pm

───── ♂♂♂ martes ─────

♏︎

Tuesday
22

☽□♄ 8:53 am
☽⚹♀ 1:55 pm
☽⚹♂ 2:58 pm
☽△♆ 4:00 pm

───── ☿☿☿ miércoles ─────

♏︎
♐︎

Wednesday
23

☽⚹♇ 1:24 am v/c
☽→♐︎ 5:29 am
♂⚹♆ 11:12 am
☉□☽ 2:32 pm
☿⚹♃ 9:06 pm
☽⚹♅ 11:17 pm

───── ♃♃♃ jueves ─────

Waning Half Moon in ♐︎ Sagittarius 2:32 pm PST

♐︎

Thursday
24

☽□♃ 3:19 am
♀⚹♆ 8:04 am
☽⚹♄ 12:45 pm
☿□♅ 6:21 pm
☽□♆ 7:24 pm v/c

───── ♀♀♀ viernes ─────

♐︎
♑︎

Friday
25

☽→♑︎ 8:27 am
☉⚹☽ 9:10 pm

───────────────────────────

ALL ASPECTS IN PACIFIC STANDARD TIME; ADD 3 HOURS FOR EST; ADD 8 HOURS FOR GMT

Night Mare

Her muzzle was gray. She whinnied, nudged me
onto her swayback. Jostled me, plodding,
down to the midnight shore. The wind mourned
in the waves lifting us suddenly like ash.

No saddle, no reins, my fists against her withers,
we soared into starlessness where memory
could enter. Hallways of lost voices,
My body the age of every tear-streaked mirror.
My mind the thorn of sorrow. Then

we flew over a pasture and the dark mare
set us down. She spoke: "You fed me handfuls
of clover here, so sweet the bees revered it.
This was the best day of my life."

"Yes," I recalled, "I was with a dear friend.
The scent of clover lingered on our palms all day
along with the tickle of your muzzle.
It was the best day of my life."

When I woke I was alone, curtains framing
the final coat of darkness. In the west a silver
crescent marked the hoofprint of the moon.

© *Joanne M. Clarkson 2020*

ኙ፟ኙ sábado

♑ **Saturday**
26

☽△♅ 3:40 am
☽⚹♃ 6:43 am
☽PrG 2:29 pm
☽⚹♆ 9:49 pm

☉☉☉ domingo

♑
♒ **Sunday**
27

☽☌♀ 1:06 am
☽☌♂ 2:05 am
☽☌♇ 6:49 am v/c
☽→♒ 10:35 am

Seeds

I don't know
what this choice
will lead to. Or the one
I made yesterday,
or even that one
five years ago,
when I walked away.

I don't know
how hardy this vine will be
how productive,
how sweet her fruit.

I only know that these seeds
are the ones in my hands
and this soil at my feet

is longing
to be the dark agent
of transformation
she was always meant to be.

What good gardener
would waste the gift of seed
for a sliver of doubt
wedged inside her mind?

I want dirt
under my
fingernails
and all my
seed packets
empty.

¤ *Emily Kedar 2019*

Night Shadows © *Barb Levine 1997*

III. SEEDS & CYCLES

Moon III: March 2–March 31

New Moon in ♓ Pisces March 2; Full Moon in ♍ Virgo March 18; Sun in ♈ Aries March 20

Holding Fire © Sheri Howe 2015

February / March

veljača / ožujak

© Jakki Moore 2015

Star Blaze

─── ☽☽☽ ponedjeljak ───

Monday
28

☽□♅ 5:50 am
☽☌♉ 2:11 pm
☽☌♄ 6:01 pm v/c

─── ♂♂♂ utorak ───

Tuesday
1

March

☽→♓ 12:53 pm
☉⚹♅ 9:05 pm

─── ☿☿☿ srijeda ───

Wednesday
2

☿☌♄ 8:33 am
☽⚹♅ 8:42 am
☉☌☽ 9:35 am
☽☌♃ 1:24 pm

New Moon in ♓ Pisces 9:35 am PST

─── ♃♃♃ četvrtak ───

Thursday
3

♂☌♇ 12:43 am
☽☌♆ 3:37 am
♀☌♇ 9:56 am
☽⚹♇ 1:03 pm
☽⚹♀ 1:15 pm
☽⚹♂ 1:45 pm v/c
☽→♈ 4:52 pm

─── ♀♀♀ petak ───

Friday
4

No exact aspects

─────────────────────────────

Universe Wishes

Infinitely comforted to learn:
As the white dwarf star
Nears the end of its billions of years lifespan
It sends out carbon seeds on a stellar wind
To create new stars, new life
Humble and majestic as a dandelion seed head
Lofting its progeny into a friendly meadow breeze
The vast incomprehensibility of the universe
Made familiar as a child making wishes
On a puff of dandelion seeds

□ Shelley Blooms 2020

Brotar desde la Oscuridad *© Annika Gemlau Asombrasdelsur 2020*

───── ♄♄♄ subota ─────

♈

Saturday
5

☽⚹♄ 3:56 am	☽□♇ 8:01 pm v/c
☉♂♃ 6:06 am	♂→♒ 10:23 pm
☽⚹♅ 11:49 am	♀→♒ 10:30 pm
♃ApH 2:10 pm	♀♂♂ 11:12 pm

───── ☉☉☉ nedjelja ─────

♈
♉

Sunday
6

☽→♉ 12:00 am	
☽□♂ 12:06 am	
☽□♀ 12:06 am	
☽♂♅ 10:38 pm	

March
Falgun

© Jan Pellizzer 2020

As Night Falls

♉

Monday
7

☽⚹♃	5:49 am
☉⚹☽	9:03 am
☽□♄	1:56 pm
☽⚹♆	8:03 pm

♉
♊

Tuesday
8

☽□♉	6:04 am
☽△♇	6:35 am v/c
☽→♊	10:39 am
☽△♂	2:40 pm
☽△♀	3:27 pm

♊

Wednesday
9

| ☿→♓ | 5:32 pm |
| ☽□♃ | 7:06 pm |

♊
♋

Thursday
10

☉□☽	2:45 am
☽△♄	2:48 am
☽□♆	8:42 am v/c
☽ApG	3:13 pm
☽→♋	11:24 pm

Waxing Half Moon in ♊ Gemini 2:45 am PST

♋

Friday
11

| ☽△♉ | 4:00 am |
| ☽⚹♅ | 11:37 pm |

List for Today:

Rescue tadpoles from the
evaporating puddle
in the driveway.
Listen to the crows in
the compost pile
and try to identify them
by their different voices.
Plant basil and calendula
and a few more
rows of lettuce.
Check blackberry canes
to see if the berries
have set.
Wonder about
action and apathy
and what bridges gaps.
Refuse to surrender belief in joy.
Listen for faint echoes of hope.
Feel the tender beat of humanity
pulsing in the world.
Feel the sun on your face.
Remember that even if you
have to move one tadpole at a time,
change is always possible.

© Molly M. Remer 2020

Oregon Flower Harvest
© *Betty LaDuke 2013*

ᚻᚻᚻ sonibar

♋

Saturday
12

☽△♃ 9:07 am
☉△☽ 8:52 pm
☽△♆ 9:25 pm

☉☉☉ robibar

♋
♌

Sunday
13

☉♂♆ 4:43 am
☽☌♇ 8:44 am v/c
☽→♌ 12:31 pm

Daylight Saving Time Begins 2:00 am PST

Spring Equinox

Day and night, dark and light are equal in length. The trees' hard "resting" buds are pliant again. Whorls, eggs, columns and frogs, motifs of ancient renewal populate our dreams and inscapes. Volumes of light flood the air revealing grime on windows, cobwebs along walls.

As we perform our rituals of spring cleaning, throw off sluggishness and tonify our livers, we can hear birdsong from every room in the house. Ecstatic of heart again, we are like haiku writers trying to contain elation in just three lines.

Even though the winds of change and uncertainty gust, when Oestra's egg of pure potential cracks open, we pluck our intentions from our vision boards, woad our brows and stride courageously out. What finds shape and strength now will determine the rest of the year.

We call on our kindreds, human and non-human. The wisdom medicine of the wild geese who fly over us morning and evening, their honking almost singing, offers us the gift of synergy. Close and familial, they've flown infinitely further because they've done it together.

Debra Hall © Mother Tongue Ink 2021

Spring Equinox © KT InfiniteArt 2020

Throwing Shadows © *Helen Seay Art 2016*

Gravity

    I go to sleep among Fireflies. The Earthworm tells me how deep within where we cannot see, they are reweaving the groundwork for life. Vultures tell how they seek death out: that's where the nourishment is. Cicadas must drink from the roots of history for a long time, before they can rise and sing. Deer tell how to lay their antlers down and give it up, trusting that new ones will grow back stronger next year. Hermit crabs are willing to walk naked on the beach, from the old shell to the new.

    Cardinals never fly away south, no matter how cold it gets, but call up the sun with their red songs each morning. Bears make the spring come by surrendering to the darkness of winter; desire wakes the groundhogs in spring. Salmon, moving impossibly uphill against the flow of time, tell me that really, they're only returning home. And Canada Geese tell how spring is nothing more than circling back to the wholeness we once knew.

    I dream the earth holds me tight—they call it gravity; I call it love.

excerpt ¤ Mindi Meltz 2019

March
Mí Márta

────── ☽☽☽ Dé Luain ──────

♌ Monday
14

☽☌♂ 12:17 am
Ψ⌂pH 1:08 am
☽☌♀ 3:00 am
☽□♅ 12:02 pm

Las Tres Princesas de la Noche
⌂ *Molly Brown 2020*

────── ♂♂♂ Dé Máirt ──────

♌
♍ Tuesday
15

☽☍♄ 3:56 am v/c
☽→♍ 9:58 pm

────── ☿☿☿ Dé Céadaoin ──────

♍ Wednesday
16

☽☍♉ 7:08 pm
☽△♅ 8:25 pm

────── ♃♃♃ Dé Ardaoin ──────

♍ Thursday
17

☿✶♅ 5:13 am
☽☍♃ 6:44 am
☽☍Ψ 4:02 pm

────── ♀♀♀ Dé Haoine ──────

♍
♎ Friday
18

☉☍☽ 12:17 am
☽△♇ 1:11 am v/c
☽→♎ 4:26 am
♀✶♄ 9:24 am
☉✶♇ 12:37 pm
☽△♂ 9:29 pm

Full Moon in ♍ Virgo 12:17 am PDT

ALL ASPECTS IN PACIFIC DAYLIGHT TIME; ADD 3 HOURS FOR EDT; ADD 7 HOURS FOR GMT

2022 Year at a Glance for ♈ Aries (March 20–April 19)

This year is about fully embodying the truth of your own values. Beyond ideas and ideals, the ways that you live and fight for what you cherish are woven into the fiber of your being, are alive in your muscles, nerves, blood, bones. 2022 will continue to slow you down so you can become more intimate with your own instincts, which sometimes move so fast you can hardly see them as they dash by. The beginning of the year starts off with potentially challenging energies for you, as deeply personal work is activated in a part of your chart that is visible, asking you to explore your public roles and how your wounding and need for love shows up in them. January will dig things up, maybe for everyone to see. Surrender to what presents itself for healing; listen humbly and consider your stamina and the stamina of your relationships. Summer is not without some challenges but can be spent in integration, cross-pollination and celebration. In all these things, your body is a guide you can come back to again and again. The last four months of the year, things will not move as directly as you may like. You won't be able to speed up with impunity yet, but will be continually pointed back to the things that require a slower pace. The more you can soften and explore deeper realms of consciousness, the easier it will be for things to move the way they need to. Use your courageous honesty to learn the difference between self-soothing illusions and the freeing power of imagination.

Maeanna Welti © Mother Tongue Ink 2021

Forward Static ¤ *RXANDRSN 2020*

--- ♄♄♄ Dé Sathairn ---

♎ 🌑

Saturday
19

☽△♀ 1:52 am
♀□♅ 4:16 am
☽△♄ 4:59 pm

--- ☉☉☉ Dé Domhnaigh ---

♎
♏ 🌑

Sunday
20

☽□♇ 5:40 am v/c
☉→♈ 8:33 am
☽→♏ 8:44 am
♅♂♃ 11:06 pm

Spring Equinox

☉→♈

Sun in ♈ Aries 8:33 am PDT

March
marzo

© *Greta Boann Perry 2019*

Life Spirals into Being

─────── ☽☽☽ lunes ───────

♏

Monday
21

☽□♂ 4:16 am
☽☍♅ 5:58 am
☽□♀ 9:33 am
♂⚹♄ 2:00 pm
☽△♃ 5:08 pm
☽△♅ 7:26 pm
☽□♄ 8:49 pm

─────── ♂♂♂ martes ───────

♏
♐

Tuesday
22

☽△♆ 12:26 am
☽⚹♇ 9:01 am v/c
☽→♐ 11:59 am
♂□♅ 1:44 pm
☉△☽ 3:52 pm

─────── ☿☿☿ miércoles ───────

♐

Wednesday
23

☽⚹♂ 10:12 am
☿♂♆ 10:44 am
☽⚹♀ 4:29 pm
☽PrG 4:34 pm
☽□♃ 8:59 pm

─────── ♃♃♃ jueves ───────

♐
♑

Thursday
24

☽⚹♄ 12:08 am
☽□♆ 3:30 am
☽□♅ 5:59 am v/c
☽→♑ 2:54 pm
☉□☽ 10:37 pm

Waning Half Moon in ♑ Capricorn 10:37 pm PDT

─────── ♀♀♀ viernes ───────

♑

Friday
25

☽△♅ 12:15 pm

─────────────────────

ALL ASPECTS IN PACIFIC DAYLIGHT TIME; ADD 3 HOURS FOR EDT; ADD 7 HOURS FOR GMT

Copper Witch

Muscle by muscle, bone by bone, she takes herself apart
scrubs her heart in the river,
grinds the knot in her back against the stones
dives into the jade pool, holds her breath
letting the water's mossy tongue taste her
until her lungs beg for air

Choose chants the river

She opens her eyes underwater, looks down at her body
hears the sun singing, feels her heart beat in unison
cuts the tether, and rises to the surface
shedding the water like a snake skin

She drinks iron from the stones
oils her joints by climbing up and down the rocks
guzzles at the spring until her thirst is quenched
bakes herself copper in the sun
until the current runs through her
clear as the first flutes of morning
every molecule awake to the music

The river rushing over the rocks singing in gospel
The choir of the pines rehearsing a requiem

excerpt © Meredith Heller 2019

ꜧꜧꜧ sábado ——————

♑
♒

Saturday
26

☽⚹♃	12:48 am	☽☌♇	3:04 pm
☿⚹♇	3:35 am	☽⚹♅	4:51 pm v/c
☽⚹♆	6:36 am	☽→♒	5:55 pm

—————— ⊙⊙⊙ domingo ——————

♒

Sunday
27

☿→♈	12:44 am
⊙⚹☽	5:34 am
☽□♅	3:38 pm
☽☌♂	10:08 pm

March / April
očujak / travanj

Sacred is Growth

ↄↄↄ ponedjeljak

♒︎
♓︎

Monday
28

☽☌♀	6:48 am
☽☌♄	7:11 am v/c
♀☌♂	12:27 pm
☿ApH	6:11 pm
☽→♓︎	9:31 pm

♂♂♂ utorak

♓︎

Tuesday
29

☽⚹♅	7:54 pm

☿☿☿ srijeda

♓︎

Wednesday
30

☽☌♃	10:24 am
☽☌♆	2:54 pm
☽⚹♇	11:37 pm v/c

♃♃♃ četvrtak

♓︎
♈︎

Thursday
31

☽→♈︎	2:30 am
☽☌♅	7:34 pm
☉☌☽	11:24 pm

New Moon in ♈︎ Aries 11:24 pm PDT

♀♀♀ petak

♈︎

Friday
1

April

☽⚹♂	3:07 pm
☽⚹♄	7:04 pm
☉☌♅	7:56 pm

Poppy Moon © Schehera VanDyke 2018

Planting Poppy Seeds with Mom

On our knees, we pushed
thousands of poppy seeds silently into the ground.
The seeds will know what to do—hoping for a petaled body,
take their coats off at the gates to the underworld.

© Jennifer Lothrigel 2020

───────── ♄♄♄ subota ─────────

♈
♉

Saturday
2

☽⚹♀ 3:24 am   ☽→♉   9:50 am
♀♂♃ 6:42 am   ♂ApH 12:06 pm
☽□♇ 6:51 am v/c ☉♂♅   4:11 pm

───────── ☉☉☉ nedjelja ─────────

♉

Sunday
3

☽♂♅ 10:47 am

───────────────────────────

Mother Tongue

I hear the sounds of the Mother Tongue
slapping
clicking
hissing
cooing
hushing
I feel her rhythms and shapes roll through
palate,
throat, teeth

They ripple through my whole body
Pumping my toes
Plumping my eyes
Vibrating every membrane
Cascading through every pore

We are
  roaring
   clamoring
    declaring
     swearing
      our allegiance
       to One and All
       swaying and sashaying
       stomping and snapping
       turning and tapping
       mapping
       our new humanity

          ¤ Sheryl J. Shapiro 2020

Sacred Heart Mandala © Elspeth McLean 2018

IV. HEART TO HEART

Moon IV: March 31–April 30

New Moon in ♈ Aries March 31; Full Moon in ♎ Libra April 16; Sun in ♉ Taurus April 19

Moon Mamas © *Nicole Miz 2002*

April
Choitro

now is the time
to turn towards all the love
that's been waiting for you
all the life that thrusts itself forth
with the river of spring's great thaw
face the sun now
and melt   palms open

excerpt ¤ Osha Waters 2019

─── ☽☽☽ sombar ───

♉
♊

Monday
4

☽□♂ 4:09 am
☽✶♃ 4:29 am
☽□♄ 4:58 am
☽✶♆ 7:36 am

☽△♇ 5:00 pm
♂♂♄ 6:51 pm
☽□♀ 6:53 pm v/c
☽→♊ 8:04 pm

─── ♂♂♂ mongolbar ───

♊

Tuesday
5

♀→♓ 8:18 am

─── ☿☿☿ budhbar ───

♊

Wednesday
6

☉✶☽ 5:32 am
☽✶☿ 2:56 pm
☽△♄ 5:26 pm
☽□♃ 5:42 pm
☽□♆ 7:54 pm
☽△♂ 8:15 pm v/c

─── ♃♃♃ brihospotibar ───

♊
♋

Thursday
7

☿✶♄ 5:37 am
☽→♋ 8:30 am
☽ApG 12:17 pm
☽△♀ 1:19 pm

─── ♀♀♀ sukrobar ───

♋

Friday
8

☿✶♂ 11:19 am
☽✶♅ 11:28 am
☉□☽ 11:47 pm

Waxing Half Moon in ♋ Cancer 11:47 pm PDT

ALL ASPECTS IN PACIFIC DAYLIGHT TIME; ADD 3 HOURS FOR EDT; ADD 7 HOURS FOR GMT

In the Wide Dark Together

Enfold me, love, into the dim falling.
Carry me close, close,
sing me with your breath.
Is it we or something larger calling?
Let us be fearless—
crave and compass depth.
Open me, love,
as I open to your bright
offering: I contain the night.

Course with me, love,
coupled and cradled.
Fire me and fill me.
I'll cavern you, crown you,
I'll croon you through me
till our breath is braided.
Flourish and flame in me
as I curl close around you.
I flower for you, love,
I am far-flung—
the night unfolds within me,
burns like a sun.

© Jennifer Highland 2012

Deep Embrace *© Abena Addo 1997*

♄♄♄ sonibar

♋
♌

Saturday
9

☽△♃ 7:36 am
☽△♆ 8:46 am
☽□☿ 4:25 pm
☽☍♇ 6:01 pm v/c
☽→♌ 9:00 pm

☉☉☉ robibar

♌

Sunday
10

☿□♇ 1:45 am
☿→♉ 7:09 pm
☽□♅ 11:25 pm

April
Mí Aibreán

─────── ☽☽☽ Dé Luain ───────

♌

Monday
11

☉△☽   4:01 pm
☽☍♄   5:50 pm

─────── ♂♂♂ Dé Máirt ───────

♌
♍

Tuesday
12

☽☍♂   3:16 am v/c
☽→♍   7:07 am
♃☌♆   7:42 am
☽△♅   1:55 pm
☉⚹♄   5:14 pm
☽☍♀ 10:27 pm

─────── ☿☿☿ Dé Céadaoin ───────

♍

Wednesday
13

☽△♅   8:15 am

─────── ♃♃♃ Dé Ardaoin ───────

♍
♎

Thursday
14

☽☍♆   3:11 am
☽☍♃   3:49 am
☽△♇ 11:11 am v/c
☽→♎   1:46 pm
♂→♓   8:06 pm

─────── ♀♀♀ Dé Haoine ───────

♎

Friday
15

No exact aspects

─────────────────────────────

ALL ASPECTS IN PACIFIC DAYLIGHT TIME; ADD 3 HOURS FOR EDT; ADD 7 HOURS FOR GMT

Dancing in Your Eyes

Joy. What a powerful feeling. To experience total bliss in a given moment. A gift. One given or received and, if you are paying attention, both at once.

Joy. An intoxicating rush of being bound by nothing and happy for all. An expression so clearly mapped out by the lines on one's face. Dancing about your eyes, playing on your cheeks.

Joy. To be found in the most delicate moments or blown in upon a wave of unbridled laughter. Pouring in through the cracks. Cleaning out the cobwebs. Taking flight.

Fros and Frappes
© *Destiney Powell 2017*

And, if you are lucky, you see that joy reflected in the face of another. A mirror of something good. Something pure.

But, best of all, you see that joy resonating throughout yourself. Feel it coursing through you. Holding you in all moments yet to come.

□ *Melissa Rees 2020*

─────── ካካካ Dé Sathairn ───────

♎︎
♏︎ ◯ **Saturday**
16

☽△♄ 6:06 am
☉☍☽ 11:55 am
☽☐♇ 2:57 pm v/c
☽→♏︎ 5:22 pm
☽△♂ 7:55 pm

─────── ⊙⊙⊙ Dé Domhnaigh ───────   Full Moon in ♎︎ Libra 11:55 am PDT

♏︎ ◐ **Sunday**
17

☽☍♅ 3:43 pm
☽△♀ 3:50 pm
☽☍♅ 4:27 pm
☿⚹♀ 6:09 pm
☿♂♅ 9:51 pm

April
abril

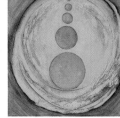

© *Janyt Piercy 2017*

Celestial Tide

─── ☽☽☽ lunes ───────

♏︎
♐︎

Monday
18

♀⚹♅ 12:15 am
☉□♇ 8:14 am
☽□♄ 8:31 am
☽△♆ 9:40 am
☽△♃ 11:36 am
☽⚹♇ 4:55 pm v/c
☽→♐︎ 7:16 pm

─── ♂♂♂ martes ───────

♐︎

Tuesday
19

☽□♂ 12:30 am
☽PrG 8:17 am
☉→♉ 7:24 pm
☽□♀ 9:33 pm

☉→♉

Sun in ♉ Taurus 7:24 pm PDT

─── ☿☿☿ miércoles ───────

♐︎
♑︎

Wednesday
20

☽⚹♄ 10:18 am
☽□♆ 11:20 am
☽□♃ 1:56 pm v/c
☽→♑︎ 8:52 pm
☉△☽ 10:43 pm

─── ♃♃♃ jueves ───────

♑︎

Thursday
21

☽⚹♂ 4:53 am
☽△♅ 8:18 pm

─── ♀♀♀ viernes ───────

♑︎
♒︎

Friday
22

☽⚹♀ 3:42 am
☽△♅ 8:13 am
☽⚹♆ 1:38 pm
☽⚹♃ 4:58 pm
☽☌♇ 8:53 pm v/c
☽→♒︎ 11:17 pm

─────────────────────

ALL ASPECTS IN PACIFIC DAYLIGHT TIME; ADD 3 HOURS FOR EDT; ADD 7 HOURS FOR GMT

2022 Year at a Glance for ♉ Taurus (April 19–May 20)

This year will push you out of your comfort zone. You've been going through that anyway, but this is a year for you to define yourself, explore, try on new roles, make new connections. Uranus continues to ask you to show the world what it looks like when stable, unchangeable Taurus embraces change. You are the one who knows in spirit the joy and freedom of the body. You are a revolution of beauty, richness, resource, and the world has a place for you in it. Pluto is calling you beyond the most familiar horizons, that you may find your place in our healing. Saturn in Aquarius is enlivening and challenging you in the work and roles others see you in. The year begins and ends with squares between Uranus and Saturn, giving you a chance to work through any friction between those public roles and how you do you. There needs to be room for you in your work, and you need space for this new, deepening authenticity and freedom. You also need to take care of the wider web of your relationships with integrity and courage. The year will be book-ended by question marks about how this is all possible. Throughout the year, make sure you stay generously connected to the deep wells of love that are there for you. This year will amplify your connections in human, animal and spiritual communities. Staying lovingly connected will nourish all the ways in which you are challenging yourself to grow.

Maeanna Welti © Mother Tongue Ink 2021

Open © Kay Kemp 2009

ħħħ sábado

≈

Saturday
23

⊙□☽   4:56 am
☽□♅   11:35 pm

☉☉☉ domingo

Waning Half Moon in ≈ Aquarius 4:56 am PDT

≈

Sunday
24

♉□♄   6:50 am
☿⚹♆   3:37 pm
☽♂♄   4:33 pm
☽□♉   5:33 pm v/c

April / May
travanj / svibanj

Our Hope for Humanity
palm to palm
we make a circuit—
loving energy looping
round our own tiny peaceful
world of now
excerpt © Erin Robertson 2020

──── ☽☽☽ ponedjeljak ────

Monday
25

☽→♓ 3:14 am
☉⚹☽ 1:08 pm
☽☌♂ 5:51 pm

──── ♂♂♂ utorak ────

♓

Tuesday
26

☽⚹♅ 4:39 am
☽☌♀ 9:50 pm
☿⚹♃ 10:11 pm
☽☌♆ 11:02 pm

──── ☿☿☿ srijeda ────

♓
♈

Wednesday
27

☽☌♃ 4:07 am
☽⚹♅ 4:35 am
☽⚹♇ 6:36 am v/c
☽→♈ 9:10 am
♀☌♆ 12:11 pm

──── ♃♃♃ četvrtak ────

♈

Thursday
28

☿△♇ 5:05 am

──── ♀♀♀ petak ────

♈
♉

Friday
29

☽⚹♄ 6:15 am
♇℞ 11:37 am
☽□♇ 2:38 pm v/c
☿→♊ 3:23 pm
☽→♉ 5:19 pm

───────────────

ALL ASPECTS IN PACIFIC DAYLIGHT TIME; ADD 3 HOURS FOR EDT; ADD 7 HOURS FOR GMT

Beltane

The Great rite, the Greening time. The trees shape-shift the land before our eyes like conjurers pulling miniature leaves out of their cuffs. So, not cowed by ecocide, nature blossoms and burgeons beyond every horizon in the usual way—we can never catch up. Rising in love under skies bluer than euphoria, we leap the bel-fire into summer.

Joy establishes an easy rhythm for us to expand into. After weeks of nurturing, we relax our watchfulness to let our plants, projects and care-lings become sky born in their own time.

We make love all night in the woods and fields to the parts of our feral, sensual selves we had forgotten about, find a patch of earth for our dance of atavistic ecstasy, wash our faces in May morning dew, bring back an armful of blossoms to decorate our windows.

When we least expect her, Sheela na gig appears flashing her genius at the global elites who are destroying the Earth, showing us how to harness our powers of irreverence, resilience and mischief.

Debra Hall © Mother Tongue Ink 2021

Moon Lodge □ Dorrie Joy 2020

Here are Her Words

Here are her words,
Written with the blackest ink from the
Sharpest point of
An antique fountain pen
Carved from the branches of this oak tree,
Where an owl now meditates
While a crow watches,
With its eye radiating wisdom
After a long journey from inside
The darkest rock cave in the forest,
Where smoky quartz and
Ancient fern fossils illuminate the still glowing
And quivering coals from the fires of the
Green witches.

Clutching her pen
As a pearl handled knife
Or an engraved iron sword,
She will not silence the chanting or
The howling of her grandmothers and their mothers,
Who in this very cave
Wove words into incantations
And danced light into the crystals.
They brought healing out from the forest and
Into the streets.
She will do the same
With her words.
They will heal
They will bring light out
From the darkest places where wisdom and magic
Still radiate.

¤ *Tonya J. Cunningham 2020*

Fierce Love © *Autumn Skye 2019*

ħħħ subota

☿ ## Saturday
30

⊙☌☽ 1:28 pm
♀☌♃ 2:14 pm
☽⚹♂ 4:23 pm
☽☌♅ 9:24 pm

New Moon in ♉ Taurus 1:28 pm PDT
Partial Solar Eclipse 1:41 pm PDT*

⊙⊙⊙ nedjelja

♉ ## Sunday
1

♀⚹♇ 3:37 am
☽□♄ 4:33 pm
☽⚹♆ 5:04 pm

May
Beltane

MOON V   *Eclipse visible SW South America, Pacific, Atlantic and Antarctica   79

Under the Ice

It is said that the sound of the cello is closest in tambour to the human voice.

This must not be the voice of any ordinary human, I think, *but one who accepts the ongoing metamorphosis of all things.*

For it feels as though the cello knows how to find the edges of our being, its music pushing into the resilient depths of what we are made of. It knows that the impermanence of life holds beauty and grief in a tangled embrace. I imagine the cello's grunts and moans surfacing from the stomachs of crystal caverns hidden in the earth. Its sound is something dying, something dancing, something flying into a thunderstorm, something birthed from a blackhole.

It is our underworld voice, echoing our richest, darkest expression.

What does one do when the cello is playing, when there is a slow dying happening, always holding the promise of rebirth?

excerpt © Kendra Ward 2020

Music Within
© Jakki Moore 2020

V. MUSE-ING

Moon V: April 30–May 30

New Moon in ♉ Taurus April 30; Full Moon in ♏ Scorpio May 15; Sun in ♊ Gemini May 20

Ravenesce © Helen Seay Art 2018

May
Boishakh

Snake Woman □ Glenda "GG" Goodrich 2020

—))) sombar —

♉
♊

Monday
2

) ⚹ ♃ 12:19 am
) △ ♇ 1:00 am
) ⚹ ♀ 3:13 am v/c
) → ♊ 3:46 am
) ☌ ♉ 8:05 am
♀ → ♈ 9:10 am

— ♂♂♂ mongolbar —

♊

Tuesday
3

) □ ♂ 7:41 am
♃ ⚹ ♇ 3:33 pm

— ☿☿☿ budhbar —

♊
♋

Wednesday
4

) △ ♄ 4:51 am
) □ ♆ 5:15 am
♂ ⚹ ♅ 8:47 am
) □ ♃ 1:37 pm v/c
) → ♋ 4:05 pm
) □ ♀ 9:57 pm

— ♃♃♃ brihospotibar —

♋

Thursday
5

☉ ☌ ♅ 12:21 am
) ApG 5:46 am
♅ ApH 8:55 am
) ⚹ ♅ 10:13 pm
☿ ⚹ ♀ 11:01 pm

— ♀♀♀ sukrobar —

♋

Friday
6

☉ ⚹) 12:03 am
) △ ♂ 12:34 am
) △ ♆ 6:12 pm

ALL ASPECTS IN PACIFIC DAYLIGHT TIME; ADD 3 HOURS FOR EDT; ADD 7 HOURS FOR GMT

Your Source and Your Shame

Being creative can lead to your darkness. When I say darkness, I don't just mean that dark Source where all things emerge, where the moon becomes the muse, where artists and dreamers go to find generative threads of Creation. I don't just mean the kind of darkness that is the Void, the Source, the Center of all Things.

I mean the darkness you want to keep hiding. Your heaviness, the parts of you kept in the shadows because it is hard to face and terrifying to feel. I mean your black night, the shadowy raven you keep hidden, caged, and tied down. And though you have rejected these parts of you, let me clarify that you want them, too. In fact, you are always wanting them, forever feeling their absence, your loneliness, and your so-called imperfection.

Creativity can lead to both types of darkness, one a prelude to the other. You see, in order to feel the fullness of your fire, in order to know the exuberance of your light, in order to radiate the bright sun that is you, your shadowy raven must be set free. This darkness must join forces with your creative expression. It must become a part of the great fountain of YOU. Keeping this darkness at bay is like cupping your hand on the fountainhead.

© Adriana Attento 2010

ᚻᚻᚻ sonibar

♋
♌

Saturday
7

☽☌♇	1:59 am	☽→♌	4:50 am
☉✶♂	2:48 am	☽✶♅	1:59 pm
☽△♃	3:25 am v/c	☽△♀	5:01 pm

☉☉☉ robibar

♌

Sunday
♉

☽□♅	10:41 am
☉□☽	5:21 pm

Waxing Half Moon in ♌ Leo 5:21 pm PDT

May
Mí Bealtaine

© Kristen Roderick 2019

Breaking the Ocean

——— ☽☽☽ Dé Luain ———

♌
♍

Monday
9

☽☍♄   5:38 am v/c
☽→♍   3:53 pm

——— ♂♂♂ Dé Máirt ———

♍

Tuesday
10

☽□☿   1:09 am
☿R   4:47 am
♃→♈   4:22 pm
☽△♅   8:27 pm

——— ☿☿☿ Dé Céadaoin ———

♍
♎

Wednesday
11

☽☍♂   5:17 am
☉△☽   7:02 am
☽☍♆   2:17 pm
☽△♇   8:59 pm v/c
☽→♎   11:34 pm

——— ♃♃♃ Dé Ardaoin ———

♎

Thursday
12

☽☍♃   12:02 am
☽△☿   7:54 am
☽☍♀   8:49 pm

——— ♀♀♀ Dé Haoine ———

♎

Friday
13

☽△♄   6:53 pm

ALL ASPECTS IN PACIFIC DAYLIGHT TIME; ADD 3 HOURS FOR EDT; ADD 7 HOURS FOR GMT

The Lineage of Fiber Art

Lineage focuses on ancestry, where we come from, the names and faces of our family tree, and what's been inherited by means of DNA. But the Latin root of *lineage* means "string, line, thread."

The practice of weaving and fiber work connects me to something beautiful and mysterious that can feel more familiar than blood.

Throughout history, fiber art helped women find their voices, tell their stories, weave their fates and cast their spells. Minerva, Artemis, the Fates, and the Valkyries were called back through the ages, blessing the makers and receivers of woven pieces.

excerpt © Kristen Roderick 2019

Mama Cañari ⌑ *Mimi Foyle 2018*

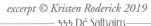

──────── ♄♄♄ Dé Satharn ────────

♎︎
♏︎

Saturday
14

☽□♇ 1:07 am v/c
☽→♏︎ 3:34 am

──────── ☉☉☉ Dé Domhnaigh ────────

♏︎

Sunday
15

Lunar Beltane

☽☍♅ 5:04 am
♀☌♃ 5:12 am
☉□♄ 11:49 am
☉✶♆ 12:15 pm

☽△♂ 6:01 pm
☽□♄ 8:38 pm
☽△♆ 8:40 pm
☉☍☽ 9:14 pm

Total Lunar Eclipse 9:11 pm PDT*
Full Moon in ♏︎ Scorpio 9:14 pm PDT

May
mayo

─────── ♌♌♌ lunes ───────

♏
♐

Monday
16

☽✶♇ 2:28 am v/c
☽→♐ 4:50 am
☽△♃ 6:33 am
☽☍♅ 10:19 am

© Shelley Anne Tipton Irish 2010

Together Under the Moon

─────── ♂♂♂ martes ───────

♐

Tuesday
17

☽△♀ 8:31 am
☽PrG 8:32 am
☽□♂ 8:51 pm
☽□♆ 8:59 pm
☽✶♄ 8:59 pm v/c
♂♂♆ 11:33 pm

─────── ☿☿☿ miércoles ───────

♐
♑

Wednesday
18

☽→♑ 5:02 am
☽□♃ 7:21 am

─────── ♃♃♃ jueves ───────

♑

Thursday
19

☉△♇ 5:11 am
☽△♅ 6:16 am
☽□♀ 1:01 pm
☿✶♃ 6:33 pm
☽✶♆ 9:41 pm

─────── ♀♀♀ viernes ───────

♑
♒

Friday
20

☽✶♂ 12:07 am
☽♂♇ 3:24 am
☉△☽ 4:59 am v/c
☽→♒ 5:53 am
☽△♅ 8:11 am
☽✶♃ 8:54 am
☉→♊ 6:22 pm

☉→♊

Sun in ♊ Gemini 6:22 pm PDT

ALL ASPECTS IN PACIFIC DAYLIGHT TIME; ADD 3 HOURS FOR EDT; ADD 7 HOURS FOR GMT

2022 Year at a Glance for ♊ Gemini (May 20–June 21)

It's a good thing you are curious about everything. This year much will happen for you in the dark and behind the scenes, and your curiosity will serve you well. Apply it to going deep instead of broad, into the richness of the dark. Your body is the road to connection with spirit, and all the ways that you can usually think your way quickly through things will not have nearly as much weight as usual. Notice how your body connects, the wild other realms it leads into. The cost of ignoring it will be higher than usual this year, and not one you want to pay. You need to find a way to both stretch beyond your usual world and to hold a space that is deeply, privately embodied. This year will push your capacity for real depth, wrapping up a long cycle of intimacy work that will get you familiar with wounding, emotional honesty, and being with what scares us about love. Spiritual practices and embodiment work can help you harmonize the energies you're working with. Make room to be with what doesn't come through easily via language, but that speaks clearly through the senses. Notice what even your flexible mind might not readily recognize as innovations in how you can live, connect and heal. The end of the year will bring some extra urgency and pressure to the themes of the year, but take time—rushing will come with consequences. Reach into what resources you deeply, and be willing to learn about many ways and rates of change.

Maeanna Welti © Mother Tongue Ink 2021

Spiritually Connected
© Patricia Wyatt 1998

ᚻᚻᚻ sábado

≈

Saturday
21

☽□♅   8:16 am
☉♂♉ 12:18 pm
☽⚹♀   7:40 pm

◉◉◉ domingo

≈
♓

Sunday
22

☽♂♄   12:19 am v/c
☽→♓   8:49 am
☽□♉   9:12 am
☉□☽   11:43 am

♂⚹♇   3:15 pm
☿PrH   4:27 pm
♉→♉   6:15 pm

Waning Half Moon in ♓ Pisces 11:43 am PDT

May
svibanj

Out of the Dark
Lift your pens, brushes, hands, voices,
Birth a new design
onto our broken world,
make it whole, watch it take form,
Together, dance and sing
Our blueprints into the wind!
excerpt ▢ Tanya Dahms 2020

──── ☽☽☽ ponedjeljak ────

 ♓

Monday
23

☉⚹♃   4:05 am
☽⚹♅ 12:54 pm
☿⚹♂   8:27 pm

──── ♂♂♂ utorak ────

♓
♈

Tuesday
24

♀⚹♄   4:06 am   ☽→♈   2:39 pm
☽♂♅   5:41 am   ♂→♈   4:17 pm
☽⚹♇   11:49 am   ☽♂♃   7:27 pm
☽⚹♅   12:50 pm   ☉⚹☽ 10:03 pm
☽♂♂   2:33 pm v/c

──── ☿☿☿ srijeda ────

♈

Wednesday
25

☿△♇   2:49 pm

──── ♃♃♃ četvrtak ────

♈
♉

Thursday
26

☽⚹♄   2:06 pm
☽♂♀   8:00 pm
☽□♇   8:20 pm v/c
☽→♉ 11:22 pm
♀□♇ 11:29 pm

──── ♀♀♀ petak ────

♉

Friday
27

No exact aspects

ALL ASPECTS IN PACIFIC DAYLIGHT TIME; ADD 3 HOURS FOR EDT; ADD 7 HOURS FOR GMT

Muse

My ear pressed close listening to the whispers of her heart, soon each whisper became a branch. Higher and higher I climbed her voice like a tree. Then as usual, my wings got tangled in my messy hair, I dropped my brush, trembled, stumbled and fell to the ground with a splatter and a plop.

But then . . . there where I landed, under a heap of knotted wings and hair, lay my brush, soaked in a new color Earth had never shown before. Just one glimpse of this color, and I knew, if everyone could truly see

Genesis
© *Autumn Skye 2018*

it we would shift the planet and return it to brand new. This one miracle, sweet ashes of Earth resumed. Returning to love in a blaze of color to fill the heart of all Earth's children. To feed the hungry, saddened, forgotten, and neglected souls.

Just one color, and only this to imagine. Here, where I fell in a messy pile of me. Ahhhhhh . . . while in her limbs I nested. In dusty feathers and twisted locks I mused . . . As anything is possible, even Just one color, stumbled upon while listening to a tree. Could shift the consciousness of me and of our planet. To me as you, you as me, and we as tree.

© *Brigidina 2016*

ᚻᚻᚻ subota

♉

Saturday
28

☽♂♅ 6:50 am
♀→♉ 7:46 am

☉☉☉ nedjelja

♉
♊

Sunday
29

☽⚹♆ 12:49 am
☽□♄ 12:51 am
♂♂♃ 3:31 am
☽♂♉ 4:15 am

☽△♇ 7:10 am v/c
☽→♊ 10:22 am
☽⚹♃ 5:12 pm
☽⚹♂ 5:55 pm

Dancing Through the Apocalypse

While the ground is still under your feet
can you feel it with your soul
and yet not be destroyed
for the grief it carries
but be buoyed by the seeds of life
still germinating within?

Can you see yet around you
the disease-riddled forest swaying
or the dwindling numbers
of geese flying South
and send your blessings with their journey
in spite of endless hits to your own heart
as the world falls apart around you?

And as the world burns
it still turns
life remains held in the balance tilted.
Even now, you are supported.
The reason for your life
moves through you all the same.
Steps only you can take will be
your dance through the apocalypse.

Shake violently
pirouette and collapse.
Get back up and find your grace
to slow dance with death
slam dance with life
interpret the song of your purpose
in whatever steps are required of you.

A million dances in each land
will keep the planet spinning.
Embrace the madness swirling around us
moving through it still.

This cacaphonic symphony is our life's work.

We mustn't sit down before the crescendo.

¤ Earthdancer 2020

VI. EARTH RESCUE

Moon VI: May 30–June 28

New Moon in ♊ Gemini May 30 ; Full Moon in ♐ Sagittarius June 14; Sun in ♋ Cancer June 21

The Bag Lady © *Denise Kester 1994*

May / June
Boishakh / Joishtho

─── ☽☽☽ sombar ───────────

♊

Monday
30

☉☌☽ 4:30 am

Family

© Susan Korsnick 2019

New Moon in ♊ Gemini 4:30 am PDT

─── ♂♂♂ mongolbar ───────────

♊
♋

Tuesday
31

☽□♆ 1:10 pm
☽△♄ 1:10 pm v/c
☽→♋ 10:49 pm

─── ☿☿☿ budhbar ───────────

♋

Wednesday
1

☽□♃ 6:35 am
☽⚹♀ 8:24 am
☽□♂ 10:31 am
☽ApG 6:12 pm

June

─── ♃♃♃ brihospotibar ───────────

♋

Thursday
2

☽⚹♅ 8:05 am

─── ♀♀♀ sukrobar ───────────

♋
♌

Friday
3

☿D 1:00 am
☽△♆ 2:05 am
☽⚹♅ 3:44 am
☽☍♇ 8:15 am v/c
☽→♌ 11:38 am
☽△♃ 8:09 pm

ALL ASPECTS IN PACIFIC DAYLIGHT TIME; ADD 3 HOURS FOR EDT; ADD 7 HOURS FOR GMT

Melt © *Sandra Stanton 2020*

♌

Saturday
4

☽△♂   3:15 am
☽□♀   3:47 am
♄R   2:47 pm
☉⚹☽   4:23 pm
☽□♅   8:46 pm

♌
♍

Sunday
5

☽☍♄   2:03 pm
☽□☿   4:12 pm v/c
☽→♍ 11:22 pm

June

Mí Meitheamh

Monday
6

Dreams and plants speak to us.
We can walk and dance in the darkness,
Our steps know the path.
From our hands, seeds grow.
We are witches, guardians of darkness,
of sacred life.

excerpt ¤ Astrid Thibert 2020

☉✷⚷ 1:44 am
☽△♀ 9:05 pm

Tuesday
7

☽△♅ 7:26 am
☉□☽ 7:48 am
☽☍♆ 11:44 pm

Waxing Half Moon in ♍ Virgo 7:48 am PDT

Wednesday
8

☽△☿ 2:55 am
☽△♇ 5:09 am v/c
☽→♎ 8:22 am
☽☍♃ 5:26 pm

Thursday
9

☽☍♂ 5:16 am
☉△☽ 6:56 pm

Friday
10

☽△♄ 5:27 am
☽□♇ 10:36 am v/c
☽→♏ 1:41 pm
☿△♇ 2:22 pm

ALL ASPECTS IN PACIFIC DAYLIGHT TIME; ADD 3 HOURS FOR EDT; ADD 7 HOURS FOR GMT

Listen

What do the animals know that we don't?
While we speak over one another
our small tongue-tied human sounds.
We can't hear their night-music:
> Milk white murky sap song
> Beading at the tips of stalks
> Broken by the musky amble
> Of bear, foraging.

The earth wails her own deafening dirge.
Listen, the geese never left this year.
I watch them fly back and forth
across a gunmetal sky,
Their scattered, illegible verse
overwriting the solace of winter rhythm.
Their harsh cry once gathered our hearts
Into the kingdom of the worthy.
But now their voices keen confusion
when we are brave enough
to quiet down and listen to their song.

What do the animals know that we don't?
Here, at the end of the movement,
At this held pause between breaths
When the seasons are not promised
To follow one after another anymore.

¤ *Emily Kedar 2019*

Virginia Maria Romero Art 2012

Mary Walks in Peace

ᚻᚻᚻ Dé Sathairn

♏ ☾ **Saturday**
11

♀☌♅ 3:57 pm
☽☍♅ 6:05 pm
☽☍♀ 6:16 pm

☉☉☉ Dé Domhnaigh

♏ ☾ **Sunday**
♐ **12**

☽□♄ 7:44 am
☽△♆ 8:01 am
☽✶♇ 12:34 pm
☽☍♉ 2:40 pm v/c
☽→♐ 3:31 pm

June
juno

♐

Monday
13

☽△♃ 12:26 am
☿→♊ 8:27 am
☽△♂ 3:05 pm

Sound the Horns: It's Juneteenth!

In 1865, Union soldiers landed in Texas with news the Civil War had ended. During the teens of June, word of mouth spread that the enslaved were now free, *2½ years after* the Emancipation Proclamation. *Finally!* On June 19th we celebrate the end of slavery in the U.S.

© Mother Tongue Ink 2020

♐
♑

Tuesday
14

⊙☍☽ 4:52 am
☽⚹♄ 7:38 am
☽□♆ 7:58 am v/c
☽→♑ 3:14 pm
☽PrG 4:37 pm

Full Moon in ♐ Sagittarius 4:52 am PDT

♑

Wednesday
15

☽□♃ 12:21 am
♂☌♝ 7:17 am
☽□♂ 4:49 pm
☽△♅ 6:10 pm

♑
♒

Thursday
16

⊙△♄ 12:13 am
☽△♀ 2:09 am
⊙□♆ 6:41 am
☽⚹♆ 7:23 am
☽☌♇ 11:41 am v/c
☽→♒ 2:44 pm
☽△♃ 7:30 pm

♒

Friday
17

☽⚹♃ 12:27 am
☽□♅ 6:37 pm
☽⚹♂ 7:35 pm

Redemption

Baptized with twinkling stars in my dark frizzy afro hair. With memories glimmering away in the spaciousness. Thrown back in time to the unknown savanna of a mythical land far far away. *They are coming, they are coming in full force from behind, and there is no escape route in sight!*

Ancestral tribes of wisdom born through pain and separation, forced here on ocean waves. The smell of dehumanization permeating the skies for seven generations. What will it take for us to dream another dream? The soft velvet darkness arising from my deep ancestral spheres soothes

Harriet Powers:
African American Ancestor
© *Toni Truesdale 1997*

my longing for belonging. As I sleep at night, I merge with those who knew that the Earth could never be owned. I recognize light shadows dancing as my Mother, Grandmother, and Great Grandmother. Priestesses just like me.

Visibly, I strain my inherited habits with a tight fist, looking the whiteness straight into the eyes. Dragon roar sisters holding hands with bleeding knuckles forming a circle of no more regrets. Stomping ahead, crawling ahead, dancing in chains, and crying for equality. The freedom, the respect, and the glory that so many of you have enjoyed exclusively for so long is now ours too.

¤ *Victoria Chimey Victoré 2020*

ħħħ sábado

♒︎
♓︎

Saturday
18

☽□♀	7:09 am	♀□ħ	2:32 pm
☽♂ħ	7:47 am	☽→♓︎	4:01 pm
☉△☽	11:50 am v/c	♀⚹♆	9:06 pm

☉☉☉ domingo

♓︎

Sunday
19

☽□☿	1:00 am
☉⚻♇	1:10 am
☽⚹♅	9:50 pm

Summer Solstice

As the sun captures the top of the sky, we crest the day with exuberance, hand ourselves over to the juice, to wild swims, the silken overlap of petal on petal, open faced flowers loved by bees, their centres easy to reach.

Cowled in heat and the verdant smells of grasses at thigh height, our eyes are drawn to the hilltops and skies beyond.

A walk up to Midsummer's summit gives us clear and far sightedness. As a cloud like the shadowy bird of midwinter passes over, we experience the dark side of the sun, remember countries on fire, lands parched, pleasure dependent on what country we belong to—if any. On our way back down, we choose what actions will draw us up to our full height.

Using the magic of Midsummer night, the enchanted song-light through the woods, we build a fire to charge up our potency, weave a garland of prayers with wildflowers and herbs for the next generations of Earth protectors, float it down river watched over by the Sidhe.

Debra Hall © Mother Tongue Ink 2021

Classic Rock
© Serena Supplee
2011

The Shift has Come

We've prayed for change,

drawing pleasure
up our spines
sourced from
earthen wells within

bathing in the bliss
of our own
sexual energy.

We've purged our pain,

doubled over
heaving human breath
back into soil

Solar Café © *Gretchen Butler 1998*

shaking our systems clean
from centuries
of misused power.

Rapping our rattles in remembrance,
drawing song out from each others' shadows,

We've called *in* our sisters, our brothers,
our siblings, our families, our tribe.

We've sung, screamed, sobbed, and sparkled with laughter.

We've waited, we've watched, we've readied ourselves . . .

Now, we walk.

◻ *Anna Ruth Hall 2019*

June
lipanj

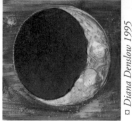

——— ☽☽☽ ponedjeljak ———

♓
♈

Monday
20

☿⚹♃ 12:44 am
☽☌♆ 12:21 pm
☽⚹♀ 4:11 pm
☽⚹♇ 5:01 pm
☉□☽ 8:11 pm v/c
☽→♈ 8:37 pm

New Moon in Cancer

Waning Half Moon in ♓ Pisces 8:11 pm PDT

——— ♂♂♂ utorak ———

♈

Tuesday
21

♀△♇ 1:23 am
☉→♋ 2:14 am
☽☌♃ 8:37 am
☽⚹☿ 11:34 am

Summer Solstice

☉→♋

Sun in ♋ Cancer 2:14 am PDT

——— ☿☿☿ srijeda ———

♈

Wednesday
22

☽☌♂ 11:58 am
♀→♊ 5:34 pm
☽⚹♄ 7:18 pm

——— ♃♃♃ četvrtak ———

♈
♉

Thursday
23

☽□♇ 1:02 am v/c
☽→♉ 4:58 am
☉⚹☽ 9:12 am

——— ♀♀♀ petak ———

♉

Friday
24

☽☌♅ 3:14 pm

___

ALL ASPECTS IN PACIFIC DAYLIGHT TIME; ADD 3 HOURS FOR EDT; ADD 7 HOURS FOR GMT

2022 Year at a Glance for ♋ Cancer (June 21–July 22)

Your relationship with community is in a long process of being shaken up and freed up. It is challenging and remaking how you know and claim your place in the ecosystems around you. The beginning of the year comes in with another round of work—the long healing of Pluto opposing Cancer, digging deep in your personal relationships since 2008. Underworlds have been traversed, cracked foundations exposed, the structures of woundings revealed. It's been a long road and you're not at the end of it, but you will be coming out freer, lighter, more alive. It's not easy to be remade in every way that you love. While you are in this shake-up, listen to your body. The dark will whisper its truths loud enough to be heard. Be with those connections that your body signals an unreserved "yes" to, human or otherwise. Experiment with how you connect with all of life so that you can be fully at home in your own skin, making that the measure of how you are weathering these years of change. It's not about the deeply rooted, established home for you just now, though you may have it, though you may love to seek and make it. What frees you comes from outside your usual sphere; what heals you happens in collaboration; what opens your deep oceans of dreaming is found beyond your own door. You can be tiny, defined by your shell—or you can be the whole ocean.

Maeanna Welti © Mother Tongue Ink 2021

────────── ♄♄♄ subota ──────────

♉
♊ Saturday
25

☽□♄   6:02 am
☽⚹♆   7:05 am
☽△♇ 12:02 pm v/c
☽→♊   4:13 pm

Aura *© Aiyana Adriazola 2019*

────────── ☉☉☉ nedjelja ──────────

♊ Sunday
26

☽☌♀ 12:03 am
☽⚹♃   6:26 am

so i ran into the thighs of the mountain

where rivers rush
and women gathered
i arrived
scattered and hungry
starving for that woman
screaming her name
at the top of my lungs
that wild woman in me
caught in the wind
who knows me
who can hold me
solid and strong
who is not afraid to be broken
for she knows to lick her wounds
and stitch them
with branches and earth
the one who wakes me at night
her yearnings raging in my chest
noxious from too much comfort
she runs outside the door naked
to be drenched in spirit
her body soaked in moonlight
to be struck by lightning
the one who lays her body
down on the earth
and holds her tight
until she feels her pulse
the one who
would trade her name
and her whole story
for one single piece

of visceral truth
the one whose mother tongue
is the great felt silence of spirit
i called for she
who hears the mountains
whisper back to her
when she sings for them
tracking her steps
in my intuitions
following her
luscious trails
she who knows the home
that was made for her
she who finds her mother's nipple
in the berry bushes
in the sweet water stream
in the wild beehive
the one who allows
the earth to love her
to move her body
like she means it
the way her secrets are told
she who dances with the sky
in fierce ecstasy
surrenders her destiny
to the greater order
weaving miracles inside her
the one who loves herself
like she loves the river
for she knows they were
from the same mother.

VII. WILD WOMAN

Moon VII: June 28–July 28

New Moon in ♋ Cancer June 28; Full Moon in ♑ Capricorn July 13; Sun in ♌ Leo July 22

The Call of the River © *Autumn Skye 2013*

June / July
Joishtho / Asharh

───── ☽☽☽ sombar ─────────────────────

♊ Monday
27

☽☌☿ 12:22 am
☿✳⚷ 4:46 am
♂✳♄ 3:28 pm
☽△♄ 6:23 pm
☽✳♂ 6:35 pm
☽□♅ 7:38 pm v/c

───── ♂♂♂ mongolbar ─────────────────

♊
♋ Tuesday
28

♆R 12:55 am
☽→♋ 4:53 am
☉□♃ 5:59 pm
☽□♃ 7:44 pm
☉☌☽ 7:52 pm
♀✳♃ 8:51 pm
☽ApG 11:10 pm

───── ☿☿☿ budhbar ─────────────────
                                    New Moon in ♋ Cancer 7:52 pm PDT

♋ Wednesday
29

☽✳♅ 4:48 pm

───── ♃♃♃ brihospotibar ─────────────

♋
♌ Thursday
30

☽△♆ 8:27 am
☽□♂ 11:16 am
☽☍♇ 1:14 pm v/c
☽→♌ 5:39 pm

───── ♀♀♀ sukrobar ─────────────────

♌ Friday   July
1

☽△♃ 8:49 am
☽✳♀ 2:59 pm
♂□♇ 7:13 pm

───────────────────────────────────

ALL ASPECTS IN PACIFIC DAYLIGHT TIME; ADD 3 HOURS FOR EDT; ADD 7 HOURS FOR GMT

Nyx

Born was I of great Chaos
(who also spawned Love).
My darkness disrupts
your sun's tiresome routine.

I come from disorder,
so disorder each day.
My shadow precedes me,
casts your noon into twilight.

The sky used to fill
with my beating black wings
dimming pale moonlight.
A witch you then called me—
a frightening sight.

**Incan Dragon Goddess
Mama Pacha**
¤ *Anna Lindberg 2016*

Now I ride a black motorcycle
down the setting sun's rays.
The moon's my silver helmet.
Star-garlands whip in my hair,
comets cruise in my sidecar.

Your time calls me Night—
but Nyx is the name that's right.

© *Lorraine Schein 2015*

ꜩꜩꜩ sonibar

♌

Saturday
2

☿△♄   3:39 am
☽□♅   5:22 am
☿□♆   1:52 pm
☽⚸♄   6:54 pm
☽✳☿   9:43 pm

◉◉◉ robibar

♌
♍

Sunday
3

☽△♂   2:59 am v/c
☽→♍   5:31 am
☿⊼♇   7:13 pm

July
Mí Iúil

My Voice
The ragged beauty of truth
will shine through,
making a stand in wild flame.
Soaring. Claiming space in
the atmosphere of everything.
excerpt © Caroline Miskenack 2019

—————— ☽☽☽ Dé Luain ——————

 ♍

Monday
4

☉✶☽ 6:03 am
☽□♀ 8:37 am
☽△♅ 4:23 pm
♂→♉ 11:04 am
☿→♋ 11:25 am
☿✶♂ 11:37 pm

—————— ♂♂♂ Dé Máirt ——————

♍
♎

Tuesday
5

☽☌♆ 6:46 am
☽△♇ 11:03 am v/c
☽→♎ 3:25 pm
☽□☿ 6:20 pm

—————— ☿☿☿ Dé Céadaoin ——————

 ♎

Wednesday
6

☽☌♃ 6:13 am
♀✶♇ 10:17 am
☉□☽ 7:14 pm
☽△♀ 10:54 pm

—————— ♃♃♃ Dé Ardaoin ——————

Waxing Half Moon in ♎ Libra 7:14 pm PDT

 ♎
♏

Thursday
7

☽△♄ 12:17 pm
☽□♇ 6:04 pm v/c
☽→♏ 10:15 pm

—————— ♀♀♀ Dé Haoine ——————

♏

Friday
8

☽☌♂ 2:06 am
☉□♃ 6:22 am
☽△☿ 10:31 am
☿□♃ 11:14 pm

ALL ASPECTS IN PACIFIC DAYLIGHT TIME; ADD 3 HOURS FOR EDT; ADD 7 HOURS FOR GMT

Japanese Goddess of Fire—Kamui Fuchi
□ *Anna Lindberg 2020*

ᚺᚺᚺ Dé Sathairn

♏ ☽ **Saturday**
9

☉△☽ 4:10 am
☽⚹♅ 5:34 am
☽□♄ 4:04 pm
☽△♆ 5:55 pm
☽⚹♇ 9:34 pm v/c

◉◉◉ Dé Domhnaigh

♏ ☾ **Sunday**
♐ **10**

☽→♐ 1:34 am
☉⚹♅ 1:39 am
☽△♃ 3:02 pm

July
julio

———— ☽☽☽ lunes ————

Monday
11

☽☌♀	2:11 pm
☽⚹♄	4:48 pm
☽□♆	6:42 pm v/c

Blueberry Moon

———— ♂♂♂ martes ————

Tuesday
12

☽→♑	2:01 am
☽△♂	10:12 am
☽□♃	3:07 pm
☿□♅	9:08 pm
♀△♄	9:27 pm

———— ☿☿☿ miércoles ————

Wednesday
13

☽PrG	2:01 am	☿⚹♅	5:17 pm
☽☌♅	4:58 am	☽⚹♆	5:57 pm
☽△♅	6:41 am	☽☌♇	9:17 pm v/c
☉☌☽	11:37 am	♀□♆	10:24 pm

Full Moon in ♑ Capricorn 11:37 am PDT

———— ♃♃♃ jueves ————

Thursday
14

☽→♒	1:13 am
☽□♂	11:38 am
☽⚹♃	2:30 pm

———— ♀♀♀ viernes ————

Friday
15

☽□♅	6:16 am
☽☌♄	3:27 pm
♀⚼♇	3:51 pm
☽△♀	9:36 pm v/c

ALL ASPECTS IN PACIFIC DAYLIGHT TIME; ADD 3 HOURS FOR EDT; ADD 7 HOURS FOR GMT

Howl

Something in you is changed,
Something wild and right:
The part of you that is animal shines
Out wetly
in the dew tonight.
You howl
and drink the midnight sap
held holy, up, in ancient laps
of ash and elm
and dewy realms
you rise and sink in cold and inky moon glow
you call out in a voice that only Crow knows.
You unfold your head and dance,
entranced with your own shadows.

© Emily Kell 2017

Watching (As the World Burns) *© Rachel Cruse 2019*

ħħħ sábado

♒︎
♓︎

Saturday
16

☽→♓︎	1:18 am
☉⊼♄	4:34 am
☿⊼♄	8:55 am
☉♂♉	12:38 pm
☽✶♂	2:37 pm

☉☉☉ domingo

♓︎

Sunday
17

☿△♆	12:52 am	☽♂♆	8:07 pm
♇PrH	6:03 am	☉△☽	8:25 pm
☽✶♅	8:01 am	☽△☿	11:39 pm
☉△♆	3:55 pm	☽✶♇	11:43 pm v/c
♀→♋︎	6:32 pm		

July
srpanj

──── ☽☽☽ ponedjeljak ────

♓   ## Monday
♈   ## 18

☿☍♇ 12:01 am
☽→♈   4:17 am
☽☐♀   5:14 am
☽☌♃   7:34 pm

Midnight © *Kym Stine 2013*

──── ♂♂♂ utorak ────

♈   ## Tuesday
            ## 19

☿ApH 2:36 am
☿→♌   5:35 am
♄R   6:26 am
☉☍♇   6:38 pm
☽⚹♄ 11:28 pm

──── ☿☿☿ srijeda ────

♈   ## Wednesday
♉   ## 20

☽☐♇   6:20 am
☉☐☽   7:19 am v/c
☽→♉ 11:23 am
☽☐♅   5:19 pm
☽⚹♀   6:17 pm

Waning Half Moon in ♈ Aries 7:19 am PDT

──── ♃♃♃ četvrtak ────

♉   ## Thursday
            ## 21

☽☌♂   9:06 am
☽☌♅ 11:14 pm

──── ♀♀♀ petak ────

♉   ## Friday
♊   ## 22

☽☐♄   9:18 am
☽⚹♆ 12:45 pm
☉→♌   1:07 pm
☽△♇   4:45 pm v/c
☽→♊ 10:11 pm
☉⚹☽ 10:58 pm

☉→♌

Sun in ♌ Leo 1:07 pm PDT

ALL ASPECTS IN PACIFIC DAYLIGHT TIME; ADD 3 HOURS FOR EDT; ADD 7 HOURS FOR GMT

2022 Year at a Glance for ♌ Leo (July 22–Aug 22)

Anything is possible with boldness, diligence, humility and joy. This year invites and awakens all of this for you. If you will embrace that which whispers up from the depths, allow it its full weight, and enrich it with your playfulness, you will be able to bring an honesty and aliveness to the day-to-day work of healing. The beginning and end of the year are both pressure cookers for how we bring our healing and our fight for freedom into a livable, joyfully sustainable reality. The planets are asking you to mind the details: notice how the routines you live, the mechanics of your days, the rhythms you keep, all affect your capacity and willingness for true transformation. The sum of these elements make up your health. The last few years have revealed your limits. This is valuable information. We can grow and work more freely and fully when we work within them. The possibilities for career growth and abundance in your public roles are huge, but need to respect your limits and the truths of your body. You need room to express your real, bravely honest emotional realities—save space for joy. Without doing the work in the day to day and in your most intimate relationships, you will get stretched thin, pulled out of yourself, and compromise the authenticity of what you offer the world. Feed your radiance from the inside. Give it rich, dark soil to grow from, and don't ask it for more than it truly wants to give.

Maeanna Welti © Mother Tongue Ink 2021

ℏℏℏ subota

  ## Saturday
23

☿△♃ 10:52 am
☽⚹♃ 3:38 pm
☽⚹☿ 4:36 pm

© Sue Ellen Parkinson 2020

The Star Catcher

⊙⊙⊙ nedjelja

 ## Sunday
24

☽△♄ 9:27 pm
♀□♃ 11:13 pm

July
Asharh

Shauna Crandall 2018

Gold Coast

♊
♋

Monday
25

☽□♅ 1:14 am v/c
☽→♋ 10:54 am

♋

Tuesday
26

☽ApG 3:22 am
☽□♃ 4:35 am
☽♂♀ 7:54 am
☿□♂ 12:13 pm
☽✶♂ 4:57 pm

♋
♌

Wednesday
27

☽✶♅ 12:36 am
☿△♄ 9:55 am
☽△♆ 1:58 pm
☽☍♇ 5:54 pm v/c
☽→♌ 11:36 pm

♌

Thursday
28

☉♂☽ 10:55 am
♃R 1:37 pm
☿□♅ 2:16 pm
☽△♃ 5:03 pm

New Moon in ♌ Leo 10:55 am PDT

♌

Friday
29

☽□♂ 8:38 am
☽□♅ 12:48 pm
☽♂♅ 4:49 pm
☽☍♄ 9:29 pm v/c

ALL ASPECTS IN PACIFIC DAYLIGHT TIME; ADD 3 HOURS FOR EDT; ADD 7 HOURS FOR GMT

Mudpearl

I had believed
If I was to become a pearl I would no longer be messy

I had believed if I tamed my imperfections
I would be loved

I had believed my wildness would strip me of my dignity

Now I see that without my wildness, imperfections and mess
I could not be part of humanity.

I am the swirl of night becoming herself in the first kiss of dusk

I am night
Before she is confident
of her blackness

I am becoming
the dark rapture
From where
everything is born
Pure
Alight
imPerfect
Messy
and Wild

© Catja Wilson 2020

Sooner or Later the Sand Gets In
© Rachel Cruse 2014

ᚻᚻᚻ sonibar

♌
♍

Saturday
30

☽→♍ 11:10 am
♉♂♄ 11:05 pm

⊙⊙⊙ robibar

♍

Sunday
31

♀□♅ 7:04 am
⊙△♃ 3:36 pm
☽⚹♀ 8:19 pm
☽△♂ 10:35 pm
☽△♅ 11:30 pm

My Body is a Calendar in the Dark

I would go as a child, from the bright lights of the Bronx into the dark unlit mountain roads of San Sebastian, Puerto Rico *y en ese oscuro inescapable*, find home, find *refugio*, find love.

It was a return to geography built from my matrilineal line of bodies; mountains and mountain women, weathered by storms but unbroken, with names that hung like constellations in my mouth: Edelmira, Gloria, Mercedes, Quintina, Estrella, Nemesia, Lisette, Carmen, Sonia, Lala, Monsa, Carmela, Minerva, Viña, Carmita, Norma, Esperanza, Constancia, Lourdes, Tita, Fela, Juana la India.

Bodies with cyclical bleeding that taught us to begin the counting of days, weeks, months and seasons, which became years, which became science. Bodies that translated the moon.

Night in San Sebastian required new vision—what lights they had would often go out. My great-grandmother, Abuela Quintina, would go out into *la oscuridad* from her wooden porch, machete in hand. I would hang back, afraid.

She would pull me out, "*No seas tan cobarde.*" Admonishing me for being cowardly, she taught me to look fearlessly into the night sky, into the mountains shrouded in *sombras*, till they became paths I could follow.

Pervasive dark became a land of discovering. She would point at *murcielagos* or the stars y *la luna, siempre, la luna.* "*Mira la hija, mira la, que bella, es tuya.*"

I follow a truth *mis antepasadas* hid inside of me like a tiny heirloom seed, so that it might survive and someday, under the right conditions, bloom again with the proper care.

Under the dark moon, I look into the night sky. My body is a calendar in the dark. I bloom, mark time, bleed with pride, over the voices of my beloved female lineage saying things like, "*No diga eso muchacha que esas cosas no se hablan delante la gente.*" Words that had been handed to them like a death sentence, a calendar marking only loss. My body now marks the full calendar of days and nights, free. Born of the tiny seed with no name they planted in my pockets.

VIII. HERITAGE

Moon VIII: July 28–August 27

New Moon in ♌ Leo July 28; Full Moon in ♒ Aquarius August 11; Sun in ♍ Virgo August 22

Song of Sophia © Shiloh Sophia McCloud 2019

August
Mí Lúnasa

The Offering

© Marla Faith 2006

---------- ⟩⟩⟩ Dé Luain ----------

 ♍
♎

Monday
1

☿⊼♆ 4:23 am
☽☍♄ 11:50 am
☽△♇ 3:29 pm v/c
♂♂♅ 4:53 pm
☽→♎ 9:05 pm

---------- ♂♂♂ Dé Máirt ----------

 ♎

Tuesday
2

Lammas / Lughnasad

♀✶♅ 5:25 am
☿⊼♇ 6:24 am
☽☍♃ 1:27 pm
☉✶☽ 5:12 pm
♀✶♂ 7:00 pm

---------- ☿☿☿ Dé Céadaoin ----------

♎

Wednesday
3

☽□♀ 10:54 am
☽△♄ 3:28 pm
☽□♇ 11:19 pm v/c
☿→♍ 11:58 pm

---------- ♃♃♃ Dé Ardaoin ----------

 ♎
♏

Thursday
4

☽→♏ 4:47 am
☽✶☿ 5:29 am

---------- ♀♀♀ Dé Haoine ----------

♏

Friday
5

☉□☽ 4:06 am
♀⊼♄ 9:23 am
☽☍♅ 2:13 pm
☽☍♂ 6:38 pm
☽□♄ 8:46 pm
☽△♀ 9:56 pm

Waxing Half Moon in ♏ Scorpio 4:06 am PDT

ALL ASPECTS IN PACIFIC DAYLIGHT TIME; ADD 3 HOURS FOR EDT; ADD 7 HOURS FOR GMT

Lammas

With the afterglow of late summer purring in our bodies and the land, the days are lulled and languorous. The communities of trees are hanging heavy canopies as their life force is directed into the berries, fruits, nuts and seeds. The mellifluous hum of the nectar gatherers, wasps and worker bees fills the air with their sybaritic symphony.

The moon is low and orange over the fields, the first fruits of our labours ripe enough to be eased from the branch and baked into a harvest loaf.

A change in the evening air signals that the halcyon days are ending. It heightens our awareness that only a small percentage of the world have cornucopias of surplus.

Summoning the medicine of dragonfly who can jump tracks, adapt with lightning ease, fly backwards and forwards into the past and future, we initiate deep wisdom circles to welcome indigenous wisdom already known. Doughnut and gift economies to close the global poverty gap and share this Love-fest from the earth, who could feed us all, mouth on mouth.

Debra Hall © Mother Tongue Ink 2021

Seed Savers © *Leah Marie Dorion 2017*

Goddesses

Deep in the rippled, rain-soaked night
dawn chokes the treetops
while holy ones speak their names
Withered winter goddesses
unafraid on the coolest night of summer
Names my great-great-grandmother's
mother's mother's mother's mother's mothers
uttered quietly:

Skadhi   Cailleach   Perchta

Gliding hunters
    Water splashers
        Thread spinners
            Stone throwers
                Pine weavers

Prancers at once young and spry, old and crumbling
shoving broken leaves, wool and dry berries
deep in their pockets like the voices of the dead in a dream

They stop me, step around
mundane thoughts
by the mirror and
frame for me the new maps they scrawl
with the crow's feet
printed careful as a queen's seal
around my eyes

© Chantel Camille Roice 2020

Feels Like Home
© Sue Tyler Design 2018

Trust © *Barbara Largent 2020*

♏︎
♐︎

Saturday
6

☽△♆ 1:08 am
☽⚹♇ 4:24 am v/c
☽→♐︎ 9:38 am
☽□♅ 5:18 pm

♐︎

Sunday
7

☽△♃ 12:12 am
♀△♆ 9:43 am
☉△☽ 11:21 am
♂□♄ 12:57 pm
☽⚹♄ 11:11 pm

August
agosto

─── ⊳⊳⊳ lunes ───

♐
♑

Monday
8

☽□♇ 3:30 am v/c
☽→♑ 11:39 am
☉△⚸ 1:01 pm
♀☌♇ 10:18 pm

New Moon Ritual
With palm to heart and heart to palm,
a sacred web is woven,
Native, Spirit, Ancestor,
each is called to bless the coven.
Goddess, Crone, Mother, Sister,
all present in the dark unknown.
excerpt □ Deneene Bell 2020

─── ♂♂♂ martes ───

♑

Tuesday
9

☽△☿ 12:51 am
☽□♃ 1:24 am
☿⊼♃ 6:06 am
☽△♅ 5:58 am

─── ☿☿☿ miércoles ───

♑
♒

Wednesday
10

☽△♂ 2:12 am
☽⚹♆ 3:45 am
☽☌♇ 6:45 am
☽☍♀ 9:39 am v/c
☽PrG 10:15 am
☽→♒ 11:45 am

─── ♃♃♃ jueves ───

♒

Thursday
11

☽⚹♃ 1:08 am
☉□♅ 5:53 am
♀→♌ 11:30 am
♂⚹♆ 2:44 pm
☽□♅ 5:47 pm
☉☍☽ 6:36 pm
☽☌♄ 10:58 pm

Lunar Lammas

Full Moon in ♒ Aquarius 6:36 pm PDT

─── ♀♀♀ viernes ───

♒
♓

Friday
12

☽□♂ 4:07 am v/c
☽→♓ 11:44 am

─────────────────────────

ALL ASPECTS IN PACIFIC DAYLIGHT TIME; ADD 3 HOURS FOR EDT; ADD 7 HOURS FOR GMT

Where We Talked of Witches

When We Meet—Evening
© KT InfiniteArt 2019

Witches
gathered quietly in
morning light
listening to our
clear questions
about the magic
they had cast
and kept
from being silenced.
Splendid ghosts, sacred ghosts,
they hovered over our lips and pens
as we voiced and then set to page guesses, memories,
wisdoms, prayers
inspired by a black cat reading a solemn book of spells. How
can a room of women create such power it changes a world?
We looked to them, their confidence
in hearts healing history's wrong.
Quietly they sang to us, their circle our circle of widening words:
survival
the call for souls' embrace, firm mouths proclaiming:
strong.

© Katharyn Howd Machan 2020

ᎭᎭᎭ sábado

♓ ◗ Saturday
13

☽☌♉ 12:02 pm
☽⚹♅ 6:49 pm

☉☉☉ domingo

♓
♈ ◗ Sunday
14

☽☌♆ 4:58 am   ☽→♈ 1:43 pm
☽⚹♂ 7:53 am   ♂△♇ 2:28 pm
☽⚹♇ 8:11 am v/c ♄PrH 2:45 pm
☉☌♄ 10:10 am   ☽△♀ 8:53 pm
☿☌♃ 10:41 am

August
kolovoz

— ☽☽☽ ponedjeljak —

♈

Monday

15

☽☌♃ 3:59 am

— ♂♂♂ utorak —

♈
♉

Tuesday

16

☽⚹♄   4:14 am
☉△☽   7:48 am
☿△♅ 10:46 am
☽□♇   1:18 pm v/c
☽→♉   7:22 pm

— ☿☿☿ srijeda —

♉

Wednesday

17

☽□♀   8:54 am
☉⚻♆ 10:57 am

— ♃♃♃ četvrtak —

♉

Thursday

18

♀△♃   1:03 am   ☽△♅ 12:37 pm
☽☌♅   7:20 am   ☽⚹♆   6:49 pm
☿⚻♄ 12:06 pm   ☉□☽   9:36 pm
☽□♄ 12:34 pm   ☽△♇ 10:32 pm

Waning Half Moon in ♉ Taurus 9:36 pm PDT

— ♀♀♀ petak —

♉
♊

Friday

19

☽☌♂   4:05 am v/c
☽→♊   5:06 am
☉⚻♇   9:09 am
☽⚹♃   8:52 pm

Inheritance

My ancestors knew
the whirl
of the cyclone
the writhing,
twisting force
the threat
of swirling knots

They knew
how to dwell
in the eye
the arc of stillness

Trials and Tribulations
© KoCo Collab 2019

They knew the briny tangles would smooth to billowy ribbons
They knew how to ride them, gliding to another shore.

◻ *Sheryl J. Shapiro 2020*

───────── ħħħ subota ─────────

♊

Saturday
20

♂→♊ 12:56 am
☽✶♀ 2:08 am

───────── ☉☉☉ nedjelja ─────────

♊
♋

Sunday
21

☽△♄ 12:03 am
♅☍♆ 12:40 am
☽☐♆ 6:46 am

☽☐♅ 7:28 am
☉✶☽ 3:06 pm v/c
☽→♋ 5:29 pm

August
Srabon

♋ Monday
22

☽□♃ 9:10 am
☽ApG 2:58 pm
☿△♇ 2:58 pm
☉→♍ 8:16 pm

☉→♍

Sun in ♍ Virgo 8:16 pm PDT

♋ Tuesday
23

☽⚹♅ 7:51 am
☽△♆ 7:26 pm
☽☍♇ 11:17 pm

♋
♌ Wednesday
24

☽⚹☿ 2:40 am v/c
☽→♌ 6:09 am
♅R 6:53 am
♀△♃ 10:31 am
☽⚹♂ 11:16 am
☽△♃ 9:10 pm

♌ Thursday
25

☽☌♀ 4:50 pm
☿→♎ 6:03 pm
☽□♅ 7:44 pm
☽☍♄ 11:55 pm v/c

♌
♍ Friday
26

☽→♍ 5:25 pm
♀□♅ 9:33 pm
☉□♂ 10:27 pm

ALL ASPECTS IN PACIFIC DAYLIGHT TIME; ADD 3 HOURS FOR EDT; ADD 7 HOURS FOR GMT

2022 Year at a Glance for ♍ Virgo (Aug. 22–Sept. 22)

Creativity has been the key to your healing. Your creativity has needed healing. You are hopefully realizing the wealth of your own joy, your own playfulness, hopefully discovering its sacredness even as you continue to root out what has blocked it. You have been working on this for years, and it's time to make sure every tendril of barrier is excavated. Keep playing about the things that are most serious. Keep creating, whether you consider yourself a "creative" or not. Start this year by letting your creativity support you in another round of calling up the deep heals. This year will be about both revolutionizing and stabilizing your routines. They can be wildly different and unique as long as they serve you well. You know your own rhythms and health best. Build your life accordingly. You may experience times when the consequences of unhealthy routines are amplified. This is a call for a creative, wing-nutty strictness. Be as diligent about what sets you free as other people are about tracking their finances. Your personal relationships have a dreamy quality about them that may be a balm for you, but it's also possible to get lost in a series of fantastical mirages instead of seeing clearly with the eyes of love. In March this dreaminess may amplify, while late summer could expose illusions with friction and dissonance. Compassion is not boundaryless, and clarity is not about score-keeping. You can soften into reality with love and still hold your form.

Maeanna Welti © Mother Tongue Ink 2021

art © Paula Franco 2018

ᚻᚻᚻ sonibar

♍

Saturday
27

☽□♂ 1:11 am
☉♂☽ 1:17 am

New Moon in ♍ Virgo 1:17 am PDT

☉☉☉ robibar

♍

Sunday
28

☽△♅ 5:47 am
♀♂♄ 11:27 am
☽♂♇ 4:27 pm
☽△♇ 8:08 pm v/c

Into Kali's Cauldron

Will the record show that we signed up for this gig?
That we willingly climbed into Kali's cauldron?
Or were we pushed?
Drawn? Coaxed? Pulled? Hoodwinked?
Suddenly submerged in Kali's chaos and impenetrable darkness
Though, truth be told, it was a gradual accumulation
One jaw-drop calamity, one soul-shuddering catastrophe after another
Striving to trust this disruption, this upside-down world challenge
To test our mettle, to burn away the well-worn comfortable parts
Our rationalizations, our excuses, our flaking expendable shell
Our eyes have been torn from their sockets
Lost in black holes of irretrievable darkness
Fighting the temptation to just surrender to Hypnos' honeyed sleep
We rally our resources:
Hands reach out to mold the overwhelming night into spark
Ears strain to glimpse tones that might fire
Noses inhale deeply to detect scents of hidden light
Tongues probe the void to discern the taste of a preternatural dawn
Our instincts on high alert, Intuition steps up to the microphone:
Trust. Kali's rollercoaster tour of Hell?
An improbably charitable blessing. Really. Truly.
A Tunnel of Love journey from which we will emerge
Scathed, yes.
But wiser, stronger, clear-eyed and ready, finally,
To do the work that must be done.

¤ *Shelley Blooms 2020*

Ceridwin's Cauldron
© *Margaret Lynn Brown 2017*

IX. RISE & RESIST

Moon IX: August 27–September 25

New Moon in ♍ Virgo August 27; Full Moon in ♓ Pisces Sept. 10; Sun in ♎ Libra Sept. 22

Moon Ease
© Corinne "Bee Bop" Trujillo 2019

August / September

Srabon / Bhadro

Say Her Name

We repeat names to give them power
We say names to give us strength
Voicing their names
transforms grief to ancestor
victim to spirit guide

excerpt © Robin D. Bruce 2020

────── ☽☽☽ Dé Luain ──────

Monday
29

☽→♎ 2:45 am
☽☌♉ 9:10 am
☽△♂ 12:50 pm
☽☍♃ 4:00 pm

────── ♂♂♂ Dé Máirt ──────

Tuesday
30

☉☌♃ 3:09 am
☽△♄ 5:13 pm
☽✶♀ 11:07 pm

────── ☿☿☿ Dé Céadaoin ──────

Wednesday
31

☽□♇ 3:43 am v/c
♀☌♆ 9:36 am
☽→♏ 10:11 am

────── ♃♃♃ Dé Ardaoin ──────

Thursday
1

September

☉✶☽ 2:19 am
♂✶♃ 4:52 am
☽☍♅ 8:06 pm
☽□♄ 11:02 pm
♀☌♇ 11:33 pm

────── ♀♀♀ Dé Haoine ──────

Friday
2

☽△♆ 5:52 am
☽✶♇ 9:22 am
☽□♀ 10:22 am v/c
☽→♐ 3:39 pm
☿☍♃ 6:49 pm

What Was Lost Was Gained © Zena Carlota 2015

ᚾᚾᚾ Dé Sathairn

Saturday
3

☽△♃	3:10 am
☽⚹♉	3:37 am
☽☍♂	5:23 am
☉□☽	11:08 am

⊙⊙⊙ Dé Domhnaigh ——— Waxing Half Moon in ♐ Sagittarius 11:08 am PDT

Sunday
4

☽⚹♄	2:49 am
☽□♆	9:32 am
☽△♀	6:51 pm v/c
☽→♑	7:02 pm
♀→♍	9:05 pm

September
septiembre

♑
Monday
5

☽□♃ 5:44 am
☽□♅ 8:21 am
☉△☽ 5:25 pm

♑
≈
Tuesday
6

☽△♅ 2:23 am
☽✶♆ 11:21 am
☽♂♇ 2:43 pm v/c
☽→≈ 8:41 pm

≈
Wednesday
7

☽✶♃ 6:45 am
☽△♅ 10:48 am
☽PrG 11:24 am
☽△♂ 1:13 pm
☉⊼♟ 6:39 pm

≈
♓
Thursday
8

☽□♅ 3:25 am
☽♂♄ 5:33 am v/c
☽→♓ 9:42 pm

♓
Friday
9

☽☍♀ 6:39 am
♀⊼♃ 3:06 pm
☽□♂ 4:08 pm
☿R 8:38 pm

ALL ASPECTS IN PACIFIC DAYLIGHT TIME; ADD 3 HOURS FOR EDT; ADD 7 HOURS FOR GMT

I Hear Her Singing

waiting on hold for unemployment
standing in line for food
she hums

counting change for medicine
protesting for reparations
she thrums

in the refugees' tent city
in the migrants' detention camp
one step away from police tape
her voice whirs and stirs

at the grave of her child
at the judge's bench
she vibrates at light speed

in places meant to reduce
her voice throbs and drones
if only deep inside her
rising like a bee bent for pollen
never out of sight of her Queen.

Night Flight ¤ *Cici Artemisia 2015*

¤ *Stephanie A. Sellers 2020*

ᚻᚻᚻ sábado

<table>
<tr><td>♓
♈</td><td>○</td><td>Saturday
10</td></tr>
</table>

☉☌☽ 2:59 am
☽⚹♅ 4:51 am
☽☌♆ 1:55 pm
☽⚹♇ 5:29 pm v/c
☽→♈ 11:47 pm

⊙⊙⊙ domingo

Full Moon in ♓ Pisces 2:59 am PDT

<table>
<tr><td>♈</td><td>○</td><td>Sunday
11</td></tr>
</table>

☉△♅ 6:09 am
☽☌♃ 9:30 am
☽☍♀ 2:52 pm
☽⚹♂ 8:56 pm

September
listopad / rujan

— ☽☽☽ ponedjeljak —

♈

Monday
12

☉⚼♄ 9:09 am
☽✶♄ 10:25 am
☽□♇ 9:53 pm v/c

White Hawk

© Amber Torrey 2020

— ♂♂♂ utorak —

♈
♉

Tuesday
13

☽→♉ 4:39 am

— ☿☿☿ srijeda —

♉

Wednesday
14

☽△♀ 1:41 am
☽☌♅ 3:34 pm
☽□♄ 5:29 pm
☉△☽ 10:31 pm

— ♃♃♃ četvrtak —

♉
♊

Thursday
15

☽✶♆ 1:47 am
☽△♇ 5:59 am v/c
☽→♊ 1:16 pm
♆PrH 7:30 pm
☽✶♃ 11:13 pm

— ♀♀♀ petak —

♊

Friday
16

☽△♅ 2:36 am
♀□♂ 11:49 am
☉☍♆ 3:21 pm
☽☌♂ 5:52 pm
☽□♀ 6:18 pm

ALL ASPECTS IN PACIFIC DAYLIGHT TIME; ADD 3 HOURS FOR EDT; ADD 7 HOURS FOR GMT

Corn Harvest
© *Dorrie Joy 2018*

Return to the Medicine Wheel

We are bones they sought to break and bury.
    the seeds that rose instead
How our ancestors cried for us, huddled in
    the medicine wheel, wailing as one,
        swaying with the winds of change
The polluted air, the poisoned blankets
    aimed at eradicating our brown
        our muscled bodies
We returned to the wheel to tell the story of
    their survival, through forage and fear,
        by covering up, by binding our bodies
           (raped   loved   sacrificed) to the color
            of privilege and power   reaching a
              hand back in the darkest night
            to say, *You too, come.*
      There is a way forward . . .   © *Xelena González 2020*

ħħħ subota

♊ Saturday
17

♀⊼♄ 12:24 am
☽△♄ 4:04 am
☽□Ψ 12:53 pm
☉□☽ 2:52 pm v/c
♂⚹♇ 8:54 pm

☉☉☉ nedjelja

Waning Half Moon in ♊ Gemini 2:52 pm PDT

♊
♋ Sunday
18

☽→♋ 12:59 am
☽□♃ 10:38 am
☽□♀ 10:56 am
♅☍♃ 3:34 pm
☉△♇ 8:58 pm

Fall Equinox

With a bouquet of decaying fungi schmiegeled in her hands like the bride of rot, the natural year breathes out.

We stand in the centre of the double spiral, a fulsome pause to orient our bodies to the slow rhythms of darkness and quietude. Like all transitions it can be a turbulent tussle with a strong emotional undertow.

Nature, our favourite village auntie, consoles us with caches of light and beauty for us to find like squirrel unearthing her nuts in the windy sunshine.

Beneath the ground mycelium thread through the leaf litter. Even if you haven't done everything you wanted to, your body at death will be a tasty smorgasbord of nutrients for the Earth they murmur. Death is also home, whispers stillness like a newly discovered place.

In the gloaming gnarled trees are hoary medicine women casting shadows onto their crochet hooks, knitting our Autumn color-lust into woolly warmth. They inspire us to create new stories with girth as we press apples, dry our herbs, root ourselves again and again in hope.

Debra Hall © Mother Tongue Ink 2021

Komorebi © Nora Bruhn 2020

Decay © Lindsay Carron 2016

Thanking Goodness

My mother taught me to, literally, *thank goodness:* write thank you notes to the host of the dinner party, return cookie tins full, look directly at aunts and uncles and acknowledge their birthday gifts.

I am the fruiting body of a vast mycelium of generosity: life feeding life; a hungry guest at life's opulent dinner party, eating my fill of cookies. Each birthday, I have been the recipient of another year's worth of life's spectacular presence. How can I say thank you to microbes in soil, plants that offer body, breath and beauty, animal sustenance and companionship, water always passing through, soothing, smoothing, the branching human tree: friends, lovers, family, ancestral roots, and blossoming generations to come, firelight, sunlight, starlight, the moon!—that patient teacher of empty and full, the beautiful, ineffable pulsing in it all. Could death really be gratitude?

Ready or not, when it comes, let me lay my good body on the good earth and in nature's perfect language gratefully feed what feeds me.

© Sophia Rosenberg 2019

September

 Bhadro

In lacuna, the space in between,
we weave voices and visions
into dreams of new possibilities
for ourselves, for our communities,
for our world—
and we prepare to rise anew.
excerpt © Kay Marie Porterfield 2020

─── ⟩⟩⟩ sombar ───

 ♋

Monday
19

⟩ApG	7:46 am
⟩⚹♀	1:53 pm
⟩⚹♅	2:43 pm
♀△♅	9:44 pm

─── ♂♂♂ mongolbar ───

♋
♌

Tuesday
20

⟩△♆	1:25 am	⟩→♌	1:37 pm
⟩☍♇	5:58 am	☿PrH	4:05 pm
☉⚹⟩	8:57 am v/c	⟩⚹♉	6:52 pm
♀⊼♄	1:11 pm	⟩△♃	10:32 pm

─── ☿☿☿ budhbar ───

♌

Wednesday
21

⟩⚹♂	11:00 pm

─── ♃♃♃ brihospotibar ───

♌

Thursday
22

Fall Equinox

⟩☐♅	2:36 am
⟩☍♄	4:07 am v/c
☉→♎	6:04 pm
☉♂♉	11:50 pm

☉→♎

Sun in ♎ Libra 6:04 pm PDT

─── ♀♀♀ sukrobar ───

♌
♍

Friday
23

⟩→♍	12:53 am
☿→♍	5:04 am

2022 Year at a Glance for ♎ Libra (Sept. 22–Oct. 23)

I hope you're not tired of digging deep. Or that if you are, you're letting yourself be resourced, giving yourself the grace of surrender, letting your body pace you just right, building magic into every routine. No big deal, you're just in the final stretch of a years-long marathon of healing your roots. This hasn't been an easy run. Pluto in Capricorn has been challenging you for 14 years, meeting you with sternness, referring you back to your own resources every time you look for someone's hand to hold, forcing you to keep your eyes on your own plate. 2022 gives you time to review and integrate, but with the added pressure and support of Uranus remaking how you do emotional honesty, intimacy, sex, and facing the scary stuff. Your connection with others doesn't go away just because Pluto tells you to do you. There is potential for a wild freedom in how deeply you can connect if you diligently attend to your creativity and self-expression—celebrate yourself like it's your job. You can be free of every lie you've learned about intimacy and sovereignty being mutually exclusive if you sit in the discomfort of being fully yourself both on your own and in your partnerships. The late summer has opportunities for confusion and blurry lines, and the potential for deep spiritual connection. Focus on bringing your spiritual practices into your routines to help you reconcile seeming paradoxes.

Maeanna Welti © Mothr Tongue Ink 2021

Spirit of Dawn © Sue Ellen Parkinson 2018

─────────── ♄♄♄sonibar ───────────

♍︎

Saturday
24

♀☍♇ 1:51 am
☽□♂ 10:50 am
☽△♅ 12:17 pm
☽☍♇ 10:10 pm

─────────── ☉☉☉ robibar ───────────

♍︎
♎︎

Sunday
25

☽☌♀ 12:24 am
☽△♄ 2:34 am
☽☌♅ 5:49 am v/c
☽→♎ 9:43 am

☉☌☽ 2:54 pm
☽☍♃ 4:45 pm
♃PrH 7:11 pm
♀△♇ 10:46 pm

New Moon in ♎ Libra 2:54 pm PDT

Skirling

And there was that time when nine of us
reclaimed the night for the women's world
of sisters and mothers and daughters.
Samhain's black wind chasing us down
alleys and ginnels and we skirled through lanes
out over the hill where scudding sky was alive
above us stars coming and going, no moon,
trees laughing and bowing and invisible witches.
hooting and howling as the magic rode up inside us—

And we were a power that night.
Nine of us, flying joyful, remembering:
this is how it is in the truthful place
of the world's women when we are together
taking dark spangles to wear on our shoulders
no secrets, no disguises—just women.
Taking power. This is the light we fly by,
each to the other, together. This is the power
to remember alone in the dark. We hold it deep
in ourselves in a roar that will shake the world.

□ *Rose Flint 2020*

*Dimensional
Travel Series 4*
© *Wendy Page 2014*

X. MAKING MAGIC

Moon X: September 25–October 25

New Moon in ♎ Libra Sept. 25; Full Moon in ♈ Aries Oct. 9; Sun in ♏ Scorpio Oct. 23

Celebration © *Toni Truesdale 2013*

Everyday Sorceress

May you make your own magic
out of weeds and wonder.
May you create your own enchantments
from the stuff of mud and memory.
May you spin your own spells
from threads of raindrops and roses.
May you breathe in the knowing
that you hold the power
to make the world anew.

© *Molly M. Remer 2019*

Sept. / Oct.

Mí Meán Fomhair / Mí Deireadh Fomhair

————— ⱭⱭⱭ Dé Luain —————

Monday
26

♀ ☌ ♀   10:59 am
☉ ☍ ♃   12:33 pm
☽ △ ♂   7:54 pm
☽ △ ♄   8:44 pm

Fortunes can be read in fallen leaves
And in the white foam runes
Of the tide, where
Between their oracular duties
And sweeping the sea floor
Begging for apples,
The mermaids have often come ashore.

excerpt © Lorraine Schein 2007

————— ♂♂♂ Dé Máirt —————

Tuesday
27

☿ △ ♇   5:56 am
☽ □ ♇   9:21 am v/c
☽ → ♏   4:14 pm
♂ △ ♄   10:48 pm

————— ☿☿☿ Dé Céadaoin —————

Wednesday
28

No exact aspects

————— ♃♃♃ Dé Ardaoin —————

Thursday
29

♀ → ♎   12:49 am
☽ ☍ ♅   12:49 am
☽ □ ♄   1:57 am
☽ △ ♆   10:03 am

☽ ✶ ♀   11:57 am
☽ ✶ ♇   2:20 pm v/c
☽ → ♐   9:03 pm
☽ ✶ ♀   11:04 pm

————— ♀♀♀ Dé Haoine —————

Friday
30

☽ △ ♃   2:38 am
☉ ✶ ☽   10:05 am

ALL ASPECTS IN PACIFIC DAYLIGHT TIME; ADD 3 HOURS FOR EDT; ADD 7 HOURS FOR GMT

Corvids © *Sandra Stanton 2020*

The Answer

Watch birds in flight.
Feathers glow gold
under white sun.

> A bird flies to the right
> the answer is *yes.*
> To the left
> the answer is *no.*

> Left is not bad.
> Sometimes *no* is the answer.

¤ *Susan Levitt 2020*

──────── ᚺᚺᚺ Dé Sathairn ────────

 ♐

Saturday

1

October

☽⚹♄	5:48 am
☽☌♂	8:03 am
♀☌♃	11:12 am
☽□♅	1:45 pm
☽□♅	2:46 pm v/c

──────── ☉☉☉ Dé Domhnaigh ────────

 ♐
 ♑

Sunday

2

☽→♑	12:38 am
♅☽	2:07 am
☽□♃	5:37 am
☽□♀	7:35 am
☉□☽	5:14 pm

Waxing Half Moon in ♑ Capricorn 5:14 pm PDT

October
octubre

—— ☽☽☽ lunes ——

Monday
3

♑

☽△♅ 7:37 am
☽⚹♆ 4:31 pm
☽△☿ 5:59 pm
☽☌♇ 8:49 pm v/c

Let Me Be Free

© *Helen Seay Art 2019*

—— ♂♂♂ martes ——

Tuesday
4

♑
♒

☽→♒ 3:20 am
☽⚹♃ 7:48 am
☽PrG 9:32 am
☽△♀ 3:04 pm
☉△☽ 11:31 pm

—— ☿☿☿ miércoles ——

Wednesday
5

♒

☽□♅ 9:57 am
☽☌♄ 11:00 am
☽△♂ 3:45 pm v/c

—— ♃♃♃ jueves ——

Thursday
6

♒
♓

☽→♓ 5:47 am
♀PrH 5:29 pm
☿△♇ 8:55 pm

—— ♀♀♀ viernes ——

Friday
7

♓

☉☍♅ 3:48 am
☽⚹♅ 12:35 pm
☽□♂ 7:40 pm
☽☌♆ 9:40 pm

———

ALL ASPECTS IN PACIFIC DAYLIGHT TIME; ADD 3 HOURS FOR EDT; ADD 7 HOURS FOR GMT

Grandma Aggie © *Teya Jacobi 2019*

ᚺᚺᚺ sábado

♓
♈

○

Saturday

♉

☽⚹♇	2:14 am
☽☍♉	4:10 am v/c
☽→♈	8:57 am
☽♂♃	12:37 pm
♇☽	2:56 pm

⊙⊙⊙ domingo

♈

○

Sunday

9

☽☍♀	7:20 am
⊙☍☽	1:55 pm
☽⚹♄	5:48 pm

Full Moon in ♈ Aries 1:55 pm PDT

October
listopad

♈
♉

Monday
10

☽⚹♂ 1:14 am
♀☍♅ 6:15 am
☽□♇ 7:02 am v/c
☽→♉ 2:04 pm
☿→♎ 4:51 pm

Time to order We'Moon 2023!
Free Shipping within the US October 10-13th!
Promo Code: Lucky13 www.wemoon.ws

♉

Tuesday
11

☉⚻♅ 2:13 am
☉△♄ 6:06 pm
♂□♆ 10:46 pm
☽♂♅ 11:20 pm

♉
♊

Wednesday
12

☿☍♃ 12:24 am
☽□♄ 12:36 am
☽⚹♆ 9:25 am
☽△♇ 2:42 pm v/c
☽→♊ 10:08 pm

♊

Thursday
13

☽⚹♃ 1:08 am
☽△☿ 4:29 am
♀⚻♅ 9:57 am
♀△♄ 11:21 pm

♊

Friday
14

☽△♄ 10:33 am
☽△♀ 11:51 am
☉△☽ 4:23 pm
☽□♆ 7:46 pm
☽♂♂ 9:11 pm v/c

ALL ASPECTS IN PACIFIC DAYLIGHT TIME; ADD 3 HOURS FOR EDT; ADD 7 HOURS FOR GMT

Inner Flame © *Melissa Stratton Pandina 2020*

Night Magic

My focus shifts to night magic,
the work I do in the dark.
With candles and cards, books and bells,
I weave my will into the fabric of the universe.

excerpt ¤ Astrea Taylor 2020

ℏℏℏ subota

♊
♋ 　🌓　 **Saturday**
15

☽→♋　9:11 am
☽□♃　11:44 am

☉☉☉ nedjelja

♋ 　🌓　 **Sunday**
16

☽□☿　12:18 am
☉⚹♆　8:39 am
☽✶♅　9:09 pm

MOON X   145

October
Ashshin

♋
♌

Monday
17

☽ApG	3:19 am	♀⚼♆	3:00 pm
☽□♀	7:14 am	☉△♂	3:05 pm
☽△♆	8:04 am	☽→♌	9:44 pm
☉□☽	10:15 am	☽△♃	11:44 pm
☽⚹♇	1:56 pm v/c		

Waning Half Moon in ♋ Cancer 10:15 am PDT

♌

Tuesday
18

♀△♂	7:20 pm
☽⚹⚨	10:15 pm

♌

Wednesday
19

☉□♇	6:33 am
☽□♅	9:17 am
☽⚹♄	10:59 am
⚨⚹⚨	6:24 pm
♀□♇	11:02 pm
☽⚹♂	11:23 pm

♌
♍

Thursday
20

♀ApH	12:45 am
☽⚹♀	2:12 am
☉⚹☽	3:35 am v/c
☽→♍	9:25 am

♍

Friday
21

☽△♅	7:19 pm

2022 Year at a Glance for ♏ Scorpio (Oct. 23–Nov. 22)

Uranus in Taurus is still working you over this year, still making space for more intimacy through challenging your favorite ways of operating. Where you go under the surface, Uranus is out in the open. Where you follow the rivers of feelings, it maps the body. Where you find relief in intensity, it seeks what calms. It disrupts by slowing down. It revolts by putting pleasure first. It gets real by refusing the logic of anything that takes us out of ourselves. Your closest partnerships and collaborations get exposed as either keeping you from yourself or as uncomfortable roads to freedom, calling you to an honesty that is simple, joyful, embodied, while still wanting you to be yourself. What does it look like to put your Scorpio powers in service of what is pleasurable, simple, straightforward, and joyful? The wisdom of your own body can ground you, take your enormous capacity for honesty and intensity, depth and passion, and turn it into soil you can fully root into. This year starts and ends with an exploration of the consequences of structures of your life not being fully livable. It will ask you to investigate your foundations of family and home, to be practical and free. It will ask you to revisit the narratives that have guided you and given you a sense of self, to look for those that instead make you free to be who you are now becoming.

Maeanna Welti © Mother Tongue Ink 2021

The Gateway Series: Transformation
© Megan Welti 2016

ħħħ sonibar

♍
♎

Saturday
22

☿⊼♅	4:24 am	☿△ħ	6:00 pm
☽♂♅	5:37 am	☽→♎	6:24 pm
☽□♂	9:27 am	☽♂♃	7:17 pm
☽△♇	11:17 am v/c	ħD	9:07 pm
☉♂♀	2:17 pm		

☉☉☉ robibar

♎

Sunday
23

♀→♏	12:52 am
☉→♏	3:36 am
♀⊼♃	8:57 am
☉⊼♃	1:20 pm

Sun in ♏ Scorpio 3:36 am PDT

Solace

Persephone is all around us now.
Her velvet darkness envelopes the harvest moon,
round and red from western winds
that are choked with smoke.
She is a primordial fortress
with many, many doors,
all ajar,
through which the deepest, oldest currents flow.
Grief has a gravity all its own
that causes us to descend
into the dark undercurrents
of her shoreless rivers, her endless tears
from which all our living roots drink.
There have been many sorrows,
many lifetimes of sorrows
but now she grieves at the altar of mass extinction
with the names of the lost
written in braille upon her skin
as the songs of the wild world lapse into silence.
Her pomegranate heart does not break.
It softens and splits,
seeding the dark with a choir of stars.
All her great waters are whispering, "Shhh…shhh,"
haunting us with the memory of the womb.
Healing us
With the memory of the womb,
even as we carve runes of shame
into the soft underbelly of the world,
desperately trying to mark our place in time
without realizing
that we are already guests
standing before her open doors,
receiving
her unending solace.

XI. SHADOW WORK

Moon XI: October 25–November 23

New Moon in ♏ Scorpio Oct. 25; Full Moon in ♉ Taurus Nov. 8; Sun in ♐ Sagittarius Nov. 22

Persephone © Megan Welti 2015

October
Mí Deireadh Fomhair

Diamond Ring

Monday
24

♎

☽△♄ 4:08 am
☽☌♅ 9:01 am
☽△♂ 4:12 pm
☽□♇ 5:36 pm v/c

Tuesday
25

♎
♏

☽→♏ 12:18 am
☉☌☽ 3:49 am
☽☌♀ 5:04 am
☿☌Ψ 9:29 am

Lunar Samhain

New Moon in ♏ Scorpio 3:49 am PDT
Partial Solar Eclipse 4:00 am PDT*

Wednesday
26

♏

☽☍♅ 6:34 am
☽□♄ 8:30 am
☽△Ψ 4:04 pm
☿△♂ 8:36 pm
☽✶♇ 9:27 pm v/c

Thursday
27

♏
♐

☽→♐ 3:54 am
☽△♃ 4:01 am
☿□♇ 6:08 am
♃→♓ 10:10 pm

Friday
28

♐

☽✶♄ 11:16 am
☽□Ψ 6:37 pm
☽☍♂ 10:59 pm

---

*Eclipse visible Europe, NE Africa, Mid East, SW Asia

Dark is the Shadow

When the moon eclipses the sun, be there for it.
Seek it, go wherever it takes you. Hurry.
Pay whatever is required to go into the Dark,
to see the light only visible from the Shadow.
Accept and claim its alien gifts rushing in for you
only now, only now.
Upheaval is but another word for change.

excerpt © Rachel Creager Ireland 2020

Eclipsed
© Tamara Phillips
2017

──── ꙮꙮꙮ Dé Sathairn ────

♐
♑

Saturday
29

☽⚹☿	5:33 am	☿△♃	10:32 am
☽□♃	6:10 am v/c	☿→♏	12:22 pm
☽→♑	6:21 am	☉⚹☽	5:20 pm
☽PrG	7:37 am	☽⚹♀	8:41 pm

──── ☉☉☉ Dé Domhnaigh ────

♑

Sunday
30

♂R	6:26 am
☽△♅	11:21 am
☽⚹♆	8:51 pm

October / November
octubre / noviembre

Monday
31

Samhain / Hallowmas

♊ ♒

☽☌♇	2:22 am
☽⚹♃	8:14 am v/c
☽→♒	8:43 am
☽□♅	2:37 pm
☉□☽	11:37 pm

Waxing Half Moon in ♒ Aquarius 11:37 pm PDT

Tuesday
1

November

♒

☽□♀	4:05 am
☽□♅	1:53 pm
☽☌♄	4:22 pm

Wednesday
2

♒ ♓

☽△♂	4:08 am v/c
♀⚼♄	10:13 am
☽→♓	11:46 am

Thursday
3

♓

☽△♅	12:43 am
☉△☽	7:01 am
☽△♀	12:43 pm
☽⚹♅	5:28 pm

Friday
4

♓ ♈

☽☌♆	3:33 am
☽□♂	8:02 am
☽⚹♇	9:33 am
☽☌♃	3:05 pm v/c
☽→♈	4:07 pm

ALL ASPECTS IN PACIFIC DAYLIGHT TIME; ADD 3 HOURS FOR EDT; ADD 7 HOURS FOR GMT

Samhain

Winter's gate. The deepest in, the darkest moon, the fertile void, the waiting womb.

Silence roots, trees unleaf, the land is stripped back to bone, bone-fires on hills, wood smoke at dusk, wet leaves in layers stuck to our boots, the spider, the web, the ancestor bread, a purple candle in the heavy-hung window for our beloved dead returning home.

The night of the shore left behind, the exposed root, the vulnerable wound. The night to be soft with our hearts, protect our scars, gather in close to the welcoming hearth.

The night the night hag rides.

With the land electrified, familiar landmarks resemble ancient sites. We untie from the loom, allow the pattern to be lost, slow to stone to speak the truth as hollow bone.

On a bigger arc than our lives will witness, beyond the sideways growing rhizomes of Patriarchy's fake news, beyond faith, deep space, the witches' broom nebula, (where wise women have always gone for a brew, always will) is the Unchanging where nothing can stop the final word being Love.

Debra Hall © Mother Tongue Ink 2021

Darkest Night © Toni Truesdale 2006

The Conversation

Death, when I don't face you,
my tree of nerves
chatters in a brittle wind.
My fear of you arises
in disguise at every turn.
You wait like a patient mother
while I wrestle, while I run.
Death, I name you friend.
Before we meet
I want to correspond,
to speak the shape you make
inside my skin, to trace
the shifting of your shape
as we draw near.
Friend, I name your coming.

Daughter, I am the moondark.
Light shines on the side of me
you cannot see.
My veil of absence
lets your gaze dive deeper
into the ebony ocean of night.
At the end of the wane
at the start of the wax,
when the dark of the moon
plunges you back to that womb,
it is I who pulse at your side.
Daughter, I am hidden
only in transparency.
Look twice at any moment,
and you will sense my presence.
And when the day arrives
that you can see my new moon face,
I'll gather you up in my arms
and whisper
that your letting go is done.

© *Susa Silvermarie 2020*

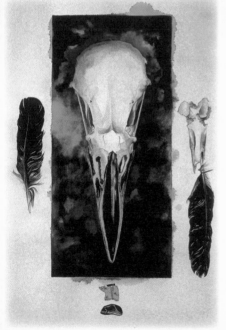

The Raven Years
□ *Catherine Firpo, PhD 2007*

Cosmic Mirror of Light © *Danielle Helen Ray Dickson 2018*

♈ ☽ **Saturday**
5

⊙⚹♃ 1:57 am
♀☍♅ 3:22 pm

♈ ☽ **Sunday**
♉ **6**

☽⚹♄ 1:43 am   ☽□♇ 2:30 pm v/c
☿⚹♃ 6:34 am   ☽→♉ 9:15 pm
☽⚹♂ 12:30 pm   ♀□♄ 11:33 pm

Daylight Saving Time Ends 2:00 am PDT

November
studeni

☽☽☽ ponedjeljak

♉

Monday
7

No exact aspects

Haya-Akitsu-Hime
Beloved Goddess of the Sea
You Who Embrace All
Embrace all of me
the wicked and the wounded
the shameful and the shamed
You Who Embrace All
Teach me to do the same
excerpt © Ellen Lorenzi-Prince 2013

♂♂♂ utorak

♉

Tuesday
8

☽☍☿ 2:43 am
☉☍☽ 3:02 am
☽☌♅ 4:47 am
☽□♄ 8:20 am
☉☌☿ 8:42 am

☽☍♀ 11:51 am
☽✶♆ 3:54 pm
♅PrH 5:07 pm
☿☍♅ 6:40 pm
☽△♇ 10:38 pm

Total Lunar Eclipse 2:59 am PST*
Full Moon in ♉ Taurus 3:02 am PST

☿☿☿ srijeda

♉
♊

Wednesday
9

☉☍♅ 12:26 am
☽✶♃ 4:00 am v/c
☽→♊ 5:37 am
☿□♄ 11:52 pm

♃♃♃ četvrtak

♊

Thursday
10

♀△♆ 4:22 am
☽△♄ 6:22 pm

♀♀♀ petak

♊
♋

Friday
11

☉□♄ 12:04 am
☽□♆ 2:03 am
☽☌♂ 5:34 am
♀⚻♂ 1:07 pm
☽□♃ 2:28 pm v/c
☽→♋ 4:22 pm

*Eclipse visible Asia, Australia, Pacific Americas. parts of Northern and Eastern Europe

Yokai Amabie © *Flora ikiGaia 2020*

♋

Saturday
12

☿△♆ 10:36 am

─────── ☉☉☉ nedjelja ───────

♋

Sunday
13

☿ApH	1:39 am	☽△♆	2:08 pm
♀⚹♇	1:41 am	☽△♅	6:25 pm
☽⚹♅	1:59 am	☽☍♇	9:35 pm
☿⊼♂	7:46 am	☽ApG	10:35 pm
☉△☽	11:22 am	☽△♀	11:54 pm

November
Kartik

―――― ☽☽☽ sombar ――――

♋
♌

Monday
14

☽△♃ 2:41 am v/c
☽→♌ 4:48 am
☿⚹♇ 6:27 pm
☉△♆ 7:43 pm

―――― ♂♂♂ mongolbar ――――

♌

Tuesday
15

♀△♃ 1:36 am
☽□♅ 2:23 pm
☉⚹♂ 5:06 pm
☽☍♄ 7:17 pm
♀→♐ 10:08 pm

―――― ☿☿☿ budhbar ――――

♌
♍

Wednesday
16

☽⚹♂ 4:12 am
☉□☽ 5:27 am
☿△♃ 7:43 am
☽□♅ 3:55 pm v/c
☽→♍ 5:03 pm
☽□♀ 7:14 pm

―――― ♃♃♃ brihospotibar ――――

Waning Half Moon in ♌ Leo 5:27 am PST

♍

Thursday
17

☿→♐ 12:42 am

―――― ♀♀♀ sukrobar ――――

♍

Friday
18

☽△♅ 1:23 am
☽☍♆ 1:12 pm
☽□♂ 1:35 pm
☉⚹♇ 1:38 pm
☽△♇ 8:26 pm
☉⚹☽ 9:00 pm

ALL ASPECTS IN PACIFIC STANDARD TIME; ADD 3 HOURS FOR EST; ADD 8 HOURS FOR GMT

Starlit © *Natasza Zurek 2017*

Love's Forge

I heard she drank the fire
I heard she tempered her sword
I heard she sat in stillness
until peace found her
I heard her heart remembered to belong.

excerpt © Meredith Heller 2019

———— ᚼᚼᚼ sonibar ————

♍ Saturday
♎ 19

☽☍♃ 12:46 am v/c
☽→♎ 2:57 am
♂□♆ 7:43 am
☽✶♅ 9:54 am
☽✶♀ 11:15 am

———— ☉☉☉ robibar ————

♎ Sunday
20

☽△♄ 2:18 pm
☽△♂ 7:37 pm
☉△♃ 8:07 pm

November
Mí na Samhna

 ⊃⊃⊃ Dé Luain

Monday
21

☽□♇ 3:14 am v/c
☽→♏ 9:16 am
☿♂♀ 2:55 pm

Unbridled © *Helen Seay Art 2015*

○○○ Dé Máirt

♏

Tuesday
22

☉→♐ 12:20 am
☽☍♅ 1:24 pm
☽□♄ 6:33 pm

☉→♐

Sun in ♐ in Sagittarius 12:20 am PST

☿☿☿ Dé Céadaoin

♏
♐

Wednesday
23

☽△♆ 12:03 am
☽⚹♇ 6:38 am
☽△♃ 10:16 am v/c
☽→♐ 12:15 pm
☉○☽ 2:57 pm
♃D 3:02 pm

New Moon in ♐ Sagittarius 2:57 pm PST

♃♃♃ Dé Ardaoin

♐

Thursday
24

☽○♀ 5:26 am
☽○☿ 6:49 am
☽⚹♄ 8:16 pm
☽☍♂ 10:36 pm
☿△♄ 10:46 pm

♀♀♀ Dé Haoine

♐
♑

Friday
25

☽□♆ 1:24 am
☽□♃ 11:22 am v/c
☽→♑ 1:18 pm
♀△♄ 4:51 pm
☽PrG 5:21 pm

ALL ASPECTS IN PACIFIC STANDARD TIME; ADD 3 HOURS FOR EST; ADD 8 HOURS FOR GMT

2022 Year at a Glance for ♐ Sagittarius (Nov. 22–Dec. 21)

This year marks the final stages of many years of deep work on self-worth for you. The magical dark is full of treasures and discoveries. The task of restoring what is sacred deserves a rich fullness of attention. All the journeys you have made into the underworld have revealed your own value, even as many scary things under the surface have been exposed. You are hopefully integrating and folding these discoveries into your abundant sense of possibility. It is important to allow this work to be detailed. It is important to have stable routines. That alone might be radical for you, but these years of Uranus in Taurus slowing you down have the potential of revolutionizing your relationship to the adventure of being in a body. Your health requires that you learn to hear your body's needs and limits as clearly as you can hear the call of wonder over the horizon. This summer's Neptune transits will ask you to soften into sensitivity and vulnerability. They'll ask you to explore the non-linear, liminal parts of your consciousness, and will likely also show you how and when you are tempted to escape or be led astray. The year closes with another square between Saturn and Uranus, re-emphasizing your health and how you nurture yourself in the day-to-day. There are a million ways to keep it interesting, and no reason not to. Be disciplined about staying curious and attentive to the intelligence of the body. Honor your body's communications.

Maeanna Welti © Mother Tongue Ink 2021

© Jo Jayson 2016

Innana—Star of
Heaven and Earth

——— ♄♄♄ Dé Sathairn ———

♑

Saturday
26

☽△♅ 3:34 pm

——— ☉☉☉ Dé Domhnaigh ———

♑
♒

Sunday
27

☽⚹♆ 2:06 am
☽☌♇ 8:43 am
☿⚹♅ 11:16 am
☽⚹♃ 12:11 pm v/c
☽→♒ 2:07 pm

A Trip to Earth

Once past bumper-to-bumper stars in the Milky Way, past the planets that incinerate upon contact or freeze your fuel cells, past the planets that don't even have water, head south toward the blue planet that floats in space like a jewel. Be sure to look for whales and silvery fish, then open the hatch and feel our sun. Dolphins will greet you with squeals, white-winged gulls will cry hello. Everybody here sings and talks, so I hope you're ready for our music.

You must be starving from eating road food for a thousand light years, so head to land for simmering plantains or maybe squash blossoms fried into rice or maybe you got here just in time for warm bread pulled from an adobe oven.

Maybe it's raining and someone calls you under their roof: maybe it's snowing and someone gives you a warm coat. When the sun comes out again, like it does without fail every day and you see your first rainbow glimmering in the sky, this is when you're going to say "Why didn't I come to Earth sooner? Why did I never see this place before?"

▢ *Stephanie A. Sellers 2020*

Falias © *Tara Luther 2017*

XII. HOME

Moon XII: November 23–December 23

New Moon in ♐ Sagittarius Nov. 23; Full Moon in ♊ Gemini Dec. 7; Sun in ♑ Capricorn Dec. 21

fille des univers © *Nolween LM 2018*

Nov. / Dec.
noviembre / diciembre

Monday
28

☉✶☽	12:06 am	♀⊼♅	6:19 pm
♂△♄	9:56 am	☽✶☿	8:26 pm
☽✶♀	4:39 pm	☽△♂	10:31 pm
☽□♅	4:48 pm	☽♂♄	10:53 pm v/c

Tuesday
29

☿☍♂	12:30 pm
☽→♓	4:15 pm
☿✶♄	8:17 pm

Wednesday
30

☉□☽	6:36 am
♂PrH	6:07 pm
☽✶♅	7:58 pm
♀☍♂	9:28 pm

Waxing Half Moon in ♓ Pisces 6:36 am PST

Thursday
1

December

☽□♂	12:42 am	☿□♆	5:08 pm
☽□♀	1:08 am	☽♂♃	6:44 pm v/c
☽□☿	6:23 am	♀✶♄	7:09 pm
☽♂♆	7:36 am	☽→♈	8:41 pm
☽✶♇	2:58 pm		

Friday
2

☉△☽	4:10 pm

ALL ASPECTS IN PACIFIC STANDARD TIME; ADD 3 HOURS FOR EST; ADD 8 HOURS FOR GMT

Shadow Work © Emily Kell 2018

Mapping a New Reality

When all the old paths
have been concreted over,
the way forgotten,

when words shape-shift
beneath your feet,
spelling another reality,

when you don't know
what to pray for anymore,
let alone to whom—then

you must abandon

the broken compasses,
burn the man-made maps
and head for home—

follow the knowing
in your bones, the aching
of your heart,

the song-line of your body.

¤ *Siobhan Mac Mahon 2017*

———————————— ᚻᚻᚻ sábado ————————————

♈ ☾ **Saturday**
3

☽⚹♂ 5:11 am ☽△♅ 7:53 pm
☽⚹♄ 9:06 am ☽□♇ 9:46 pm v/c
☽△♀ 12:57 pm ♀□♆ 11:12 pm
♆D 4:14 pm ☉△⚷ 11:13 pm

———————————— ☉☉☉ domingo ————————————

♈ ☾ **Sunday**
♉ **4**

☽→♉ 3:38 am

December
prosinac

Let her guide you deep
into night's holy magic:
You too belong here,
creature of the night,
goddess of Mystery,
sacred daughter,
Welcome Home.
excerpt ¤ Johanna Elise 2020

☽☽☽ ponedjeljak

♉

Monday
5

☽☌♅ 9:38 am
☽□♄ 5:53 pm
☽⚹♆ 10:36 pm
☿□♃ 11:05 pm

♂♂♂ utorak

♉
♊

Tuesday
6

☽△♇ 6:51 am
☽⚹♃ 11:02 am v/c
☽→♊ 12:48 pm
☿→♑ 2:08 pm

☿☿☿ srijeda

♊

Wednesday
7

☉⚻♅ 2:34 pm
☉☍☽ 8:08 pm
☽☌♂ 8:18 pm
☉☍♂ 9:41 pm

♃♃♃ četvrtak

Full Moon in ♊ Gemini 8:08 pm PST

♊
♋

Thursday
8

☽△♄ 4:41 am
☽□♆ 9:13 am
☽☍♀ 9:29 pm
☽□♃ 10:13 pm v/c
☽→♋ 11:49 pm

♀♀♀ petak

♋

Friday
9

♀□♃ 4:55 am
☽☍☿ 7:55 am
♀→♑ 7:54 pm

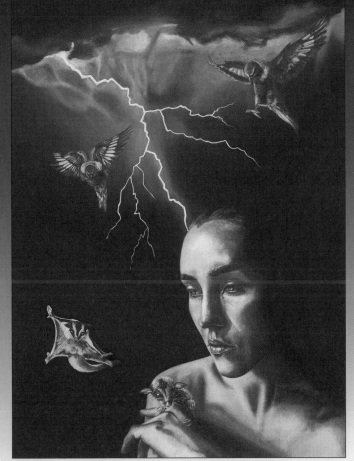

Cauda Pavonis © *Zoë Rayne 2018*

ħħħ subota

♋ ◐ **Saturday**
10

☽⚹♅ 7:17 am
☽△♆ 9:18 pm

───── ⊙⊙⊙ nedjelja ─────

♋ ◑ **Sunday**
♌ **11**

☽☍♇ 6:11 am
☽△♃ 10:49 am v/c
☽→♌ 12:09 pm
☽ApG 4:23 pm

MOON XII   167

December
Ogrohaeon

Bridge of Change

© *Visual Lifesavers Art 2015*

---))) sombar ---

 ♌

Monday
12

☉✶♄ 10:12 am
☽✶♂ 5:04 pm
☽□♅ 7:47 pm

--- ♂♂♂ mongolbar ---

♌

Tuesday
13

☽☍♄ 6:09 am
☉△☽ 7:52 am v/c

--- ☿☿☿ budhbar ---

 ♌
♍

Wednesday
14

☽→♍ 12:45 am
☉□♆ 9:10 am
☽△♀ 12:32 pm

--- ♃♃♃ brihospotibar ---

♍

Thursday
15

☿□♃ 9:21 pm
☽△☿ 1:02 am
☽□♂ 3:29 am
☽△♅ 7:41 am
☿☌♂ 7:11 pm

--- ♀♀♀ sukrobar ---

♍
♎

Friday
16

☽☍♆ 9:40 pm
☉□☽ 12:56 am
☽△♇ 6:25 am
☽☍♃ 11:13 am v/c
☽→♎ 11:49 am

Waning Half Moon in ♍ Virgo 12:56 am PST

ALL ASPECTS IN PACIFIC STANDARD TIME; ADD 3 HOURS FOR EST; ADD 8 HOURS FOR GMT

Where are You From?

The dreaded question . . .
Where are you from?
Leaves me baffled at times.
Do you want to know where I presently reside?
Or where I was born and raised?
Or where my heart calls home?
Do you want to know where my ancestors came from?
Or are you looking for an explanation
for my mocha skin and kinky hair?
All of these answers are different.
I want to reply to this question:
I come from the stars, from a planet of Light
I am the result of thousands of years of Love.
I am a child of the Universe.
The Earth is my mother,
The Sky is my father.
And I am home wherever I go.

© *Mahada Thomas 2020*

───────── ʔʔʔ sonibar ─────────

Saturday
17

♌

☽□♀	5:28 am
☽△♂	11:44 am
☿△♅	1:36 pm
☽□♅	5:25 pm

───────── ☉☉☉ robibar ─────────

Sunday
18

♌
♏

☽△♄	3:31 am
☉⚹☽	2:02 pm
☽□♇	2:35 pm v/c
☽→♏	7:30 pm

Winter Solstice

The shortest day, the longest night, the stars brought closer by the primordial dark.

The Sun stands still as we hunker-down like heavy bears in our hibernacula, put down what we are braced against, bring everyone inside, sit down to every meal as a feast, share our gifts from the tree of life, bauble and sparkle against all that is drear, wreath the door with the green that never dies, drift like snowbanks into lazy peace.

On Midwinter's morning as the lambent glow of magic sidles closer, we go out in good company with a flask of something spiced to stand in sacred waiting for the birth of something precious, for Deer Mother to carry the sun back on her uplifted antlers.

In this moment the ancient stirs in us, illuminating our heart's deepest chambers, renewing our strength to challenge the injustices we were born into, born to stem.

Everything we care about pivots on this one thing, the life and light that have left the world, the love we will be returning.

Debra Hall © Mother Tongue Ink 2021

Mushroom Lights in the Night ¤ Mathilda Berg 2020

Mushroom Magic ¤ *Diane Norrie 2020*

dark moon in winter

tap tightened
the sound of dripping water
is absorbed by thick flannel silence
lights off
this cabin is a wedge of stillness
that disappears in dark forest
lamp black, coal black, soot black
ink black, boot black, bone black
as above, so below
the loft is woodstove warm
cat already folded on the bed
winter woollens peeled
I am a love-letter to sleep
I slide into the envelope of sheets
and whisper
home

December

Mí na Nollag

☽☽☽ Dé Luain

Nocturnal Journey

© Jenny Hahn 2017

♏ 

Monday
19

♀□⚷ 8:23 am
♀⚻♂ 9:37 am
♂✶⚷ 2:38 pm
☽✶♀ 5:21 pm
☽☍♅ 10:33 pm

♂♂♂ Dé Máirt

♏ ♐ 

Tuesday
20

☽✶☿ 3:58 am
♃→♈ 6:32 am
☽□♄ 8:41 am
☽△♆ 11:01 am
☽✶♇ 6:45 pm v/c
☽→♐ 11:12 pm
☽△♃ 11:19 pm

☿☿☿ Dé Céadaoin

♐ 

Wednesday
21

☉→♑ 1:48 pm
☉□♃ 4:50 pm
☽☍♂ 5:48 pm

Winter Solstice

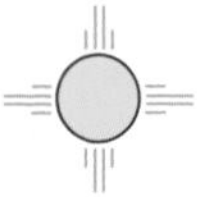

☉→♑

Sun in ♑ Capricorn 1:48 pm PST

♃♃♃ Dé Ardaoin

♐ ♑ 

Thursday
22

♀△♅ 1:48 am
☽✶♄ 10:19 am
☽□♆ 12:16 pm v/c
☽→♑ 11:49 pm

♀♀♀ Dé Haoine

♑ 

Friday
23

☽□♃ 12:13 am
⚷D 12:40 am
☉☌☽ 2:17 am

New Moon in ♑ Capricorn 2:17 am PST

All aspects in Pacific Standard Time; add 3 hours for EST; add 8 hours for GMT

2022 Year at a Glance for ♑ Capricorn (Dec. 21–Jan. 20)

Things are, and have been, very serious . . . for some time . . . with big consequences . . . calling for hard work. You do all of those things well, even if you think you should be doing more. To the degree that you define yourself by your ability to achieve and be responsible, these years have been asking you to heal, to transform narratives of scarcity and austerity into a fuller, more alive expression of your diligence, discipline and ability to build what lasts. We need this liberated version of you. We need you to lead with the you that has been into the depths of your own trauma, met yourself with compassion and had the courage to be vulnerable as well as effective. These years since 2008 have been a showcase of how Capricorn energy, so rewarded by the dominant culture, has also given and received woundings. You are exploring all these things, consciously or not, in a very personal way. You are more than what society wants from you and rewards you for. You do not have to be boxed into a small, rigid, lifeless definition of reality in order to be the realistic, strategic, practical person you are. A revolution of self-worth is available to you, in which you get to define what discipline means and what it's good for—in which you get to decide what you're in service to, and what

the legacy of that service will be. Focus on pleasure, play, and joyful embodiment to make room for the loving vitality that will shape your personal revolution and be a gift to our collective one.

Maeanna Welti © Mother Tongue Ink 2021

───────────── ♄♄♄ Dé Sathairn ─────────────

♑
≈

Saturday
24

D△♆ 12:02 am
DPrG 12:22 am
D♂♅ 4:16 am
D♂♅ 11:32 am
D⚹♆ 11:48 am

☿⚹♆ 5:16 pm
D♂♇ 7:11 pm v/c
D→≈ 11:14 pm
D⚹♃ 11:56 pm

consciencia global
© Annika Gemlau Asombrasdelsur 2019

───────────── ☉☉☉ Dé Domhnaigh ─────────────

≈

Sunday
25

D△♂ 3:34 pm
D□♅ 11:35 pm

The Place Between Light and Dark

The trapeze swings out
and you have to let go.
In between can be a hard place,
meant to teach you to trust
in something more than your own mind.

When your hands
slip from the bar—
do you see the one
whose wrists you can grasp
flying toward you in the night?

The heart yearns to soar,
but you can't remember
how to be free.
Always hanging on so tight, afraid of the ride:
thrilling, risky, a little dangerous.

A gift lies buried beneath it all.
Unwrap yourself from all you know,
let go and rise into the air,
into the deathless, exhilarating
moment of surrender where everything—is all right.

Where love surrounds you, holds you,
and a net, woven blue light, as wide
as your willingness to forgive,
waits—
with infinite patience.

¤ *Elise Stuart 2015*

XIII. LACUNA

Moon XIII: December 23–January 21

New Moon in ♑ Capricorn Dec. 23; Full Moon in ♋ Cancer Jan. 6; Sun in ♒ Aquarius Jan. 20

Joy
© Natalie Bulan 2020

Dec. 2022 / Jan. 2023
diciembre / enero

Fountainhead

© Danielle Helen Ray Dickson 2013

—— ☽☽☽ lunes ——

Monday
26

☽☌♄ 10:19 am v/c
☽→♓ 11:34 pm

—— ♂♂♂ martes ——

♓

Tuesday
27

☉⚹☽ 9:23 am
☽□♂ 3:54 pm

—— ☿☿☿ miércoles ——

♓

Wednesday
28

♀⚹♆ 12:32 am
☽⚹♅ 1:02 am
☽☌♆ 2:05 am
☽⚹♀ 3:25 pm
☽⚹☿ 4:43 pm
☽⚹♇ 10:20 pm v/c

—— ♃♃♃ jueves ——

♓
♈

Thursday
29

☿R 1:31 am
☽→♈ 2:36 am
☽☌♃ 4:11 am
☿☌♀ 5:58 am
☉□☽ 5:20 pm
☽⚹♂ 7:17 pm

Waxing Half Moon in ♈ Aries 5:20 pm PST

—— ♀♀♀ viernes ——

♈

Friday
30

☉⚻♂ 3:21 pm
☽⚹♄ 6:52 pm
☽□♅ 10:00 pm

ALL ASPECTS IN PACIFIC STANDARD TIME; ADD 3 HOURS FOR EST; ADD 8 HOURS FOR GMT

Diamond

She bends into the night
tendrils curving to cradle the light.
The sky, a shimmering curtain
     falls pooling against the earth.
She digs her toes deep
     into the mud of living.

She bends in to the night.
Her arms the silhouette
     your human eyes can just make out
in the flare of passing giants.

She bends in the night,
folds it into veins and arteries
wraps in the songs of starlight
passes the rhythm through body
down along ever-branching roots
spreading, delivering, pulsing it to soil.

She bends in the night,
     sews another year of messages
into her next ring of bark.

¤ Heidi Denkers 2016

ℏℏℏ sábado

♈ ♉

Saturday
31

☽□♀ 2:59 am
☽□♇ 4:44 am v/c
☽→♉ 9:08 am
♀♂♇ 9:25 pm

⊙⊙⊙ domingo

♉

Sunday
1

January 2023

⊙△☽ 5:42 am
☽♂♅ 1:52 pm
☿⚹♆ 10:42 pm

January
prosinac

© Suzanne Grace Michell 2015

Let There Be Peace

♉
Ⅱ

Monday
2

☽□♄	4:15 am	♀→♒	6:09 pm
☽△♅	4:30 am	☽→Ⅱ	6:44 pm
☽✳︎♆	4:53 am	☽△♀	6:48 pm
☉□♃	8:02 am	☽✳︎♃	9:37 pm
☽△♇	2:16 pm v/c		

Ⅱ

Tuesday
3

☽♂♂	11:47 am

Ⅱ

Wednesday
4

♀✳︎♃	1:08 am
☽△♄	3:54 pm
☽□♆	4:07 pm v/c

Ⅱ
♋

Thursday
5

☽→♋	6:15 am
☉△♅	8:43 am
☽□♃	9:50 am

♋

Friday
6

☽✳︎♅	12:30 pm
☉☌☽	3:08 pm
☽☌☿	5:36 pm

Full Moon in ♋ Cancer 3:08 pm PST

ALL ASPECTS IN PACIFIC STANDARD TIME; ADD 3 HOURS FOR EST; ADD 8 HOURS FOR GMT

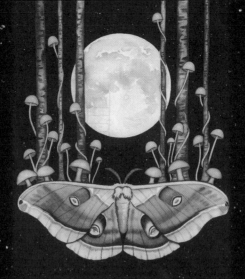

Night Flight © Liz Darling 2018

Longing for Darkness

After the sun finally gives up
the sky to the moon
and my children are dreaming

I sit in an empty, unlit room
soaking in the silky sounds
of silence. My body breathes again.

In this darkness, I am found.

□ Erin Kundrie 2020

──── ♄♄♄ subota ────

♋
♌

Saturday
7

☽△♆	4:30 am
☉♂☿	4:57 am
☽☍♇	2:23 pm v/c
☽→♌	6:40 pm
☽△♃	11:00 pm

──── ☉☉☉ nedjelja ────

♌

Sunday
8

☿PrH	12:34 am
☽ApG	1:20 am
☽☍♀	8:52 am
☽⚹♂	11:19 am
☿△♅	3:23 pm

WE'MOON EVOLUTION: A COMMUNITY ENDEAVOR

We'Moon is rooted in womyn's community. The datebook was originally planted as a seed in Europe where it sprouted on women's lands in the early 1980s. Transplanted to Oregon in the late '80s, it flourished as a cottage industry on We'Moon Land near Portland in the '90s and early 2000s, and now thrives in rural Southern Oregon.

The first We'Moon was a handwritten, pocket-size women's diary and handbook in Gaia Rhythms, translated in five languages! It was self-published under the name of Mother Tongue Ink, by me and my partner Nada in 1981, in France—in collaboration with friends from Kvindelandet ("women's land") in Denmark. We'Moon was inspired by our experience of living there together in a lively international community of 20–40 lesbian feminists in the late 1970's.

The first five editions of We'Moon were created by friends in different countries in Europe, voluntarily, as a "labor of love"— publicized mostly by word-of-mouth and distributed by backpack over national borders. When I returned to America with We'Moon, it changed to a larger, more user-friendly format as we entered the computer age. We grew into the business of publishing by the seat of our pants—starting with a little seed money, we recycled the proceeds into printing the next We'Moon, each year. By the early '90s, we finally sold enough copies to be able to pay for our labor. We'Moon Company was incorporated (dba) Mother Tongue Ink, and it has grown abundantly with colorful new fruits ever since! For a full listing of current We'Moon publications: (see pp 233–235).

Whew! It was always exciting, and a lot more work than we ever imagined! We learned how to do what was needed. We met and overcame major hurdles that brought us to a new level each time. The publishing industry has transformed: independent distributors, women's bookstores and print-based publications have declined. Nonetheless, We'Moon's loyal and growing customer base continues to support our unique womyn-created products. This home-grown publishing company is staffed by a resilient and highly skilled multi-generational team—embedded in women's community—who inspire, create, produce and distribute We'Moon year in and year out.

Every year, We'Moon is created by a vast web of womyn. Our Call for Contributions goes out to thousands of women, inviting art and writing on that year's theme (see p. 236). Women are invited to attend Selection Circles to review submissions and give feedback. In 2020, the pandemic and social distancing requirements turned those circles into virtual Zoom meetings . . . which had the beneficial effect of extending our outreach world-wide! The We'Moon Creatrix then collectively selects, designs, edits, and weaves the material together in the warp and woof of natural cycles through the thirteen Moons of the year. All the activity that goes into creating We'Moon is the inbreath; everything else we do to get it out into the world to you is the outbreath in our annual cycle. To learn more about the herstory of We'Moon, the art and writing that have graced its pages, and the Spirit that has breathed through it for 41 years now, check out the Anthology: *In the Spirit of We'Moon* (see page 233).

WE'MOON SISTER ORGANIZATIONS

We'Moon Land *is a residential women's land community—a sanctuary for women and nature.*

One of the first womyn's lands communities in Oregon, **We'Moon Land,** has been held by and for womyn since 1973. Generations of lesbians have made home here in community with women and nature—living in woman-built houses, growing organic food, on 52 beautiful acres of forests and fields, an hour from Portland. Founded on feminist values, ecological practices and earth-based women's spirituality, we are becoming a more diverse, generationally interwoven community of women-loving-women, friends and family, sharing a vision of creative spirit-centered life on the land. We host individual and group retreats, visitors, camping, workshops, land workdays, seasonal holydays, circles, and celebrations by and for women. We welcome committed lesbian feminists to join us: women with community skills, who want to live and work on the land—and carry it on in the Spirit of We'Moon. We will be celebrating our 50th Anniversary/ Land Dyke Gathering in 2023!

We'Moon Homestead is our resident non-profit organization that collectively manages We'Moon Land and community. We'Mooniversity is a tax-exempt organization that co-sponsors projects and events on the land, and aspires to become a hub—on land and online—as a networking resource for women's spirituality, community, culture, and consciousness. www.wemoonland.org, www.wemooniversity.org, wemoon.ws

Musawa ¤ Mother Tongue Ink 2021

ENTER THE WE'MOON TAROT

Wild Card
© *Jakki Moore 2013*

The *We'Moon Tarot* is coming out at last—along with *We'Moon 2022: The Magical Dark!* "You can't hurry the Goddess, She's always right on time!" We are at an auspicious confluence of the end of one cycle of We'Moon themes and the beginning of another. Both the Fool (in the previous cycle of Tarot-based themes) and the Dark Moon (in the new cycle of Moon phase themes) converge at this point, where mystery stirs the cauldron of creation, magically birthing Spirit into Form. In a We'Moon- centered version of Tarot, the dominant paradigm shifts to a more matrilineal life-affirming world view: in Her image.

The images on the We'Moon Tarot cards are drawn exclusively from art published in We'Moon, spanning two decades on each side of the turn of this century. This new Tarot deck provides a spectacular view of an extraordinary period in our personal and planetary lives—from the unique, diverse feminist perspective of We'Moon creative culture and earth-based women's spirituality. Having been part of creating the We'Moon datebook from the beginning, I am grateful to be able to draw from the full spectrum of original We'Moon art as my pallet for creating a We'Moon Tarot deck: in the Mother Tongue.

Tarot is a time-honored divinatory tool for seeking guidance: a map of consciousness for tracking the trajectory of your life's path, on your life's path, artistically rendered to spark your intuition into revealing hidden meanings relevant to the question at hand. The structural design rests on the universal patterns of Mother Nature—and human nature—as represented by the four ("mater-real") elements in the Minor Arcana suits:

Earth (physical/body) / **Water** (emotional/heart)
Fire (energetic/action) / **Air** (mental/mind)

The Major Arcana consists of a fifth suit, the ("ether-real") element of Spirit. The numbers on the cards mark your progression in the ongoing life cycles you are living through.

Whether you are new to Tarot, or an experienced Tarot card reader, the booklet that comes with the boxed set of 78 cards provides invaluable keys for interpreting the cards. This exquisite collection of We'Moon art introduces you to a whole Council of We'Moon familiars, empowered spirit'real we'moon you can converse with, in consulting your inner guidance.

Musawa ▫ Mother Tongue Ink 2021

STAFF APPRECIATION

Deep gratitude. Recognition of small blessings. Large blessings. Meeting each other where we're at. Patience. Passionate resistance. In the making of this book over the last year, the We'Moon staff (along with the rest of the world) experienced a roller coaster of a year: 2020. Throughout all of the turmoil, this group was amazingly resilient! We learned how to use the virtual meeting technology to accomplish what we would normally do in person. We worked double-time to accommodate customers who couldn't visit brick and mortar stores to fulfill their We'Moon needs, and we advertised those stores, too, who were able to offer their goods in safe ways throughout the shutdowns.

As the US reels from the blatant injustices and killing of our black and brown brothers and sisters, we rally as we are able, with calls to support those who are on the front lines, both in the tangible realms as well as energetic fields.

We commiserated, shared fears, sometimes made light in order to bear the weight. We suffered our own personal challenges and losses. We encouraged each other. We fell down and got back up. I am proud to be part of this group of women who create We'Moon, who prioritize spirit and community. We're so appreciative of the support you all showed us throughout this time. May we all be blessed with continued passion and compassion, fortitude and resilience in the years to come. Blessings of deep healing to us all.

Barbara Dickinson © Mother Tongue Ink 2021
In sweet remembrance of Ricky the Schipperke, our constant shipping house companion.
Our little "Shipperke" pictured here with Susie, is sorely missed.

WE'MOON ANCESTORS

We honor wemoon who have gone between the worlds of life and death recently, beloved contributors to wemoon culture who continue to bless us from the other side. We appreciate receiving notice of their passing.

Debra White Plume (1954–2020), a member of the Oglala Lakota tribe, was an activist committed to protect traditional tribal life and land. She began this sacred work in 1973 at Wounded Knee when activists were demanding that tribal treaties be honored. In 1999, Debra cofounded Owe Aku ("Bring Back the Way"), working to protect treaty rights. She was concerned about her people's water supply, threatened especially by pipeline projects (Keystone XL and Dakota Access), and she was a leader of the anti-pipeline protests at Standing Rock in 2016."Water is the domain of the women in our nation. And so, it's our privilege and our obligation to protect water."

E. Margaret Burbridge (1919–2020), British-American, was an astrophysicist and one of the foremost astronomers in the world, opening career doors for women in the field. She was the first woman to be Director of the Royal Greenwich Observatory. Her work made a huge impact on the history of modern astronomy, with innovative contributions to the theory of quasars and to determining measurements of galaxies. She was a passionate student of the stars and co-authored an especially influential paper on the formation of all heavy elements by nuclear fusion inside the stars.

Ffiona Morgan (1941–2020) Her life's work was devoted to Goddess-centered spirituality. In 1984 she created the *Daughters of the Moon Tarot*, one of the first oracular card decks offering artful entry into the magic of Goddess divination. She traveled world-wide, teaching Tarot and astrology, writing and consulting, offering ritual as an ordained Dianic High Priestess. Her creativity gifted women's communities with visual arts, singing, and drumming; her activist passions focused on feminist and environmental issues.

Florence Howe (1929–2020) has been called "The Mother of Women's Studies." She changed the cultural landscape with her co-founding in 1970 of the Feminist Press, which became a powerful platform for socially conscious women writers, past and present, whose voices had been overlooked in American literature. Teacher, editor, activist, visionary, Florence Howe was a force of nature, dedicated to feminism and social justice at a time when the women's movement was birthing a new era. She resourced the emerging field of Women's Studies with her vigorous mentorship and with publications that she ushered into bookstores, libraries, classrooms, study halls, and book bags.

Jade River (1950–2020) devoted her life to serving the spiritual awakening and empowerment of women. Her most fervent hope was that "no woman should ever feel alone." She co-created *Of a Like Mind*, a widely circulated spiritual newsletter that assisted women in creating community, and authored *Tying the Knot: a Gender-Neutral Guide to Handfastings or Weddings for Pagans and Goddess Worshippers*. She co-founded the Re-formed Congregation of the Goddess-International in 1983 and served as its Consistery Executive until her passing. Within RCG-I she created the Women's Theological Institute for women seeking to deepen their studies and understanding of the Goddess; nearly 50 women have been ordained after graduation. She is honored throughout the international goddess movement for her creativity and vast wisdom.

Janine Canan (1942–2020) was a wise, prolific, and bright spirit whose writings were published in We'Moon over many years, and in hundreds of other books, journals, and anthologies. Poet, essayist, holistic psychiatrist, story teller, translator, and editor, she offered brilliant reflections on gender, nature, art. She wrote poignant devotions to the divine feminine, and lucid challenges to an unexamined consciousness. "I hope my poems will stir the mind, the heart, and the inner eye of whoever may discover them, awakening him/her to a new awareness of life." And so they do, Janine.

Katherine Johnson (1918–2020) defied conventions of what a Black girl child growing up in West Virginia in the 1920s and '30s might do. She loved numbers, and counted everything. Fascinated and brilliant with math, she sped through school, starting high school at 13 and college at 15. Math called to her always, and she eventually became a research mathematician for NASA, working on critical research projects to enable space travel. She authored or coauthored 26 research projects, designing plans for orbital spacecraft, using high math geometries to send astronauts into space and back. She was hailed, along with other Black women in NASA, in the movie "Hidden Figures."

Lenn Keller (1950–2020), a photographer and filmmaker, co-founded the San Francisco Bay Area Lesbian Archives. Her collection of photos, flyers, articles, videotapes, memorabilia of every kind from the activist days of the 1970s and '80s forms the core of this archival wealth. Lenn was one of the leaders among black lesbian activists challenging racism and oppressive gender roles. In later life, she focused on preserving her collection of historical moments that documented a social revolution and a thriving lesbian subculture. Her work was first publicly exhibited in "*Fierce Sistas: the art, activism and community of lesbians of color, 1975–2000*" which sparked the creation of the Lesbian Archives in 2014.

Lesley "Ellen" Moore (1947–2020) was a community activist, who co-founded the first intentional women's land community in Oregon, with her sister Musawa in 1973—which became We'Moon Land 15 years later. Meanwhile, Lesley (a farmer and a mama bear, at heart) had started a rabbit farm, adopted a child, and moved to Maine (via an underground journey of migratory homelessness—common to lesbian mothers before legal protections). There she joined a community dedicated to serving rural homeless people (Mandela Farm and H.O.M.E, inc)—founded in the early '70s by two sisters (nuns)—where she found her life partner, and her true calling!

Phyllis Lyon (1924–2020) was an extraordinary trailblazer, energizing lesbian culture, women's liberation and gay rights for decades. In 1955, she and her partner, Del Martin, co-founded the Daughters of Bilitis, the first social and political organization for lesbians. They published *The Ladder*, the first nationally distributed lesbian publication, from 1956–72, and in 1972 published *Lesbian Woman*, a book of non-fiction writing foundational to lesbian feminism. Phyllis and Del continued their passion for progressive politics, with special fervor for women's rights, ending discrimination against gays & lesbians, countering domestic abuse. In 2008, after 55 years as life partners, they were the first gay couple to be legally married.

Ruth Bader Ginsburg (1933–2020) was a diminutive woman who wrought gigantic changes in US jurisprudence, moving heaven and earth, bit by bit, to end legal discrimination against women. She was a brilliant student, one of only nine women in their class of 500, the first female member of the *Harvard Law Review*, and eventually the first tenured female professor at Columbia. During the '70s she led the ACLU's fight against gender discrimination, winning six landmark cases before the US Supreme Court. By the time she was appointed to the Court in 1993, Ruth had worked a revolution in the legal struggle for women's equality: hundreds of state and federal laws restricting what women could do had been overruled. As a Supreme Court judge, she continued, in her methodical, steady way, to be an icon for feminist justice, sometimes arguing for gender fairness statutes that also required equal rights for men. Her stamina and determination to serve, despite recurrent illness, is legendary. A true Amazon among us.

© COPYRIGHTS AND CONTACTING CONTRIBUTORS

Copyrights for most of the work published in We'Moon belong to each individual contributor. Please honor the copyrights: ©: <u>do not reproduce without the express permission of the artist, author, publisher or Mother Tongue Ink,</u> depending on whose name follows the copyright sign. Some wemoon prefer to free the copyright on their work: ¤: <u>this work may be passed on among women who wish to reprint it "in the spirit of We'Moon."</u> In all cases, give credit to the author/artist and to We'Moon, and send each a copy. If the artist has given permission, We'Moon may release contact information. Contact mothertongue@wemoon.ws or contact contributors directly.

CONTRIBUTOR BYLINES AND INDEX
SEE PAGE 236 FOR INFO ABOUT HOW YOU CAN BECOME A WE'MOON CONTRIBUTOR!

recognize their own sacred heart and cosmic divinity, and through this recognition, may we remember our innate grace. autumnskyeart.com, FB: Autumn-Skye, Etsy: AutumnSkyeART **p. 49, 79, 89, 103**

Barbara Dickinson (Sunny Valley, OR) is trundling happily along on this adventure of life, ever curious, always learning, constantly course-correcting. May we all harvest every last drop of joy from each moment. **p. 4, 25, 183**

Barb Levine (Corvallis, OR) I live a quiet life searching for meaning and connection through nature and relationships, painting, gardening, mandalas, and family. Like women everywhere, I hope to be a tiny spark that allows love, beauty, and healing into the world. **p. 45, 54**

Barbara Largent (Bend, OR) I'm an earth-loving mama, energy healer, and physician. I work in many media, my art flowing with motion and emotion. I create art because it makes me healthy and whole. You can find my work at barbaralargenthealing.com **p. 119**

Beate Metz (Berlin, Germany) was an astrologer, feminist, translator & mainstay of We'Moon's German edition & the European astrological community. **p. 207**

Bethroot Gwynn (Myrtle Creek, OR) 26 years as We'Moon's Special Editor & 46 at Fly Away Home women's land, growing food, theater & ritual. For info about spiritual gatherings, summertime visits send SASE to POB 593, Myrtle Creek, OR 97457. For info about her new book of poetry and plays, *Preacher Woman for the Goddess*, see p. 233. **p. 25, 27**

Betty LaDuke (Ashland, OR) "Your creations are filled with joy, delight, and hope, all of which we desperately need right now."—Gov Kate Brown, 2020. Bettyladuke.com **p. 31, 59**

Brigidina (Elgin, IL) I am a TreeSister and my Sacred Earth Art is created using natural pigments, sacred cedar & rose oils, peace fire coals, honey, and waters from 54 sacred sites. Brigidina.com and Treesisters.org **p. 89**

Caroline Miskenack (Courtenay, BC) is an artist, poet, nurse, and Intentional Creativity teacher and coach, guiding others on their healing journeys. She is a member of the Co-Creation Circle at Musea-Center for Intentional Creativity. Visit her at carolinemiskenack.com **p. 106**

Catherine Firpo, PhD (San Mateo, CA) My emphasis includes the magnificence and mystery of the creative process that each person embodies. I believe this allows fierce new perspectives and global intelligence to come forward, with conscious awareness and compassion, into our beloved world. **p. 154**

Catja Wilson (Salt Spring Island, BC) was born in the beautiful land of South Africa. She is an artist and bodyworker, fascinated by sorrow, love, loss and the nature of the heart. **p. 113**

Chantel Camille Roice (Portland, OR) is a swamp witch living amidst her books and candles, making art and scrawling poetry in vintage ruffles all night long. You can find her work, as well as links to her social media and shop at stillwaterteacupillustration.com **p.118**

Christine Irving (Denton, TX) is a poet, priestess, and ritualist. Her work combines the contemporary and mythic in poetry books like *Return to Innana, Sitting on the Hag Seat,* and her novel *Magdalene A.D.* Find Christine and her other works at christineirving.com **p. 30, 31**

Cici Artemisia (Lyle, WA) is an artist and musician living in the Pacific Northwest USA, enjoying her last lifetime on earth. ciciart.com p.131

Corinne "Bee Bop " Trujillo (Denver, CO) Playing on the tightrope between child-like and wise crone, my work strives to inspire womyn to be their own. Learn more at corinnebeebop.com IG: @corinnebeebop. **p. 29, 127**

Danielle Helen Ray Dickson (Nanaimo, BC) considers her art to have the power to heal people, change lives and shed light on the world in a new way. She infuses this into her work with each intentional brush stroke. Danielledickson.com **p.155, 176**

Debra Hall (Garroch Glen, Scotland) I am a soulmaker, artist, author and poet. I am currently writing a book called *her whole nature* to celebrate women's full blooded, fully embodied spiritual nature. I always like to hear from We'Moon friends— debra. ha@hotmail.co.uk, herwholenature.com **p. 22, 45, 60, 77, 98, 117, 134, 153, 170**

Deneene Bell (Guerneville, CA) I am a mother-writer-teacher-yogini-bitch-fighter-goddess living in the redwoods north of San Francisco. Amidst these magical trees, near a great river, I nurture little spirits + words, practice and facilitate yoga, and hold womyn's circles. Wildsageyoga.com **p. 120**

Denise Kester (Ashland, OR) is a mixed media printmaking artist, renowned teacher and founder/artistic director of Drawing on the Dream, an art distribution company. Announcing the new book *Drawing on the Dream—Finding My Way by Art.* drawingonthedream.com **p. 91**

Destiney Powell (Murfreesboro, TN) is a visual artist specializing in the visual storytelling of black culture through colorful paintings. Learn more: poeticallyillustrated.net **p. 73**

Diana Celeste (Panajachel, Guatemala) is a clairvoyant, a healer, a mother of five living in the magic of Lake Atitlán, her volcanos, and the lovely Mayan people. **p. 66**

Diana Denslow (Poulsbo, WA) is a mother, artist, crone, and cat lady now emerging from four or five years of sabbatical. Diana can be reached at dianaherself66@gmail.com and her artwork can now be seen on Etsy at etsy.com/shop/MysticVisionsGallery **p. 27, 100**

Diane Norrie (Coquitlam, BC) Visual artist and teacup reader. I live in the Fraser River Valley in Small Red Salmon BC. I am strongly influenced by a spiritual connection. It makes my work constantly changing and evolving. **p. 171**

Dianne Adel (Woodacre, CA) is a healer who has spent the last three decades devoted to spiritual and somatic practices that empower women and guide them in trusting and knowing we are divine in nature and inherently unbroken. She is also an equine bodyworker and author. **p. 37**

Dorrie Joy (Avalon, UK) is a prolific, intuitive artist working in many mediums. Grandmother, builder, Moon lodge dweller. She is committed to active decolonization, and teaches traditional craft and ancestral skills. Books, prints, wild craft, original art: dorriejoy.co.uk **p. 77, 133**

Earthdancer (Golconda, IL) is a forest dweller and protector of the Shawnee National Forest, and co-creator and multi-tasking mystic at Interwoven Permaculture Farm. FB: The Poetry of Earthdancer, interwovenpermaculture.com **p. 90**

Elise Stuart (Silver City, NM) is a poet + writer who loves giving voice to youth. She has taught tons of poetry workshops in schools. Her first poetry book and memoir, *My Mother + I, We Talk Cat,* was published in 2017. **p. 49, 174**

Ellen Lorenzi-Prince (Lebanon, OH) is an artist, poet, and priestess. Her devotion to the mysterious finds expression most often through tarot. Her *Tarot of the Crone, Dark Goddess Tarot, Minoan Tarot,* and *Greek Goddess Tarot* are her offerings to the ancient ones. Darkgoddesstarot.com **p. 156**

Elspeth McLean (Pender Island, BC) uses colour, pattern, and symbology in her artwork to create vibrant, uplifting pieces. She hopes her art connects the viewer with their inner child. "Express and celebrate the colours of your soul." elspethmclean.com **p. 68**

Emily Kedar (Toronto, ON) is a writer and therapist. She welcomes contact through emilykedar.com **p. 54, 95**

Emily Kell (Boulder, CO) Witchy fem visions. IG: @emilythefunkypriestess, website: emilykell.com **p. 109, 165**

Erin Kundrie (Berkeley, CA) is an author, teacher, and herbal alchemist. Find out more about her work at CedarRoseTemple.com **p. 179**

Erin Robertson (Louisville, CO) teaches outdoor writing classes (wildwriters.org). Her poetry has been published in the *North American Review, Poet Lore*, SageGreenJournal. com and *FUNGI Magazine*. Erinrobertson.org, robertsonrambles.com **p. 76**

Flora ikiGaia (Leeuwarden, Holland) gets inspired by the spirited natural world, permaculture and the magic of plants, fungi and mystical beings. Her wild wish is to inspire people to reconnect with nature and themselves. Visit ikigai.art, IG: @ikigaiaart or fb.com/ikiGaiaArt **p.157**

Glenda "GG" Goodrich (Salem, OR) is an Artist, Art Doula and SoulCollage® Facilitator. She offers workshops that encourage. glendagoodrich.com **p. 82**

Greta Boann Perry (Oakland, CA) since childhood, has been deeply connected with Mother Earth, and ocean sailor country. Artist, potter, tree planter, forest protector, meditation teacher and painter. About which healers, shaman say, "your paintings are full of life energy, healing power." HealingSpiritScapes.com **p. 64**

Gretchen Butler (Cazadero, CA) My book, *Deep Time: An art Odyssey*, explores evolutionary ramifications of the sun and earth's carbon connection with stars. Scientific information inspires imagination. See more at gretchenbutlerwildartcafe.com **p. 99**

Gretchen Lawlor (back from Mexico to Whidbey Island, WA) We'Moon oracle, now mentor to new oracles & astrologers. Astrology is my great passion—the stars my friends, my loves, my allies. Let me help connect you to these wise guides. Readings in person, skype or zoom. 206-698-3741 (call or text) light@whidbey.com; gretchenlawlor.com **p. 15, 20**

Heather Roan Robbins (Ronan, MT): ceremonialist, counselor, and astrologer for over 40 years, creator of the *Starcodes Astro-Oracle* deck, author of *Moon Wisdom, Everyday Palmistry*, and several children's books, writes the weekly Starcodes column for *We'Moon* and the *Santa Fe New Mexican* and works with people in person in MT and by phone or zoom. Roanrobbins.com **p. 8, 12, 204, 205**

Heidi Denkers (Renton, WA) A small town girl with MA in Expressive Arts Therapy, Heidi loves words, colors, ideas. Trained at the Cunning Crow Apothecary in Seattle where she now lives As an Art Witch, find her on IG: @therarewildheidi & FB group: CreativeStrength. **p. 177**

Helen Seay Art (Tetonia, ID) is a visionary artist creating art with intention, spirit and love. She lives in the Tetons with her Love and animals, growing food, dancing and smiling. Contact her through her website helenseayart.com or helen.seay@gmail.com **p. 19, 61, 81, 142, 160**

Helena Arturaleza (The Netherlands) "Rebirth Earth" is a self-portrait that I hope inspires the viewer to look deeper within to witness beliefs that keep us from being truly empowered. Look at them with patience, presence and anticipation. So we can be inspired, vulnerable and in alignment with our chakras and our sexuality. Together we can birth a new earth. And so it is. arturaleza.art **p. 11**

Ingrid Johnston (Seattle, WA) is a mystic, healer and guide. She spends time communing with the divine and working with people to bring transformation and deeper connection to their lives. Find out more at ingridsacredhealing.com **p. 146**

Jakki Moore (Oslo, Norway) Irish Jakki is an international artist and story-teller currently based in Norway. She feels very blessed to be able to work at what she loves to do. She would love to hear from you. Jakkiart.com **p. 1, 56, 80, 182**

Jan Pellizzer (Grass Valley, CA) I am blessed to have found my Creative Spirits and nurture them with inspiration from the beauty around me. Life is better lived in color. FB: pellizzerjan, fineartamerica.com/profiles/jan-pellizzer/shopp. **p. 58**

Janet Newton (Peoria, IL) is a recently retired design/multimedia teacher who is finally enjoying time to pursue her love of art. She has completed two Tarot decks of original artwork. **p. 41, 43**

Janyt Piercy (Campbell River, BC) I have had a passion for art my whole life. I work in many mediums, from my home on beautiful Vancouver Island. Contact me @ Janyt.piercy@gmail.com or on Facebook. **p. 74**

Jeanne K. Raines (Churubusco, IN) is a sometimes artist who was caught by Medusa and remains ensnared; she's also a retired Mental Health Counselor and Massage Therapist. jeannekraines@gmail.com • **p. 33**

Jennifer Highland (Plymouth, NH) writes, hikes, tends her vegetable garden, and practices Osteopathy. **p. 46, 71**

Jennifer Lothrigel (Lafayette, CA) is a spiritual coach, poet and visual artist in the San Francisco Bay area. Connect with her online at Jenniferlothrigel.com or by email: JenniferLothrigel@gmail.com **p. 67**

Jenny Hahn (Kansas City, MO) captures the inward journey through bold, colorful expression using acrylic paint. As cofounder of Creative Nectar Studio, she holds space for others to reclaim their creativity using painting as a tool for mindfulness and self-discovery. Jennyhahnart.com **p. 46, 172**

Jo Jayson (Harrison, NY) is a self-taught, intuitive painter, teacher and author, internationally acclaimed for her work on the Sacred Feminine and author of the award-winning oracle deck and book *Self-Love Through the Sacred Feminine.* Through her paintings she teaches self-healing, and self-development to women worldwide. Jojayson.com **p. 36, 161**

Joanne M. Clarkson (Port Townsend, WA) Her fifth poetry collection, *The Fates,* won Bright Hill Press' annual contest. She is a poet, a nurse and enjoys reading palms and Tarot. See more at JoanneClarkson.com **p. 53**

Johanna Elise (Salt Spring Island, BC) is a teacher for children, a writer and a singer, blessed to live on this beautiful island with many kindred human and animal spirits. **p. 166**

K.A.K Lecky (High Point, NC) looks like a ghost and smells like a forest. She is neither. Yet. kackleckyillustration@gmail.com, kakleckyillustration.com **p. 48**

Karen L. Culpepper (Fort Washington, MD) is a momma, creative, dreamer, herbalist, and practitioner. She loves depth in her relationships, sunshine, being in salt water and laughter. Let's connect: klcccollective.ck.page/60473ddeac, IG @klcccollective, hello@klcccollective.com **p. 18**

Katharyn Howd Machan (Ithaca, NY) author of 32 published poetry collections and Professor of Writing at Ithaca College, directed the Feminist Women's Writing Workshops, Inc. In 2021, she edited *Adrienne Rich: A Tribute Anthology* deeply mourning the poet's death. (Split Oak Press) faculty.ithaca.edu/machan **p. 41, 121**

Kay Kemp (Bastrop, TX) creates heart-inspired paintings and mixed media collage. Visionary art celebrates Sacred Feminine to inspire empowerment and transformation. Spiritworks4u.com & kaykemp.com **p. 75**

Kay Marie Porterfield (Littleton, CO) Her work has appeared in *The Sun, Eastern Iowa Review, Two Hawks Quarterly, Hippocampus,* and a number of other publications. **p. 136**

Kendra Ward (Charlotte, VT) LAc., MAOM, is an acupuncturist, teacher, and writer whose work weaves feminine and earth-based sensibilities, always seeking the rapture of what makes us come utterly alive. Learn more about her at kendraward. com **p. 80**

KoCo Collab (Denver, CO) is the coalescence of artists Aiko Szymczak and Corinne "Bee Bop" Trujillo. Our mission is to reflect feminine essence through the use of universal languages and cross-cultural imagery using color theory, ethnically ambiguous portraiture and archetypes. We weave our travels, heritages and personal stories to depict the modern woman's mind. kococollab.com **p. 123**

Kristen Roderick (Toronto, ON) is a ceremonialist, writer, mama and rites of passage guide. When she's not designing courses, she's foraging through the woods looking for mushrooms or apprenticing herself to the ancient ways of weaving the fibre art. Spiritmoving.org **p. 84, 85**

KT InfiniteArt (Freeport, NY) Creatrix, artist, writer inspired by sensuality and spirit. IG @KTInfiniteArt Check out more artwork. Prints available: InfiniteArtWorld.com **p. 10, 60, 121**

Kym Stine (Shrewsbury, PA) is a healing arts practitioner and visionary artist. She channels and paints customized soul portraits, Transformative Art. Artist, speaker, author. FB: Soul Vision Art by Kym Stine. etsy.com/shop/soulvisionart Artbykym@gmail.com **p. 110**

Leah Marie Dorion (Prince Albert, SK) An interdisciplinary Métis artist, Leah's paintings honour the spiritual strength of Aboriginal women, the Sacred Feminine. She believes women play a key role in passing on vital knowledge for all humanity, which is deeply reflected in her artistic practice. Visit her at leahdorion.ca **p. 117**

Leah Markman (Eugene, OR) A Tarot enthusiast, astrology lover and leather craftswoman. She spends her time in the sunshine with her dog, horse and VW Bus. Visit her etsy for more writings and leatherwork! Etsy.com/shop//DreamtenderLeather IG: DreamtenderLeather **p. 24**

Lillie Falco-Adkins (San Francisco, CA) Witch, healer, researcher, diviner, and nascent herbalist helping to heal our female lineages by learning and re-membering the divine feminine and women's sacred work. Find me at wildishsoulsong.com and IG: @wildsoulsong **p. 122**

Linda James (Seattle, WA) is an intuitive watercolor painter, educator, and flower essence practitioner creating her life in the wonderous environment of the Pacific Northwest. Lindajamesart.com **p. 202**

Lindsay Carron (Los Angeles, CA) Lindsay's drawings and murals are a vibrant ode to the spirit of this planet and tell a story brimming with hope. Her work is dedicated to social and environmental justice and resilience. lindsaycarron.com **p. 135**

Liz Darling (Pittsburg, KS) is a visual artist and teacher. Deliberate and intricate, Darling creates precise compositions that center on themes of spirituality, transience, the divine feminine, and the natural world. Lizdarlingart.com **p. 12, 179**

Lorraine Schein (Sunnyside, NY) is a writer whose work has appeared in *VICE, Terraform, Wild Musette, Fiddler's Green Magazine, Tragedy Queens: Stories Inspired by Lana del Rey & Sylvia Plath* and *Eighteen*. Her poetry book *The Futurist's Mistress* is at mayapplepress.com **p. 105, 140**

Maeanna Welti (Portland, OR—unceded Chinook land) is a writer, astrologer and witch. She is the author of the *Healing Wheel Samhain to Samhain* workbook. Maeanna offers readings, coaching, support for ancestral and personal healing, and teaches astrology and the fundamentals of witchcraft. maeannawelti.com IG: @queenmaeanna **p.11, 39, 51, 63, 75, 87, 101, 111, 125, 137, 147, 161, 173**

Mahada Thomas (Okanagan Falls, BC) is a healing artist, writer, soul singer, spirit dancer, and Munay-Ki EarthKeeper. She shares her healing journey to inspire others. Contact her at mahadathomas@yahoo.ca. Check out her youtube channel: Mahada Thomas Healing Arts, or visit mahadathomas.com **p. 169**

Mandalamy Arts (Topeka, KS) Amy is an artist, psychologist, and life learner & homeschooling mom. She finds inspiration from nature, wildlife, stargazing, hiking, travel, yoga, art, and music. She can be found on FB and IG as Mandalamy Arts **p. 232**

Margaret Lynn Brown (Brevard, NC) is a writer, historian, and avid hiker. All of the images she records are as discovered on a trail with no staging. margaretlynnbrown.com **p. 126**

Marla Faith (Nashville, TN) is an artist, poet, and educator. Visit her gallery of uplifting colorful art at marlafaith.com. Her three books of art & poetry are *Art of the Divine: Buddhist, Hindu and Earth Gods and Goddesses; The Diver and the Pearl*; and *Listening to the Bones*. **p. 116**

Marnie Recker (Tofino, BC) I am a photographer and painter. My photographs are time capsules of people, places, light and love. I create paintings to honour the spirit of creativity and to celebrate the wondrous beauty of being alive. Learn more at Marnierecker.com **Front Cover**

Mary Ancilla Martinez (Torrance, CA) is a New Mexican born artist who paints the liminal . . . those in between spaces . . . the misty and mystical, wild and free ethereal places where unseen greets seen, where dark weaves light, and land meets sea and sky. Maryancilla.com **p. 52**

Mathilda Berg (Norresundby, Denmark) Art is the outlet for my inner spirit. My wish is to give the viewer a visual experience wherein the story is created in the mind's eye. There, it is only the imagination that sets the limits. Mathildaberg.com, mathilderness@gmail.com **p. 170**

Megan Welti (Clarksbrug, MA) is an artist, poet and energy worker living in Western Massachusetts with her husband, four children, and many fur babies. You can find prints of her original watercolors at redrootrising. squarespace.com **p. 32, 147, 148, 149**

Melissa Coss Aquino, PhD (Bronx, NY) is a Puerto Rican writer from the Bronx and an Associate Professor of English at Bronx Community College, CUNY. Her upcoming novel, *Carmen and Grace*, is about a girl gang from the Bronx encountering the Feminine Divine. melissacossaquino.com **p. 28, 114**

Melissa Kae Mason, "MoonCat!" (EARTH) Traveling Astrologer, Artist, Radio DJ, Photographer, Jewelry Creator, PostCard Sender, Goddess Card Inventor, Seer of Patterns, Adventurer and Home Seeker. See www.LifeMapAstrology.com Contact: LifeMapAstrology@gmail.com **p. 206**

Melissa Rees (Gardiner, MT) is a woman of the Rockies who thrives in and is inspired by moments of wildness and boundless laughter. Poet, dancer, organic farmer and lover of the land and sky that has given so much. **p. 73**

Melissa Stratton Pandina (Westboro, MA) is a painter whose work is inspired by living magic. Twenty years ago, she delved into Shamanism after encountering a chronic illness. Her work is inspired by folklore. Deshria.com Paintings. Prints. Classes. **p. 145**

Meredith Heller (Tiburon, CA) is a poet, educator, and author of three poetry collections, *Songlines, River Spells,* and *Yuba Witch,* and a book, *Write a Poem, Save Your Life.* She teaches writing workshops nationally on Zoom for women and kids. meredithheller.com **p. 65, 159**

Mimi Foyle (Rio Guaycuyacu, Ecuador) My passion is for the rivers, forests, and people with whom I live and work for the well-being of self, planet, and all-our-relations. With gratitude. guaycuyacu@gmail.com guaycuyacu.net **p. 85**

Mindi Meltz (Hendersonville, NC) is the author of two novels—*Beauty,* and *Lonely in the Heart of the World*—and an upcoming fairy-tale trilogy. She creates personal Animal Wisdom Card decks customized for individuals' power animals and life journeys. mindimeltz.com **p. 61**

Molly Brown (Bolinas, CA) is a painter, botanical art teacher, shamanic practitioner, herbal potion maker and lover of nature, dance, chocolate and feeling grateful. mollybrown777@gmail.com mollybrownartist.org **p. 62**

Molly M. Remer MSW, D.Min (Rolla, MO) is a poet, priestess, teacher, and artist who lives in central Missouri. She is the creator of *Story Goddesses* and the Publisher of *Woman Runes.* Brigidsgrove.com **p. 59, 139**

Musawa (Estacada, OR & Tesuque, NM) I have been hatching the We'Moon Tarot deck for ages, it seems—re-living every stage in my own Fool's journey, in the process—so I'm glad it's now finally coming out! I am looking forward to starting a whole new creative cycle personally, and in We'Moon . . . as in the World at large: we can only hope! **p. 180, 182, 198**

Natalie Bulan (Sussex, UK) My artwork is inspired by meditations arising from the body, somatic movement, Craniosacral Therapy, and Nature. "Visions of Health." IG: @nataliebulan.art, nataliekeegan.co.uk **p. 175**

Natasza Zurek (Naramata, BC) is mother to two children, a full time artist and avid trail runner. Her artwork is a commitment to the thriving and beautification of our commons of air, water and information ecology. IG: natka01 nataszazurekart.com **p. 159**

Nell Aurelia (Devon, UK) is a writer, mother and performance artist, living on the edge of Dartmoor. Contact: nell.aurelia.admiral@yahoo.co.uk or go to: thesingingdark.wordpress.com **p. 158**

Nicole Miz (Alpharetta, GA) is a Clairvoyant Intuitive Reader, Reiki Master Healer and a Spiritual Artist. She creates art to express the higher realms and feelings of love, unity, and compassion. nicolemiz.com **p. 69**

Nolween LM (France) is a French painter and author of *L'oracle du chemin intérieur.* She enjoys working on the feminine, healing and awakening, She desires to transmit through her creations harmony, serenity, and respect for every part of life. nolwenhozho.wixsite.com/del-pueblo **p. 163**

Nora Bruhn (San Francisco, CA) I find myself with one foot in the city and the other in the forests, deserts and waterways of California. I paint large scale murals of flowers cast in dramatic lighting. A perfect ménage of nature, femininity and sexuality. Currently enjoying the sweet and subversive act of leaving huge, sensuous {()} petals everywhere I go. Find me at konorebi.com. **p. 134**

Osha Waters (Niwot, CO) is a mama, birth and death doula, art and poetry diviner, devotee of the wild, and cultural change agent who supports the dismantling of oppressive systems and individual patterns in the name of collective liberation and love. kcwatersg@gmail.com **p. 70**

Patricia Wyatt (Santa Fe, NM) My paintings offer each of us a quiet moment to consider our paths, to remember our place at the circle and to know that we are the individual threads that complete one fabric. The women in *Spiritually Connected* are part of my collection of women from all over the world entitled *On Common Ground*. patriciawyattarts@comcast.net Patriciawyatt.com **p. 87**

Paula Franco (Cuidad de Buenos Aires, Argentina) is an Italo-Argentine Artist Shaman woman, visual and visionary illustrator, teacher in sacred art, writer and poet, astrologer, tarot reader, and creator of goddess cards and coloring book: *The Ancestral Goddess* and *Heaven and Earth*. Ladiosaancestral.com **p. 125**

Penn King (Dania Beach, FL) Let us honour That which created us and shine like stars in that Truth. Blessings **p. 24**

Rachel Creager Ireland (Austin, TX) is good at building campfires and remembering dreams. She self-published *Flight of Unknown Birds: Poems About the Wilderness and the Weirdness Within*. She blogs at veronicasgarden.wordpress.com **p. 151**

Rachel Cruse (Duncan, BC) Artist of the in-between moments. Learn more at Rachelcruse.com **p. 109, 113**

Robin D. Bruce (Boulder, CO) is a healer, teacher, writer, and singer, opening portals to spirit and wellness. Find her books, music, and healing tools at robindbruce.com **p. 128**

Robin Lea Quinlivan (Thomas, WV) is an oil painter who lives in the wilds of the Appalachian Mountains of West Virginia, where she co-owns an art gallery. She is inspired by love for the natural world, as well as the mutable nature and interconnectedness of all things. Robinquinlivan.etsy.com **p. 18**

Rosa Jimenez (Eugene, OR) My fulfilling work as a licensed massage therapist in this incredible location has left room in my life to pursue fun through the art forms that have inspired me over the years. rosashealingtouchmassage.qwestoffice.net **p. 150**

Rose Flint (Somerset, UK) is a poet, priestess and ceremonialist for the Goddess Conference in Glastonbury. She has published seven collections including *Mapping the Borders*, a prize-winning selection of her eco-poetry. poetrypf.co.uk/roseflintpage **p. 138**

RXANDRSN (Atlanta, GA) My art is about harmonizing the duality within self—a complicated balancing act, as it means hiding many aspects of self that don't fit the mold of our culture. My findings are translated into process sketches which evolve into biomorphic and culturally reflective mixed media pieces. rxann.n.wundrland@gmail.com, IG: @rxandrsn, rxannnwundrland.wixsite.com/rxandrsn **p. 63**

S.I Zimmerman (Medford, OR) Living in the Pause Art and Designs. **p. 8**

Sandra Pastorius (Ashland, OR) has been a practicing Astrologer since 1979, and a Featured Writer for We'Moon since 1990. Look for her collected We'Moon essays, "Galactic Musings" under Resources at wemoon.ws. With Sun in Gemini, she delights in blending the playful and the profound. Sandra offers individual and couples charts, readings and transit updates in person or by phone. Email her about astrology classes at: sandrapastorius@gmail.com. Read more articles here: wemoon.ws/blogs/sandras-cosmic-trip. Peace Be! **p. 14, 16, 208**

Sandra Stanton (Farmington, ME) continues to explore empathic connections between people, other species, and Mother Earth. World Goddesses & tree lore combine in *The Green World Oracle*, with Kathleen Jenks, published by Schiffer. Goddessmyths.com, sandrastantonart.com **p. 93, 141**

Sandy Bot-Miller (St. Cloud, MN) loves playing with words, fibers and oil pastels. She creates to nurture her own well-being and to connect with others in making the world a better place for all. sandybotmiller@gmail.com **p. 22**

Sarah Satya (Salt Spring Island, BC) Devoted to praising the sacredness of life, the preciousness of hearts, to stand in wonder of Earth and protect Her and Her creatures. I am open to collaborations that support this vision. sarahtralala.art@gmail.com **p. 102**

Schehera VanDyke (Bolinas, CA) Inspired by the sea, I go there for perspective, peace of mind, and fresh thoughts. I have seen the most profound beauty and magic on the beaches, in the waves, between the sky and water. My artwork is nature inspired. Art is healing, magic, essential and relevant. Art is life! scheheradesign.com **p. 67**

Serena Supplee (Moab, UT) The beauty, truth and freedom of canyons and rivers pulse through her. Serena paints with watercolors and oils, working from her drawings rather than photos, trusting her creative process. serenasupplee.com **p. 98**

Shauna Crandall (Driggs, ID) Her art explores the role of women in nature, society, history and myth, utilizing various media appropriate to express the theme. See more of her art at shaunacrandallart.com or contact her at skcrandall@yahoo.com **p. 112**

Shelley Anne Tipton Irish (Seattle, WA) When I paint, I feel like a choreographer pausing the dance of shadow, light, and color at the precise moment where all of them are in their full expression. Art is my life ritual. Gallerysati.com **p. 86, 108**

Shelley Blooms (Cleveland, OH) is a Spirit Pilgrim, ever on the trail of cosmic breadcrumbs by which the muses choose to amuse the noodle, through picture, poem, kit and caboodle. **p. 57, 126**

Sheri Howe (Alexander, NC) Artist & Teacher. My work is a moment of contemplation, an offering, a prayer. It reflects my experience with all that is ancient, mysterious, powerful, sustaining and beautiful in the world and our interconnectedness. Sherihowe. com, etsy.com/shop/SheriHoweArt **p. 55**

Sheryl J. Shapiro (Seattle, WA) seeks to explore and reveal the depths of her Judaic roots, whispers from nature, and the complex beauty of community. ruachhalev@gmail.com **p. 68, 123**

Shiloh Sophia McCloud (Sonoma, CA) is a visionary artist, author, and curator. For over 27 years she has worked with sacred art through Intentional Creativity®. Her global community teaches medicine painting and offers a virtual museum for women. Musea.org, shilohsophia.com **p. 115**

Siobhan Mac Mahon (Leeds, UK) is an Irish Poet, Seer and Word Witch, whose work celebrates the return of the Sacred Feminine and our deep connection to the Earth. **p. 165**

Sophia Faria (Victoria, BC) A bridge of many worlds, Sophia is a Somatic Sex Educator, Copywriter, Content Creator, and Tantric Yoga Teacher. She grounds herself in valuable knowledge in the areas of erotic embodiment, empowered relationships and sacred sexuality. Soulfoodsex.com **p. 42**

Sophia Rosenberg (Lasqueti Island, BC) Thanks We'Moon for years supporting women writers and artists and for building alternative culture! Sophiarosenberg.com, Bluebeatle Studio on Etsy **p. 135, 171, Back Cover**

Stephanie A. Sellers (Fayetteville, PA) is a homesteader and poet who supports women who have been shunned by their biological relatives at sednasdaughters.com, on FB, and in her book *Family Mobbing: Healing Global Crisis for Women and Girls.* **p. 131, 162**

Sue Ellen Parkinson (Willits, CA) is a visionary artist who paints the Sacred Feminine. Her work has led her on a journey that has profoundly changed her life. In her icons, she focuses on creating life affirming, empowering images of women. Sueellenparkinson.com, miracleofyourlife.com **p. 34, 111, 137**

Sue Tyler Design (Tetonia, ID) Western artist, teacher and Earth advocate, has lived in the West her entire life. Her experience in the mountains and with animals fuel her inspiration. She has spent 30 years exploring, teaching, and sharing inspiration with others. Suetyler.com **p. 118**

Susa Silvermarie (Ajijic, Mexico) I write this in 2020 just four months into the global shift. Identity isn't singular anymore. I'm doing my part by offering *Poems for Flourishing* to the world. Perhaps by now you can visit me in Ajijic, Mexico. Susasilvermarie.com **p. 154**

Susan Baylies (Durham, NC) sells her lunar phases as cards, larger print charts and posters at snakeandsnake.com Email her at sbaylies@gmail.com **p. 228**

Susan Korsnick (York, PA) Fine artist, illustrator, and designer, creator and guidess of Come Home to Your Self events for women and girls, my message is LOVE, beauty, connection, empowerment, the knowledge that the everyday can be sacred. Susankorsnick.com, instagram and LinkedIN **p. 92**

Susan Levitt (San Francisco, CA) is an astrologer, tarot reader, and feng shui consultant. Her publications include *Taoist Astrology* and *Introduction to Tarot.* Follow her lunar astrology blog for new Moon and full Moon updates at susanlevitt.com **p. 19, 141, 199**

Suzanne Grace Michell (Sacramento, CA) I am passionate about, and delighted by, the interplay between the Divine, humanity, the natural world, and creativity. These connections inspire my life and art. It is a joy to share my work with you. RockMama.com **p. 4, 178**

Tamara Phillips (Vancouver, BC) creates watercolour artwork that celebrates the natural world and our connection to it. TamaraPhillips.ca **p. 47, 151**

Tanya Dahms (Regina, SK) is a scientist, writer, dancer and mother who cherishes the community of Mother Gaia. **p. 88**

Tara Luther (Chicago, IL) is a contemporary oil painter. Her work explores themes of mysticism, and multidimensional awareness. Tara received her Masters in Counseling in the Arts from Alder University. She's practiced astrology for 20 years, often using astrological archetypes in her art. TaraLuther.com IG: @TaraLuther22 **p.162**

Teya Jacobi (Loveland, CO) is a retired attorney and newspaper photographer living in the Colorado Rockies where she hikes and photographs nature. **p. 143**

Toni Truesdale (Biddeford, ME) Artist, muralist, teacher and illustrator, Toni celebrates women, the natural environment and the diversity of the world's cultures. Email: tonitruesdale@gmail.com, blog: tonitruesdale@blogspot.com, FB: toni truesdale art. Prints and cards available through tonitruesdale.com **p. 97, 139, 153**

Tonya J. Cunningham (Lake Forest Park, WA) I'm grateful for the gift of time given to me to create poems, watercolors, and daydreams. Although my spirit wishes to spend its day beachcombing, as a mother and teacher, I strive to inspire empathy and hope. TJpoet@comcast.net **p. 78**

Vasalisa (Guanajuato, Mexico) is a Mexican painter exploring realist expressions of archetypical emotions. She learned painting at an early age, taught by her maternal grandmother, and has continued her studies with international masters. vasalisart@gmail.com, vasalisart.com, IG: @vasalisart **p. 51**

Victoria Chimey Victoré (Delhi, NY) a.k.a. Lama Chimey, is a Swedish-American WOC, Budddist Meditation & Dharma Teacher, Ordained Minister, Performing Artist & Publisher of *Sky Dancer World*. She works globally and can be reached at skydancerworld.com or via social media. **p. 97**

Virginia Maria Romero Art (Las Cruces, NM) As an artist who is deeply concerned about protecting wildlife, I strive to make sure that my art helps educate and motivate people to protect nature. virginiamariaromero.com **p. 95**

Visual Lifesavers Art (Vancouver, WA) I love color and light, and play with that in my artwork. I often feel like a conduit as the flow of color and shape decide what they would like to become. More artwork by Jennifer Smith can be found at etsy.com/shop/VisualLifesaversArt **p. 168**

Wendy Page (Victoria, BC) *Dimensional Travel Series # 4* is just one of ten in the series. From the depths of the darkness comes my connection with source, each level a healing. My work is an invitation to go within . . . to realize there IS more . . . and to never stop looking sark_53@telus.net **p. 138**

Wilma L. Hoffman (Klamath, CA) Native born into the Northern California coastal tribes Tolowa and Yurok, Wilma creates original artwork. She currently resides in the Pacific Northwest Coastal area producing art & spending time with family. **p. 3**

Xelena González (San Antonio, TX) authored the award-winning picture books *All Around Us* and *Where Wonder Grows*. She manifested the divination deck *Loteria Remedios*, featuring powerful icons from her Mestiza culture. She journals daily on the pages of We'Moon. cincopuntos.com/product/where-wonder-grows **p. 133**

Zena Carlota (Raleigh, NC) is a musician, storyteller and visual artist working at the intersections of ritual and psychotherapy. As future arts therapist, she weaves movement, sound and visual arts into ceremony inspired by the folkloric traditions of the African Diaspora. Zenacarlota.com **p. 129**

Zoë Rayne (Sydney, Australia) is an oil painter from The Dandenong Ranges, Australia whose paintings portray the interweaving of magic, ritual and myth throughout her life. Her paintings are a reclamation of ancestral and old ways of being found in myth, story and folklore." Zoerayne.com, IG: @zoe_rayne **p. 167**

Errors/Corrections

In *We'Moon 2021* we accidentally printed Helena Artualeza's byline in Spanish! She was our back cover artist. Find her byline on page 189, and more about her on our "Errata and Corrigenda" web page.

We appreciate all the feedback we get, so please let us know if you find anything amiss. Please visit our "Errata and Corrigenda" web page near the beginning of the year to see any corrections published for this issue of We'Moon.

WE'MOON SKY TALK

Gaia Rhythms: We show the natural cycles of the Moon, Sun, planets and stars as they relate to Earth. By recording our own activities side by side with those of other heavenly bodies, we may notice what connection, if any, there is for us. The Earth revolves around her axis in one day; the Moon orbits around the Earth in one month ($29^1/_2$ days); the Earth orbits around the Sun in one year. We experience each of these cycles in the alternating rhythms of day and night, waxing and waning, summer and winter. The Earth/Moon/Sun are our inner circle of kin in the universe. We know where we are in relation to them at all times by the dance of light and shadow as they circle around one another.

The Eyes of Heaven: As seen from Earth, the Moon and the Sun are equal in size: "the left and right eye of heaven," according to Hindu (Eastern) astrology. Unlike the solar-dominated calendars of Christian (Western) patriarchy, We'Moon looks at our experience through both eyes at once. The **lunar eye of heaven** is seen each day in the phases of the Moon, as she is both reflector and shadow, traveling her $29^1/_2$-day path around the Earth in a "Moon" Month (from each new moon to the next, 13 times in a lunar year). Because Earth is orbiting the Sun at the same time, it takes the Moon $27^1/_3$ days to go through all the signs of the Zodiac—a sidereal month. The **solar eye of heaven** is apparent at the turning points in the Sun's cycle. The year begins with Winter Solstice (in the Northern Hemisphere), the dark renewal time, and journeys through the full cycle of seasons and balance points (solstices, equinoxes and the cross-quarter days in between). The **third eye** of heaven may be seen in the stars. Astrology measures the cycles by relating the Sun, Moon and all other planets in our universe through the backdrop of star signs (the zodiac), helping us to tell time in the larger cycles of the universe.

Measuring Time and Space: Imagine a clock with many hands. The Earth is the center from which we view our universe. The Sun, Moon and planets are like the hands of the clock. Each one has its own rate of movement through the cycle. The ecliptic, a 17° band of sky around the Earth within which all planets have their orbits, is the outer band of the clock where the numbers are. Stars along the ecliptic are grouped into constellations forming the signs of the zodiac—the twelve star signs are like the twelve numbers of the clock. They mark the movements of the planets through the 360° circle of the sky, the clock of time and space.

Whole Earth Perspective: It is important to note that all natural cycles have a mirror image from a whole Earth perspective—seasons occur at opposite times in the Northern and Southern Hemispheres, and day and night are at opposite times on opposite sides of the Earth as well. Even the Moon plays this game—a waxing crescent moon

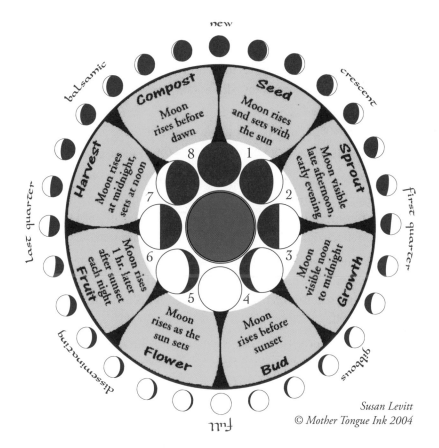

new

crescent

balsamic

Compost
Moon rises before dawn

Seed
Moon rises and sets with the sun

Sprout
Moon visible late afternoon, early evening

Harvest
Moon rises at midnight, sets at noon

Growth
Moon visible noon to midnight

Fruit
Moon rises 1 hr. later after sunset each night

Last quarter

first quarter

Flower
Moon rises as the sun sets

Bud
Moon rises before sunset

8
1
2
3
4
5
6
7

disseminating

gibbous

full

Susan Levitt
© Mother Tongue Ink 2004

in Australia faces right (☽), while in North America, it faces left (☾). We'Moon uses a Northern Hemisphere perspective regarding times, holy days, seasons and lunar phases. Wemoon who live in the Southern Hemisphere may want to transpose descriptions of the holy days to match seasons in their area. We honor a whole Earth cultural perspective by including four rotating languages for the days of the week, from different parts of the globe.

Whole Sky Perspective: It is also important to note that all over the Earth, in varied cultures and times, the dome of the sky has been interacted with in countless ways. The zodiac we speak of is just one of many ways that hu-moons have pictured and related to the stars. In this calendar we use the Tropical zodiac, which keeps constant the Vernal Equinox point at 0° Aries. Western astrology primarily uses this system. Vedic or Eastern astrology uses the Sidereal zodiac, which bases the positions of signs relative to fixed stars, and over time the Vernal Equinox point has moved about 24° behind 0° Aries.

Musawa © Mother Tongue Ink 2008

ASTROLOGY BASICS

Planets: Like chakras in our solar system, planets allow for different frequencies or types of energies to be expressed. See Mooncat's article (pp.206–207) for more detailed planetary attributes.

Signs: The twelve signs of the zodiac are a mandala in the sky, marking off 30° segments of a circle around the earth. Signs show major shifts in planetary energy through the cycles.

Glyphs are the symbols used to represent planets and signs.

Sun Sign: The Sun enters a new sign once a month (on or around the 21st), completing the whole cycle of the zodiac in one year. The sun sign reflects qualities of your outward shining self.

Moon Sign: The Moon changes signs approximately every 2 to $2^1/_2$ days, going through all twelve signs of the zodiac every $27^1/_3$ days (the sidereal month). The Moon sign reflects qualities of your core inner self.

Moon Phase: Each calendar day is marked with a graphic representing the phase of the Moon.

Lunar Quarter Phase: At the four quarter-points of the lunar cycle (new, waxing half, full and waning half moons), we indicate the phase, sign and exact time for each. These points mark off the "lunar week."

Day of the Week: Each day is associated with a planet whose symbol appears in the line above it (e.g., ☽☽☽ for Moon: Moonday)

Eclipse: The time of greatest eclipse is given, which is near to, but not at the exact time of the conjunction (☉☌☽) or opposition (☉☍☽). See "Eclipses" (p. 14).

Aspects (□ △ ☍ ☌ ✶ ⊼) are listed in fine print under the Moon sign each day, and show the angle of relationship between different planets as they move. Daily aspects provide something like an astrological weather forecast, indicating which energies are working together easily and which combinations are more challenging.

Transits are the motion of the planets and the moon as they move among the zodiacal constellations and in relationship to one another.

Ingresses (→): When the Sun, Moon and planets move into new signs.

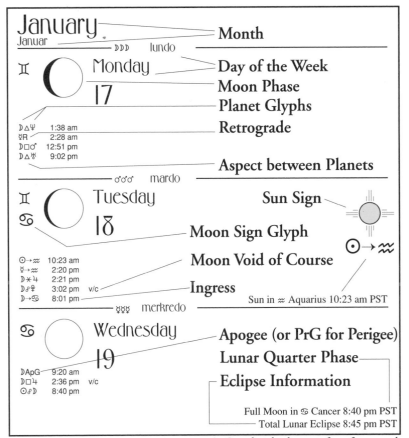

Sample calendar page for reference only

Moon "Void of Course" (D v/c): The Moon is said to be "void of course" from the last significant lunar aspect in each sign until the Moon enters a new sign. This is a good time to ground and center yourself.

Super Moon is a New or Full Moon that occurs when the Moon is at or within 90% of perigee, its closest approach to Earth. On average, there are four to six Super Moons each year. Full Super Moons could appear visually closer and brighter, and promote stronger tides. Personally, we may use the greater proximity of Super Moons to illuminate our inner horizons and deepen our self-reflections and meditations.

Apogee (ApG): The point in the Moon's orbit that is *farthest* from Earth. At this time, the effects of transits may be less noticeable immediately, but may appear later. Also, **Black Moon Lilith,** a hypothetical center point of the Moon's elliptical orbit around the Earth, will be conjunct the Moon.

Perigee (PrG): The point in the Moon's orbit that is *nearest* to Earth. Transits with the Moon, when at perigee, will be more intense.

Aphelion (ApH): The point in a planet's orbit that is *farthest* from the Sun. At this time, the effects of transits (when planets pass across the path of another planet) may be less noticeable immediately, but may appear later.

Perihelion (PrH): The point in a planet's orbit that is *nearest* to the Sun. Transits with planets, when they are at perihelion, will be more intense.

Lunar Nodes: The most Northern and Southern points in the Moon's monthly cycle when it crosses the Sun's ecliptic or annual path, offering to integrate the past (South) and future (North) directions in life.

Direct or Retrograde (D or R): These are times when a planet moves forward (D) or backward (R) through the signs of the zodiac (an optical illusion, as when a moving train passes a slower train that appears to be going backward). When a planet is in direct motion, planetary energies are more straightforward; in retrograde, planetary energies turn back in on themselves and are more involuted. See "Mercury Retrograde" (p. 14).

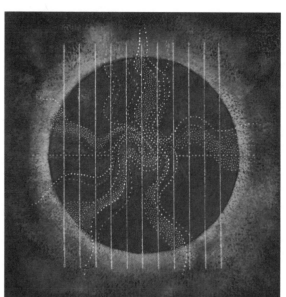

© *Mother Tongue Ink 2000*

Spirit+Matter 3
© *Linda James 2013*

SIGNS AND SYMBOLS AT A GLANCE

PLANETS

Personal Planets are closest to Earth.
⊙ **Sun**: self radiating outward, character, ego
☽ **Moon**: inward sense of self, emotions, psyche
☿ **Mercury**: communication, travel, thought
♀ **Venus**: relationship, love, sense of beauty, empathy
♂ **Mars**: will to act, initiative, ambition
Asteroids are between Mars and Jupiter and reflect the awakening of feminine-defined energy centers in human consciousness.
Social Planets are between personal and outer planets.
♃ **Jupiter**: expansion, opportunities, leadership
♄ **Saturn**: limits, structure, discipline
Note: The days of the week are named in various languages after the above seven heavenly bodies.
⚷ **Chiron**: is a small planetary body between Saturn and Uranus representing the wounded healer.
Transpersonal Planets are the outer planets.
♅ **Uranus**: cosmic consciousness, revolutionary change
♆ **Neptune**: spiritual awakening, cosmic love, all one
♇ **Pluto**: death and rebirth, deep, total change

ZODIAC SIGNS

♈ Aries
♉ Taurus
♊ Gemini
♋ Cancer
♌ Leo
♍ Virgo
♎ Libra
♏ Scorpio
♐ Sagittarius
♑ Capricorn
♒ Aquarius
♓ Pisces

ASPECTS

Aspects show the angle between planets; this informs how the planets influence each other and us. We'Moon lists only significant aspects:
☌ CONJUNCTION (planets are 0–5° apart)
Linked together, energy of aspected planets is mutually enhancing.
☍ OPPOSITION (planets are 180° apart)
Polarizing or complementing, energies are diametrically opposite.
△ TRINE (planets are 120° apart)
Harmonizing, energies of this aspect are in the same element.
□ SQUARE (planets are 90° apart)
Challenging, energies of this aspect are different from each other.
⁎ SEXTILE (planets are 60° apart)
Cooperative, energies of this aspect blend well.
⚻ QUINCUNX (planets are 150° apart)
Variable, energies of this aspect combine contrary elements.

OTHER SYMBOLS

☽ v/c–Moon is "void of course" from last lunar aspect until it enters new sign.
ApG–Apogee: Point in the orbit of the Moon that's farthest from Earth.
PrG–Perigee: Point in the orbit of the Moon that's nearest to Earth.
ApH–Aphelion: Point in the orbit of a planet that's farthest from the Sun.
PrH–Perihelion: Point in the orbit of a planet that's nearest to the Sun.
D or R–Direct or Retrograde: Describes when a planet moves forward (D) through the zodiac or appears to move backward (R).

CONSTELLATIONS OF THE ZODIAC

These stations of the zodiac were named thousands of years ago for the constellations that were behind them at the time. The signs of the zodiac act like a light filter, coloring the qualities of life force. As the Sun, Moon and other planets move through the zodiac, the following influences are energized:

♒ **Aquarius** (Air): Community, ingenuity, collaboration, idealism. It's time to honor the philosophy of love and the power of community.

♓ **Pisces** (Water): Introspection, imagination, sensitivity and intuition. We process and gestate our dreams

♈ **Aries** (Fire): Brave, direct, rebellious, energized. Our inner teenager comes alive; our adult self needs to direct the energy wisely.

♉ **Taurus** (Earth): Sensual, rooted, nurturing, material manifestation. We slow down, get earthy, awaken our senses, begin to build form, roots, and stubborn strength.

♊ **Gemini** (Air): Communication, networking, curiosity, quick witted. We connect with like minds and build a network of understanding.

♋ **Cancer** (Water): Family, home, emotional awareness, nourishment. We need time in our shell and with our familiars.

♌ **Leo** (Fire): Creativity, charisma, warmth, and enthusiasm. Gather with others to celebrate and share bounty.

♍ **Virgo** (Earth): Mercurial, curious, critical, and engaged. The mood sharpens our minds and nerves, and sends us back to work.

♎ **Libra** (Air): Beauty, equality, egalitarianism, cooperation. We grow more friendly, relationship oriented, and incensed by injustice.

♏ **Scorpio** (Water): Sharp focus, perceptive, empowered, mysterious. The mood is smoky, primal, occult, and curious; still waters run deep.

♐ **Sagittarius** (Fire): Curiosity, honesty, exploration, playfulness. We grow more curious about what's unfamiliar.

♑ **Capricorn** (Earth): family, history, dreams, traditions. We need mountains to climb and problems to solve.

adapted from Heather Roan Robbins' Sun Signs and Sun Transits
© *Mother Tongue Ink 2016*

MOON TRANSITS

The Moon changes signs every 2½ days. The sign that the Moon is in sets the emotional tone of the day.

♒ Moon in Aquarius calls us to the circle and away from private concerns; it reminds us of the sacredness of collaboration and collectivity. It's time to search for new allies, to network, and to live our philosophy.

♓ Moon in Pisces makes us aware, sometimes painfully, of our emotions. It heightens compassion,. intuition. We may have to strengthen boundaries. Explore the temple of imagination.

♈ Moon in Aries accesses our fire; temper, impatience and passion. We feel an urgency to focus, but we can lose our empathy. It's time to do what truly makes us feel alive, to initiate projects and set boundaries.

♉ Moon in Taurus slows us down; roots grow deep in this stubborn, creative, sensual time. It's time to cultivate our earthly resources: garden, home, and body. Plant seeds in fertile loam, listen to the Earth's magic.

♊ Moon in Gemini speeds our thoughts and nerves. It's time to weave words: talk, listen, laugh, sing and write. Network, negotiate, rearrange; juggle possibilities; just don't get spread too thin.

♋ Moon in Cancer reconnects us with our emotions. We may get overwhelmed and defensive, or we can nourish ourselves and reconnect with our true feelings. Water is healing; bathe, hydrate, make soup.

♌ Moon in Leo gets us into the heart of the action. It's time to let our light shine, express ourselves and appreciate other's unique stories. Celebrate, ritualize, dramatize. Share with true Leonine generosity.

♍ Moon in Virgo sharpens our minds and nerves. It helps us digest information and assess the situation. Invoke Virgoan compassion and brilliant problem-solving. Clean, organize, edit, weed and heal.

♎ Moon in Libra warms our hearts and heightens our aesthetics. Beauty, fairness and balance feed us. We want everyone to get along, and we become allergic to discord in the culture and with our beloveds.

♏ Moon in Scorpio turns us inward, deepens our curiosity and focus, but gives us attitude. We need privacy, as moods may be prickly. Clear the deadwood of soul or garden. Seek deep, refreshing contemplation.

♐ Moon in Sagittarius gets us moving around the globe, or into our minds. It loans us fresh (often tactless) honesty, an adventurous spark, philosophical perspective and easy rapport with the natural world.

♑ Moon in Capricorn whets our ambition and tests our sense of humor. It's time to put sweat-equity into our dreams; organize, build, manifest. Set clear short-term goals and feel the joy of accomplishment.

adapted from Heather Roan Robbins' Moon Signs and Moon Transits

© Mother Tongue Ink 2020

Know Yourself—Map of Planetary Influences

Most people, when considering astrology's benefits, are familiar with their Sun Sign; however, each of the planets within our solar system has a specific part to play in the complete knowledge of "The Self." Here is a quick run-down of our planets' astrological effects:

☉ **The Sun** represents our soul purpose—what we are here on Earth to do or accomplish, and it informs how we go about that task. It answers the age-old question "Why am I here?"

☽ **The Moon** represents our capacity to feel or empathize with those around us and within our own soul as well. It awakens our intuitive and emotional body.

☿ **Mercury** is "The Thinker," and involves our communication skills: what we say, our words, our voice, and our thoughts, including the Teacher/Student, Master/Apprentice mode. Mercury affects how we connect with all the media tools of the day—our computers, phones, and even the postal, publishing and recording systems!

♀ **Venus** is our recognition of love, art and beauty. Venus is harmony in its expressed form, as well as compassion, bliss and acceptance.

♂ **Mars** is our sense of "Get Up and GO!" It represents being in motion and the capacity to take action and do. Mars can also affect our temperament.

♃ **Jupiter** is our quest for truth, living the belief systems that we hold and walking the path of what those beliefs say about us. It involves an ever-expanding desire to educate the Self through knowledge toward higher law, the adventure and opportunity of being on that road—sometimes literally entailing travel and foreign or international culture, language and/or customs.

♄ **Saturn** is the task master: active when we set a goal or plan then work strongly and steadily toward achieving what we have set out to do. Saturn takes life seriously along the way and can be rather stern, putting on an extra load of responsibility and effort.

⚷ **Chiron** is the "Wounded Healer," relating to what we have brought into this lifetime in order to learn how to fix it, to perfect it, make it the best that it can possibly be! This is where we compete with ourselves to better our own previous score. In addition, it connects to our health-body—physiological and nutritional.

♅ **Uranus** is our capacity to experience "The Revolution," freedom to do things our own way, exhibiting our individual expression or even "Going Rogue" as we blast towards a future collective vision. Uranus inspires individual inclination to "Let me be ME" and connect to an ocean of humanity doing the same.

♆ **Neptune** is the spiritual veil, our connection to our inner psychology and consciousness, leading to the experience of our soul. Psychic presence and mediumship are influenced here too.

♇ **Pluto** is transformation, death/rebirth energy—to the extreme. In order for the butterfly to emerge, the caterpillar that it once was must completely give up its life! No going back; burn the bridge down; the volcano of one's own power explodes. Stand upon the mountaintop and catch the lightning bolt in your hand!

Ascendant or Rising Sign: In addition, you must consider the sign of the zodiac that was on the horizon at the moment of your birth. Your Rising sign describes how we relate to the external world and how it relates back to us—what we look like, how others see us and how we see ourselves.

It is the combination of all of these elements that makes us unique among all other persons alive! We are like snowflakes in that way! Sharing a Sun sign is not enough to put you in a singular category. Here's to our greater understanding! Know Yourself!

Melissa Kae Mason, MoonCat! © Mother Tongue Ink 2011

GODDESS PLANETS: CERES, PALLAS, JUNO AND VESTA

"Asteroids" are small planets, located between the inner, personal planets (Sun to Mars) that move more swiftly through the zodiac, and the outer, social and collective planets (Jupiter to Pluto) whose slower movements mark generational shifts. Ceres, Pallas, Juno and Vesta are faces of the Great Goddess who is reawakening in our consciousness now, quickening abilities so urgently needed to solve our many personal, social, ecological and political problems.

⚳ **Ceres** (Goddess of corn and harvest) symbolizes our ability to nourish ourselves and others in a substantial and metaphoric way. As in the Greek myth of Demeter and Persephone, she helps us to let go and die, to understand mother-daughter dynamics, to re-parent ourselves and to educate by our senses.

⚵ **Juno** (Queen of the Gods and of relationships) shows us what kind of committed partnership we long for, our own individual way to find fulfillment in personal and professional partnering. She wants partners to be team-workers, with equal rights and responsibilities.

⚴ **Pallas** (Athena) is a symbol for our creative intelligence and often hints at the sacrifice of women's own creativity or the lack of respect for it. She brings to the fore father-daughter issues, and points to difficulties in linking head, heart and womb.

⚶ **Vesta** (Vestal Virgin/Fire Priestess) reminds us first and foremost that we belong to ourselves and are allowed to do so! She shows us how to regenerate, to activate our passion, and how to carefully watch over our inner fire in the storms of everyday life.

excerpt Beate Metz © Mother Tongue Ink 2009

See p. 215 for Asteroid Ephemeris

Ephemeris 101

A Planetary Ephemeris provides astronomical data showing the daily positions of celestial bodies in our solar system.

The planets have individual and predictable orbits around the sun and pathways through the constellations that correlate with the astrological signs of the Zodiac. This regularity is useful for sky viewing and creating astro charts for a particular date.

The earliest astrologers used these ephemeris tables to calculate individual birth and event charts. These circular maps plot planetary positions and the aspects—angles of relationships—in a "state of the solar system" as a permanent representation of a moment in time. The ephemeris can then be consulted to find when real-time or "transiting" planets will be in the same sign and degree as planets in the birth or event chart. For instance, use the ephemerides to follow the Sun through the houses of your own birth chart, and journal on each day the Sun conjuncts a planet. The sun reveals or sheds light on a sign or house, allowing those qualities to shine and thrive. Ephemerides can also be used to look up dates of past events in your life to learn what planets were highlighted in your chart at that time. In addition, looking up dates for future plans can illuminate beneficial timing of available planetary energies.

Read across from a particular date, ephemerides provide the sign and degree of all the Planets, the Sun and Moon and nodes of the Moon on that day. The lower box on the page offers a quick look at Astro data such as, when a planet changes sign (an ingress occurs), aspects of the outer planets, their retrograde periods and much more. The larger boxes represent two different months as labeled. Signs and Symbols at a Glance (p. 203) is a handy key to the planet, sign and aspects glyphs.

Sandra Pastorius © Mother Tongue Ink 2018

Moon: O hr=Midnight and Noon=12PM

Planet Glyphs (p. 203)

R=Planet Retrogrades shown in shaded boxes

Ingress: January 1st the Sun moves into 10° Capricorn

Day	Sid.Time	☉	0 hr ☽	Noon ☽	True ☊	☿
1 Tu	6 41 26	10♑15 21	12♏21 35	18♏49 44	26♋52.2	23♐51.2
2 W	6 45 22	11 16 31	25 14 11	1♐35 10	26R 50.0	25 19.2
3 Th	6 49 19	12 17 42	7♐52 52	14 07 28	26 47.6	26 47.7
4 F	6 53 15	13 18 52	20 19 08	26 28 04	26 45.5	28 16.7
5 Sa	6 57 12	14 20 03	2♑34 27	8♑38 27	26 43.9	29 46.2
6 Su	7 01 08	15 21 14	14 40 17	20 40 08	26 42.9	1♑16.2
7 M	7 05 05	16 22 25	26 38 13	2♒34 48	26D 42.6	2 46.7
8 Tu	7 09 01	17 23 36	8♒30 08	14 24 32	26 42.9	4 17.6

Mars Ingress Aries January 1 @ 2:21 PM

Astro Data	Dy Hr Mn	Planet Ingress	Dy Hr Mn	Last Aspe	
♂0N	2 0:56	♂ ♈	1 2:21	1 22:27	♀
♅ D	6 20:28	☿ ♑	5 3:41	4 17:43	☿
☊ D	7 0:06	♀ ♐	7 11:19	7 6:21	♀

2022 Planetary Ephemeris

LONGITUDE — January 2022

Day	Sid.Time	☉	0 hr ☽	Noon ☽	True ☊	☿	♀	♂	⚳	♃	♄	♅	♆	♇
1 Sa	6 42 30	10♑31 41	15♐28 04	23♐01 07	1♊12.4	28♑10.9	23♑17.7	13♐05.9	28♉37.9	0♓32.7	11♒54.2	10♉57.2	20♓40.1	25♑56.1
2 Su	6 46 27	11 32 52	0♑35 49	8♑11 00	1R 09.7	29 35.2	22R 47.7	13 48.6	28R 32.3	0 44.5	12 00.7	10R 56.3	20 41.2	25 58.0
3 M	6 50 23	12 34 03	15 45 21	23 17 39	1 04.9	0♒57.1	22 16.1	14 31.3	28 27.2	0 56.4	12 07.2	10 55.5	20 42.3	25 59.9
4 Tu	6 54 20	13 35 14	0♒46 38	8♒11 13	0 58.5	2 16.1	21 43.1	15 14.1	28 22.4	1 08.3	12 13.8	10 54.7	20 43.4	26 01.9
5 W	6 58 17	14 36 25	15 30 24	22 43 24	0 51.3	3 31.7	21 08.8	15 56.8	28 18.1	1 20.4	12 20.4	10 54.0	20 44.5	26 03.8
6 Th	7 02 13	15 37 35	29 49 37	6♓48 40	0 44.3	4 43.2	20 33.6	16 39.7	28 14.2	1 32.5	12 27.1	10 53.3	20 45.7	26 05.8
7 F	7 06 10	16 38 45	13♓40 22	20 24 43	0 38.4	5 50.1	19 57.6	17 22.5	28 10.7	1 44.7	12 33.8	10 52.6	20 46.9	26 07.8
8 Sa	7 10 06	17 39 55	27 01 54	3♈32 13	0 34.1	6 51.5	19 21.1	18 05.4	28 07.7	1 57.0	12 40.5	10 52.1	20 48.2	26 09.7
9 Su	7 14 03	18 41 04	9♈56 06	16 14 04	0D 31.9	7 46.7	18 44.4	18 48.3	28 05.0	2 09.4	12 47.3	10 51.5	20 49.4	26 11.7
10 M	7 17 59	19 42 13	22 26 44	28 34 41	0 31.5	8 34.8	18 07.6	19 31.3	28 02.8	2 21.8	12 54.1	10 51.1	20 50.7	26 13.7
11 Tu	7 21 56	20 43 21	4♉38 36	10♉39 09	0 32.4	9 15.0	17 31.2	20 14.3	28 01.0	2 34.4	13 00.9	10 50.6	20 52.0	26 15.6
12 W	7 25 52	21 44 29	16 36 59	22 32 44	0 33.7	9 46.3	16 55.2	20 57.3	27 59.6	2 47.0	13 07.8	10 50.3	20 53.4	26 17.6
13 Th	7 29 49	22 45 37	28 27 02	4♊20 27	0R 34.5	10 07.9	16 20.0	21 40.4	27 58.6	2 59.7	13 14.6	10 49.9	20 54.8	26 19.6
14 F	7 33 45	23 46 43	10♊13 33	16 06 48	0 33.9	10R 18.9	15 45.8	22 23.5	27D 58.0	3 12.4	13 21.5	10 49.7	20 56.2	26 21.6
15 Sa	7 37 42	24 47 50	22 00 41	27 55 34	0 31.3	10 18.7	15 12.8	23 06.6	27 57.8	3 25.3	13 28.5	10 49.5	20 57.6	26 23.5
16 Su	7 41 39	25 48 55	3♋51 50	9♋49 47	0 26.1	10 07.0	14 41.3	23 49.8	27 58.1	3 38.1	13 35.4	10 49.3	20 59.1	26 25.5
17 M	7 45 35	26 50 00	15 49 39	21 51 38	0 18.4	9 43.4	14 11.4	24 33.0	27 58.7	3 51.1	13 42.4	10 49.2	21 00.6	26 27.5
18 Tu	7 49 32	27 51 05	27 55 55	4♌02 37	0 08.6	9 08.3	13 43.3	25 16.3	27 59.8	4 04.1	13 49.4	10D 49.1	21 02.1	26 29.5
19 W	7 53 28	28 52 09	10♌11 50	16 23 37	29♉57.3	8 22.3	13 17.2	25 59.6	28 01.3	4 17.2	13 56.4	10 49.1	21 03.6	26 31.5
20 Th	7 57 25	29 53 12	22 38 02	28 55 09	29 45.5	7 26.4	12 53.2	26 42.9	28 03.1	4 30.4	14 03.5	10 49.2	21 05.2	26 33.5
21 F	8 01 21	0♒54 15	5♍15 00	11♍37 40	29 34.5	6 22.1	12 31.5	27 26.3	28 05.4	4 43.6	14 10.5	10 49.3	21 06.8	26 35.4
22 Sa	8 05 18	1 55 18	18 03 14	24 31 47	29 25.1	5 11.4	12 12.0	28 09.7	28 08.0	4 56.9	14 17.6	10 49.4	21 08.4	26 37.4
23 Su	8 09 15	2 56 20	1♎03 28	7♎38 25	29 18.1	3 56.5	11 55.0	28 53.1	28 11.1	5 10.2	14 24.7	10 49.6	21 10.0	26 39.4
24 M	8 13 11	3 57 21	14 16 50	20 58 54	29 13.9	2 39.6	11 40.4	29 36.6	28 14.5	5 23.6	14 31.8	10 49.9	21 11.7	26 41.4
25 Tu	8 17 08	4 58 22	27 44 48	4♏34 44	29D 12.0	1 23.1	11 28.2	0♑20.1	28 18.3	5 37.1	14 38.9	10 50.2	21 13.4	26 43.3
26 W	8 21 04	5 59 22	11♏28 53	18 27 20	29 11.9	0 09.2	11 18.6	1 03.7	28 22.5	5 50.6	14 46.0	10 50.5	21 15.1	26 45.3
27 Th	8 25 01	7 00 23	25 30 10	2♐37 20	29R 12.3	28♑59.9	11 11.5	1 47.3	28 27.1	6 04.1	14 53.2	10 50.9	21 16.8	26 47.2
28 F	8 28 57	8 01 22	9♐48 41	17 03 58	29 12.0	27 56.6	11 06.9	2 30.9	28 32.0	6 17.7	15 00.3	10 51.4	21 18.6	26 49.2
29 Sa	8 32 54	9 02 21	24 22 45	1♑44 27	29 09.7	27 00.7	11D 04.8	3 14.6	28 37.3	6 31.4	15 07.5	10 51.9	21 20.4	26 51.2
30 Su	8 36 50	10 03 20	9♑08 22	16 33 36	29 04.7	26 12.8	11 05.1	3 58.3	28 43.0	6 45.1	15 14.7	10 52.5	21 22.2	26 53.1
31 M	8 40 47	11 04 17	23 59 12	1♒24 06	28 56.8	25 33.6	11 07.8	4 42.1	28 49.0	6 58.9	15 21.9	10 53.1	21 24.0	26 55.0

LONGITUDE — February 2022

Day	Sid.Time	☉	0 hr ☽	Noon ☽	True ☊	☿	♀	♂	⚳	♃	♄	♅	♆	♇
1 Tu	8 44 44	12♒05 14	8♒47 13	16♒07 28	28♉46.5	25♑03.1	11♑12.9	5♑25.8	28♉55.5	7♓12.7	15♒29.1	10♉53.8	21♓25.9	26♑57.0
2 W	8 48 40	13 06 09	23 23 49	0♓35 22	28R 34.8	24R 41.3	11 20.3	6 09.6	29 02.2	7 26.5	15 36.3	10 54.5	21 27.7	26 58.9
3 Th	8 52 37	14 07 04	7♓41 21	14 41 10	28 23.0	24 27.9	11 30.0	6 53.5	29 09.3	7 40.4	15 43.5	10 55.3	21 29.6	27 00.8
4 F	8 56 33	15 07 57	21 34 24	28 20 49	28 12.4	24D 22.7	11 41.8	7 37.4	29 16.8	7 54.4	15 50.7	10 56.1	21 31.5	27 02.7
5 Sa	9 00 30	16 08 49	5♈00 22	11♈33 10	28 04.0	24 25.1	11 55.8	8 21.3	29 24.6	8 08.3	15 57.9	10 57.0	21 33.5	27 04.6
6 Su	9 04 26	17 09 39	17 59 30	24 19 44	27 58.2	24 34.7	12 11.8	9 05.2	29 32.7	8 22.4	16 05.0	10 57.9	21 35.4	27 06.5
7 M	9 08 23	18 10 28	0♉34 23	6♉44 00	27 55.1	24 50.9	12 29.9	9 49.2	29 41.2	8 36.4	16 12.2	10 58.9	21 37.4	27 08.4
8 Tu	9 12 19	19 11 16	12 49 14	18 50 46	27D 53.9	25 13.2	12 49.8	10 33.2	29 50.0	8 50.5	16 19.4	11 00.0	21 39.3	27 10.3
9 W	9 16 16	20 12 02	24 49 17	0♊45 29	27R 53.8	25 41.3	13 11.7	11 17.2	29 59.1	9 04.6	16 26.6	11 01.0	21 41.3	27 12.1
10 Th	9 20 13	21 12 47	6♊40 06	12 33 48	27 53.7	26 14.5	13 35.4	12 01.2	0♊08.6	9 18.7	16 33.8	11 02.2	21 43.4	27 14.0
11 F	9 24 09	22 13 30	18 27 15	24 21 05	27 52.2	26 52.5	14 00.8	12 45.3	0 18.3	9 32.9	16 41.0	11 03.4	21 45.4	27 15.8
12 Sa	9 28 06	23 14 11	0♋15 53	6♋12 12	27 48.6	27 34.9	14 28.0	13 29.5	0 28.4	9 47.1	16 48.2	11 04.6	21 47.4	27 17.6
13 Su	9 32 02	24 14 51	12 10 31	18 11 15	27 42.2	28 21.3	14 56.7	14 13.6	0 38.8	10 01.4	16 55.3	11 05.9	21 49.5	27 19.4
14 M	9 35 59	25 15 30	24 14 44	0♌21 17	27 33.0	29 11.3	15 27.1	14 57.8	0 49.5	10 15.6	17 02.5	11 07.2	21 51.6	27 21.2
15 Tu	9 39 55	26 16 07	6♌31 07	12 44 21	27 21.2	0♒04.8	15 58.9	15 42.0	1 00.4	10 29.9	17 09.6	11 08.6	21 53.7	27 23.0
16 W	9 43 52	27 16 42	19 01 04	25 21 18	27 07.7	1 01.3	16 32.2	16 26.3	1 11.7	10 44.2	17 16.8	11 10.0	21 55.8	27 24.8
17 Th	9 47 48	28 17 16	1♍44 58	8♍11 59	26 53.6	2 00.7	17 06.9	17 10.6	1 23.2	10 58.5	17 23.9	11 11.5	21 57.9	27 26.6
18 F	9 51 45	29 17 48	14 42 13	21 15 31	26 40.2	3 02.8	17 43.0	17 54.9	1 35.0	11 12.9	17 31.0	11 13.0	22 00.0	27 28.3
19 Sa	9 55 42	0♓18 19	27 51 42	4♎30 36	26 28.6	4 07.3	18 20.4	18 39.2	1 47.1	11 27.3	17 38.1	11 14.6	22 02.1	27 30.0
20 Su	9 59 38	1 18 48	11♎12 05	17 56 00	26 19.8	5 14.1	18 59.0	19 23.6	1 59.5	11 41.7	17 45.1	11 16.2	22 04.3	27 31.8
21 M	10 03 35	2 19 16	24 42 16	1♏30 49	26 14.1	6 23.0	19 38.8	20 08.0	2 12.1	11 56.1	17 52.2	11 17.9	22 06.5	27 33.5
22 Tu	10 07 31	3 19 43	8♏21 37	15 14 39	26 11.2	7 33.9	20 19.8	20 52.5	2 25.0	12 10.5	17 59.2	11 19.6	22 08.6	27 35.1
23 W	10 11 28	4 20 08	22 09 58	29 07 33	26 10.4	8 46.7	21 01.9	21 36.9	2 38.2	12 24.9	18 06.3	11 21.3	22 10.8	27 36.8
24 Th	10 15 24	5 20 32	6♐07 25	13♐09 35	26 10.4	10 01.3	21 45.0	22 21.4	2 51.6	12 39.4	18 13.3	11 23.1	22 13.0	27 38.5
25 F	10 19 21	6 20 55	20 13 58	27 20 27	26 09.8	11 17.5	22 29.2	23 06.0	3 05.3	12 53.8	18 20.2	11 25.0	22 15.2	27 40.1
26 Sa	10 23 17	7 21 17	4♑28 49	11♑38 48	26 07.6	12 35.3	23 14.3	23 50.6	3 19.2	13 08.3	18 27.2	11 26.9	22 17.4	27 41.7
27 Su	10 27 14	8 21 37	18 50 00	26 01 54	26 02.7	13 54.6	24 00.4	24 35.2	3 33.4	13 22.8	18 34.1	11 28.8	22 19.6	27 43.3
28 M	10 31 11	9 21 55	3♒13 56	10♒25 26	25 54.9	15 15.4	24 47.3	25 19.8	3 47.8	13 37.3	18 41.0	11 30.8	22 21.9	27 44.9

Astro Data Dy Hr Mn	Planet Ingress Dy Hr Mn	Last Aspect Dy Hr Mn	☽ Ingress Dy Hr Mn	Last Aspect Dy Hr Mn	☽ Ingress Dy Hr Mn	☽ Phases & Eclipses Dy Hr Mn	Astro Data
☽0N 8 22:52	☿ ♒ 2 7:11	1 8:17 ♆ □	♑ 1 23:03	1 11:02 ♄ ☌	♓ 2 11:01	2 18:35 ● 12♑20	1 January 2022
☊ D 9 18:02	☊ ♉R 18 18:22	3 16:22 ♇ ☌	♒ 3 22:45	4 9:42 ♇ ⚹	♈ 4 14:58	9 18:12 ☽ 19♈27	Julian Day # 44561
☊ R 13 4:21	☉ ♒ 20 2:40	5 0:46 ♂ ⚹	♓ 6 0:18	6 17:22 ♇ □	♉ 6 22:54	17 23:50 ○ 27♋51	SVP 4♓57'23"
☿ R 14 11:43	♂ ♑ 24 12:54	7 22:24 ♇ ⚹	♈ 8 5:27	9 4:49 ♇ △	♊ 9 10:28	25 13:42 ☾ 5♏33	GC 27♐08.8 ⚵ 16♓27.5
⚳ D 14 21:21	☿ ♑R 26 3:06	10 7:24 ♇ □	♉ 10 14:48	11 8:24 ☉ △	♋ 11 23:28		Eris 23♈41.7R ⚴ 17♑23.0
♅ D 18 15:28		12 19:40 ♇ △	♊ 13 3:09	14 10:28 ☿ ☍	♌ 14 11:18	1 5:47 ● 12♒20	⚷ 8♈30.4 ⚶ 24♐31.6
☽0S 23 14:33	⚳ ♊ 9 2:14	15 2:23 ♂ ☍	♋ 15 16:12	16 16:58 ☉ ☍	♍ 16 20:44	8 13:51 ☽ 19♉46	☽ Mean ☊ 29♉31.7
☊ D 25 13:48	☿ ♒ 14 21:55	17 23:50 ☉ ☍	♌ 18 4:04	18 23:21 ♇ △	♎ 19 3:52	16 16:58 ○ 28♌00	
☊ R 27 6:18	☉ ♓ 18 16:44	20 8:17 ♂ △	♍ 20 14:03	21 5:03 ♇ □	♏ 21 9:20	23 22:34 ☾ 5♐17	1 February 2022
♀ D 29 8:47		22 19:47 ♂ □	♎ 22 22:04	23 9:25 ♇ ⚹	♐ 23 13:30		Julian Day # 44592
☿ D 4 4:14		24 22:11 ♇ □	♏ 25 3:58	25 3:26 ♆ □	♑ 25 16:29		SVP 4♓57'17"
☽0N 5 7:02		27 5:29 ☿ ⚹	♐ 27 7:36	27 14:51 ♇ ☌	♒ 27 18:37		GC 27♐08.9 ⚵ 25♓29.4
☊ D 8 13:39		28 19:01 ♆ □	♑ 29 9:10				Eris 23♈43.5 ⚴ 29♑37.0
☊ R 9 6:14	☽0S 19 19:22	31 4:45 ♇ ☌	♒ 31 9:44				⚷ 9♈16.1 ⚶ 10♑58.2
♃⚹♅ 18 0:14	♃∠∠23 22:18						☽ Mean ☊ 27♉53.3

*Giving the positions of planets daily at midnight, Greenwich Mean Time (0:00 UT)
Each planet's retrograde period is shaded gray.

March 2022

LONGITUDE

Day	Sid.Time	☉	0 hr ☽	Noon ☽	True ☊	☿	♀	♂	⚳	♃	♄	♅	♆	♇
1 Tu	10 35 07	10♓22 12	17♒35 39	24♒43 50	25♉44.7	16♒37.6	25♑35.1	26♑04.4	4♊02.4	13♓51.8	18♒47.9	11♉32.8	22♓24.1	27♑46.5
2 W	10 39 04	11 22 28	1♓49 15	8♓51 09	25R 33.0	18 01.1	26 23.8	26 49.1	4 17.3	14 06.3	18 54.8	11 34.8	22 26.3	27 48.0
3 Th	10 43 00	12 22 41	15 48 55	22 41 57	25 21.1	19 25.9	27 13.2	27 33.8	4 32.4	14 20.9	19 01.6	11 36.9	22 28.6	27 49.5
4 F	10 46 57	13 22 53	29 29 50	6♈12 15	25 10.1	20 52.0	28 03.4	28 18.5	4 47.8	14 35.4	19 08.4	11 39.1	22 30.8	27 51.1
5 Sa	10 50 53	14 23 03	12♈49 00	19 20 04	25 01.2	22 19.3	28 54.3	29 03.3	5 03.3	14 49.9	19 15.2	11 41.3	22 33.1	27 52.5
6 Su	10 54 50	15 23 11	25 45 31	2♉05 34	24 54.9	23 47.9	29 45.9	29 48.1	5 19.1	15 04.4	19 21.9	11 43.5	22 35.4	27 54.0
7 M	10 58 46	16 23 16	8♉20 33	14 30 51	24 51.3	25 17.6	0♒38.1	0♒32.9	5 35.1	15 18.9	19 28.6	11 45.7	22 37.6	27 55.4
8 Tu	11 02 43	17 23 20	20 37 01	26 39 33	24D 50.0	26 48.5	1 31.0	1 17.7	5 51.3	15 33.5	19 35.3	11 48.0	22 39.9	27 56.9
9 W	11 06 39	18 23 22	2♊39 07	8♊36 20	24 50.1	28 20.6	2 24.6	2 02.5	6 07.7	15 48.0	19 41.9	11 50.4	22 42.2	27 58.3
10 Th	11 10 36	19 23 21	14 31 52	20 26 25	24R 50.7	29 53.9	3 18.7	2 47.4	6 24.3	16 02.5	19 48.5	11 52.8	22 44.4	27 59.7
11 F	11 14 33	20 23 19	26 20 41	2♋15 19	24 50.6	1♓28.3	4 13.4	3 32.3	6 41.2	16 17.0	19 55.1	11 55.2	22 46.7	28 01.0
12 Sa	11 18 29	21 23 14	8♋11 00	14 08 22	24 48.9	3 03.9	5 08.6	4 17.2	6 58.2	16 31.5	20 01.6	11 57.6	22 49.0	28 02.3
13 Su	11 22 26	22 23 07	20 07 59	26 10 25	24 45.1	4 40.7	6 04.4	5 02.1	7 15.4	16 46.0	20 08.1	12 00.1	22 51.3	28 03.7
14 M	11 26 22	23 22 58	2♌16 10	8♌25 37	24 38.9	6 18.6	7 00.7	5 47.0	7 32.8	17 00.4	20 14.5	12 02.6	22 53.6	28 05.0
15 Tu	11 30 19	24 22 47	14 39 10	20 57 02	24 30.5	7 57.7	7 57.5	6 32.0	7 50.3	17 14.9	20 20.9	12 05.2	22 55.8	28 06.2
16 W	11 34 15	25 22 33	27 19 25	3♍46 23	24 20.5	9 38.0	8 54.8	7 17.0	8 08.1	17 29.3	20 27.2	12 07.8	22 58.1	28 07.5
17 Th	11 38 12	26 22 18	10♍17 56	16 53 58	24 10.0	11 19.5	9 52.5	8 02.0	8 26.0	17 43.8	20 33.6	12 10.4	23 00.4	28 08.7
18 F	11 42 08	27 22 00	23 34 16	0♎18 35	23 59.8	13 02.2	10 50.7	8 47.0	8 44.1	17 58.2	20 39.8	12 13.1	23 02.7	28 09.9
19 Sa	11 46 05	28 21 40	7♎06 36	13 57 56	23 51.2	14 46.1	11 49.3	9 32.1	9 02.4	18 12.6	20 46.0	12 15.7	23 04.9	28 11.0
20 Su	11 50 02	29 21 19	20 52 11	27 48 55	23 44.7	16 31.3	12 48.3	10 17.2	9 20.9	18 27.0	20 52.2	12 18.5	23 07.2	28 12.2
21 M	11 53 58	0♈20 55	4♏47 44	11♏48 15	23 40.7	18 17.7	13 47.8	11 02.3	9 39.5	18 41.4	20 58.3	12 21.2	23 09.5	28 13.3
22 Tu	11 57 55	1 20 30	18 50 05	25 52 56	23D 39.2	20 05.3	14 47.6	11 47.4	9 58.3	18 55.7	21 04.4	12 24.0	23 11.7	28 14.4
23 W	12 01 51	2 20 03	2♐56 30	10♐00 33	23 39.4	21 54.3	15 47.8	12 32.5	10 17.2	19 10.0	21 10.4	12 26.8	23 14.0	28 15.5
24 Th	12 05 48	3 19 34	17 04 53	24 09 18	23 40.4	23 44.5	16 48.4	13 17.7	10 36.3	19 24.4	21 16.4	12 29.6	23 16.2	28 16.5
25 F	12 09 44	4 19 04	1♑13 39	8♑17 46	23R 41.1	25 36.0	17 49.3	14 02.9	10 55.6	19 38.6	21 22.4	12 32.5	23 18.5	28 17.6
26 Sa	12 13 41	5 18 32	15 21 29	22 24 36	23 40.7	27 28.8	18 50.5	14 48.1	11 15.0	19 52.9	21 28.2	12 35.4	23 20.7	28 18.6
27 Su	12 17 37	6 17 58	29 26 56	6♒28 13	23 38.5	29 22.8	19 52.1	15 33.3	11 34.5	20 07.1	21 34.1	12 38.3	23 23.0	28 19.5
28 M	12 21 34	7 17 22	13♒28 11	20 26 31	23 34.1	1♈18.2	20 54.0	16 18.5	11 54.2	20 21.4	21 39.8	12 41.3	23 25.2	28 20.5
29 Tu	12 25 31	8 16 45	27 22 52	4♓16 53	23 28.0	3 14.8	21 56.2	17 03.7	12 14.1	20 35.5	21 45.5	12 44.3	23 27.4	28 21.4
30 W	12 29 27	9 16 05	11♓08 12	17 56 26	23 20.8	5 12.6	22 58.7	17 49.0	12 34.1	20 49.7	21 51.2	12 47.3	23 29.6	28 22.3
31 Th	12 33 24	10 15 24	24 41 16	1♈22 24	23 13.3	7 11.7	24 01.5	18 34.3	12 54.2	21 03.8	21 56.8	12 50.3	23 31.8	28 23.1

April 2022

LONGITUDE

Day	Sid.Time	☉	0 hr ☽	Noon ☽	True ☊	☿	♀	♂	⚳	♃	♄	♅	♆	♇
1 F	12 37 20	11♈14 40	7♈59 33	14♈32 33	23♉06.4	9♈11.8	25♒04.5	19♒19.5	13♊14.5	21♓17.9	22♒02.3	12♉53.3	23♓34.0	28♑24.0
2 Sa	12 41 17	12 13 55	21 01 16	27 25 40	23R 00.8	11 13.0	26 07.8	20 04.8	13 34.9	21 32.0	22 07.8	12 56.4	23 36.2	28 24.8
3 Su	12 45 13	13 13 08	3♉45 45	10♉01 40	22 57.1	13 15.2	27 11.3	20 50.1	13 55.5	21 46.0	22 13.2	12 59.5	23 38.4	28 25.6
4 M	12 49 10	14 12 18	16 13 36	22 21 48	22D 55.3	15 18.3	28 15.0	21 35.4	14 16.2	22 00.0	22 18.6	13 02.6	23 40.6	28 26.3
5 Tu	12 53 06	15 11 26	28 26 37	4♊28 28	22 55.2	17 22.1	29 19.0	22 20.7	14 37.0	22 13.9	22 23.9	13 05.8	23 42.7	28 27.1
6 W	12 57 03	16 10 33	10♊27 47	16 25 05	22 56.4	19 26.4	0♓23.3	23 06.0	14 58.0	22 27.8	22 29.1	13 09.0	23 44.9	28 27.8
7 Th	13 01 00	17 09 36	22 20 55	28 15 52	22 58.1	21 31.2	1 27.7	23 51.4	15 19.0	22 41.7	22 34.2	13 12.1	23 47.0	28 28.4
8 F	13 04 56	18 08 38	4♋10 33	10♋05 34	22 59.7	23 36.0	2 32.4	24 36.7	15 40.2	22 55.5	22 39.3	13 15.3	23 49.1	28 29.1
9 Sa	13 08 53	19 07 38	16 01 34	21 59 11	23R 00.6	25 40.8	3 37.2	25 22.0	16 01.5	23 09.3	22 44.4	13 18.6	23 51.2	28 29.7
10 Su	13 12 49	20 06 35	27 59 02	4♌01 43	23 00.3	27 45.1	4 42.3	26 07.4	16 22.9	23 23.1	22 49.3	13 21.8	23 53.3	28 30.3
11 M	13 16 46	21 05 29	10♌07 50	16 17 53	22 58.6	29 48.8	5 47.5	26 52.7	16 44.5	23 36.8	22 54.2	13 25.1	23 55.4	28 30.8
12 Tu	13 20 42	22 04 22	22 32 23	28 51 44	22 55.6	1♉51.5	6 52.9	27 38.1	17 06.1	23 50.4	22 59.0	13 28.3	23 57.5	28 31.4
13 W	13 24 39	23 03 12	5♍16 15	11♍46 12	22 51.5	3 52.8	7 58.5	28 23.4	17 27.9	24 04.0	23 03.8	13 31.6	23 59.6	28 31.9
14 Th	13 28 35	24 02 00	18 21 44	25 02 53	22 47.0	5 52.4	9 04.3	29 08.8	17 49.8	24 17.6	23 08.5	13 34.9	24 01.6	28 32.3
15 F	13 32 32	25 00 46	1♎49 33	8♎41 33	22 42.6	7 50.0	10 10.3	29 54.1	18 11.7	24 31.1	23 13.1	13 38.2	24 03.6	28 32.8
16 Sa	13 36 29	25 59 29	15 38 35	22 40 11	22 38.8	9 45.2	11 16.4	0♓39.5	18 33.8	24 44.5	23 17.6	13 41.6	24 05.6	28 33.2
17 Su	13 40 25	26 58 11	29 45 53	6♏55 02	22 36.1	11 37.7	12 22.7	1 24.8	18 56.0	24 57.9	23 22.1	13 44.9	24 07.6	28 33.6
18 M	13 44 22	27 56 51	14♏07 01	21 21 08	22D 34.8	13 27.1	13 29.1	2 10.2	19 18.3	25 11.2	23 26.4	13 48.3	24 09.6	28 33.9
19 Tu	13 48 18	28 55 29	28 36 40	5♐52 55	22 34.6	15 13.2	14 35.7	2 55.6	19 40.6	25 24.5	23 30.8	13 51.6	24 11.5	28 34.2
20 W	13 52 15	29 54 05	13♐09 13	20 24 56	22 35.5	16 55.8	15 42.5	3 40.9	20 03.1	25 37.8	23 35.0	13 55.0	24 13.5	28 34.5
21 Th	13 56 11	0♉52 40	27 39 31	4♑52 28	22 36.8	18 34.5	16 49.4	4 26.3	20 25.7	25 51.0	23 39.2	13 58.4	24 15.4	28 34.8
22 F	14 00 08	1 51 13	12♑03 21	19 11 48	22 38.1	20 09.2	17 56.5	5 11.7	20 48.4	26 04.1	23 43.2	14 01.8	24 17.3	28 35.1
23 Sa	14 04 04	2 49 44	26 17 33	3♒20 20	22R 38.9	21 39.7	19 03.7	5 57.1	21 11.1	26 17.1	23 47.2	14 05.2	24 19.2	28 35.3
24 Su	14 08 01	3 48 14	10♒20 00	17 16 25	22 38.9	23 05.8	20 11.0	6 42.4	21 34.0	26 30.1	23 51.2	14 08.7	24 21.1	28 35.5
25 M	14 11 58	4 46 42	24 09 28	0♓59 07	22 38.0	24 27.3	21 18.5	7 27.8	21 56.9	26 43.1	23 55.0	14 12.1	24 22.9	28 35.6
26 Tu	14 15 54	5 45 08	7♓45 18	14 27 59	22 36.4	25 44.3	22 26.0	8 13.2	22 20.0	26 55.9	23 58.8	14 15.5	24 24.8	28 35.7
27 W	14 19 51	6 43 33	21 07 11	27 42 52	22 34.4	26 56.5	23 33.7	8 58.5	22 43.1	27 08.7	24 02.4	14 19.0	24 26.6	28 35.8
28 Th	14 23 47	7 41 56	4♈15 04	10♈43 47	22 32.2	28 03.8	24 41.6	9 43.9	23 06.3	27 21.5	24 06.0	14 22.4	24 28.4	28 35.9
29 F	14 27 44	8 40 17	17 09 04	23 30 57	22 30.2	29 06.3	25 49.5	10 29.2	23 29.6	27 34.2	24 09.5	14 25.9	24 30.1	28R 35.9
30 Sa	14 31 40	9 38 37	29 49 31	6♉04 50	22 28.8	0♊03.7	26 57.5	11 14.5	23 53.0	27 46.8	24 13.0	14 29.3	24 31.9	28 35.9

Astro Data	Dy Hr Mn
☽0N	4 16:08
☊D	8 8:23
☊R	10 10:37
☽0S	19 2:18
☉0N	20 15:35
☊D	22 8:13
☊R	25 5:50
☿0N	29 5:57
☽0N	1 0:46
☊D	4 13:06
♃⚺♄	6 3:25
☊R	9 6:43
♃☌♆	12 14:44
☽0S	15 11:35
☊D	18 14:01

Planet Ingress	Dy Hr Mn
♂ ♒	6 6:24
♀ ♒	6 6:31
☿ ♓	10 1:33
☉ ♈	20 15:35
☿ ♈	27 7:46
♀ ♓	5 15:19
☿ ♉	11 2:11
♂ ♓	15 3:07
☉ ♉	20 2:25
☿ ♊	29 22:24
☊ R23	12:14
☽ 0N28	7:51
♇ R29	18:38

Last Aspect Dy Hr Mn		☽ Ingress	Dy Hr Mn
1 2:02	♄ ☌	♓	1 20:55
3 21:46	♂ ⚹	♈	4 0:54
6 4:03	♇ □	♉	6 8:01
8 14:36	♇ △	♊	8 18:41
10 16:44	♆ □	♋	11 7:25
13 15:45	♇ ☍	♌	13 19:33
15 10:57	♄ ☍	♍	16 5:00
18 8:12	♇ △	♎	18 11:27
20 12:41	♇ □	♏	20 15:46
22 16:02	♇ ⚹	♐	22 19:00
24 13:00	☿ □	♑	24 21:55
26 23:52	☿ ⚹	♒	27 0:56
28 14:12	♄ ☌	♓	29 4:33
31 6:38	♇ ⚹	♈	31 9:32

Last Aspect Dy Hr Mn		☽ Ingress	Dy Hr Mn
2 13:52	♇ □	♉	2 16:51
5 1:54	♀ □	♊	5 3:05
7 3:16	♂ △	♋	7 15:31
10 1:02	♇ ☍	♌	10 4:01
12 10:18	♂ ☍	♍	12 14:09
14 18:13	♇ △	♎	14 20:47
16 21:58	♇ □	♏	17 0:24
18 23:56	♇ ⚹	♐	19 2:18
20 20:57	♃ □	♑	21 3:53
23 3:54	♇ ☌	♒	23 6:18
25 0:35	☿ □	♓	25 10:16
27 13:37	♇ ⚹	♈	27 16:11
29 21:40	♇ □	♉	30 0:20

☽ Phases & Eclipses Dy Hr Mn	
2 17:36	● 12♓07
10 10:47	☽ 19♊50
18 7:19	○ 27♍40
25 5:38	☾ 4♑33
1 6:26	● 11♈31
9 6:49	☽ 19♋24
16 18:56	○ 26♎46
23 11:58	☾ 3♒19
30 20:29	● 10♉28
30 20:42:37	● P 0.640

Astro Data

1 March 2022
Julian Day # 44620
SVP 4♓57'14"
GC 27♐08.9 ⚴ 5♈22.0
Eris 23♈53.7 ⚵ 10♒45.5
⚷ 10♈32.2 ⚶ 25♑13.7
☽ Mean ☊ 26♉24.3

1 April 2022
Julian Day # 44651
SVP 4♓57'11"
GC 27♐09.0 ⚴ 17♈34.0
Eris 24♈11.5 ⚵ 22♒46.8
⚷ 12♈17.3 ⚶ 9♒53.0
☽ Mean ☊ 24♉45.8

*Giving the positions of planets daily at midnight, Greenwich Mean Time (0:00 UT)
Each planet's retrograde period is shaded gray.

2022 Planetary Ephemeris

LONGITUDE — May 2022

Day	Sid.Time	☉	0 hr ☽	Noon ☽	True ☊	☿	♀	♂	⚳	♃	♄	♅	♆	♇
1 Su	14 35 37	10♉36 55	12♉17 01	18♉26 13	22♉28.0	0♊56.0	28♓05.7	11♓59.8	24♊16.4	27♓59.3	24♒16.3	14♉32.8	24♓33.6	28♑35.9
2 M	14 39 33	11 35 12	24 32 38	0♊36 26	22D 27.8	1 43.2	29 13.9	12 45.1	24 40.0	28 11.7	24 19.6	14 36.2	24 35.3	28R 35.9
3 Tu	14 43 30	12 33 26	6♊37 54	12 37 17	22 28.1	2 25.1	0♈22.2	13 30.4	25 03.6	28 24.1	24 22.7	14 39.7	24 37.0	28 35.8
4 W	14 47 27	13 31 39	18 34 56	24 31 13	22 28.8	3 01.8	1 30.7	14 15.7	25 27.3	28 36.4	24 25.8	14 43.2	24 38.6	28 35.7
5 Th	14 51 23	14 29 50	0♋26 30	6♋21 15	22 29.6	3 33.3	2 39.2	15 00.9	25 51.1	28 48.7	24 28.8	14 46.6	24 40.3	28 35.6
6 F	14 55 20	15 27 59	12 15 55	18 11 00	22 30.5	3 59.4	3 47.8	15 46.2	26 14.9	29 00.8	24 31.7	14 50.1	24 41.9	28 35.4
7 Sa	14 59 16	16 26 06	24 07 02	0♌04 32	22 31.1	4 20.2	4 56.5	16 31.4	26 38.9	29 12.9	24 34.5	14 53.6	24 43.5	28 35.2
8 Su	15 03 13	17 24 11	6♌04 06	12 06 16	22 31.5	4 35.6	6 05.3	17 16.6	27 02.9	29 24.9	24 37.2	14 57.0	24 45.0	28 35.0
9 M	15 07 09	18 22 14	18 11 38	24 20 45	22R 31.6	4 45.9	7 14.2	18 01.7	27 26.9	29 36.8	24 39.9	15 00.5	24 46.6	28 34.7
10 Tu	15 11 06	19 20 15	0♍34 10	6♍52 23	22 31.5	4R 50.9	8 23.1	18 46.9	27 51.0	29 48.6	24 42.4	15 04.0	24 48.1	28 34.5
11 W	15 15 02	20 18 15	13 15 53	19 45 04	22 31.3	4 50.9	9 32.2	19 32.0	28 15.2	0♈00.3	24 44.9	15 07.4	24 49.6	28 34.2
12 Th	15 18 59	21 16 12	26 20 16	3♎01 43	22 31.2	4 45.9	10 41.3	20 17.1	28 39.5	0 11.9	24 47.2	15 10.9	24 51.0	28 33.8
13 F	15 22 56	22 14 08	9♎49 32	16 43 45	22D 31.1	4 36.3	11 50.5	21 02.2	29 03.8	0 23.5	24 49.5	15 14.3	24 52.5	28 33.5
14 Sa	15 26 52	23 12 02	23 44 13	0♏50 39	22 31.1	4 22.1	12 59.7	21 47.3	29 28.2	0 35.0	24 51.6	15 17.8	24 53.9	28 33.1
15 Su	15 30 49	24 09 54	8♏02 37	15 19 32	22R 31.2	4 03.9	14 09.0	22 32.3	29 52.7	0 46.3	24 53.7	15 21.2	24 55.3	28 32.7
16 M	15 34 45	25 07 45	22 40 42	0♐05 16	22 31.2	3 41.8	15 18.5	23 17.3	0♋17.2	0 57.6	24 55.7	15 24.6	24 56.6	28 32.2
17 Tu	15 38 42	26 05 34	7♐32 18	15 00 48	22 31.1	3 16.3	16 27.9	24 02.3	0 41.7	1 08.8	24 57.6	15 28.1	24 57.9	28 31.8
18 W	15 42 38	27 03 22	22 29 44	29 58 06	22 30.9	2 48.0	17 37.5	24 47.3	1 06.4	1 19.9	24 59.4	15 31.5	24 59.2	28 31.3
19 Th	15 46 35	28 01 09	7♑24 53	14♑49 13	22 30.4	2 17.3	18 47.1	25 32.2	1 31.0	1 30.9	25 01.1	15 34.9	25 00.5	28 30.8
20 F	15 50 31	28 58 54	22 10 17	29 27 24	22 29.7	1 44.7	19 56.8	26 17.2	1 55.8	1 41.8	25 02.7	15 38.3	25 01.8	28 30.2
21 Sa	15 54 28	29 56 39	6♒40 01	13♒47 44	22 29.1	1 10.8	21 06.6	27 02.0	2 20.6	1 52.6	25 04.2	15 41.7	25 03.0	28 29.7
22 Su	15 58 25	0♊54 22	20 50 17	27 47 31	22D 28.6	0 36.4	22 16.4	27 46.9	2 45.4	2 03.3	25 05.7	15 45.1	25 04.2	28 29.1
23 M	16 02 21	1 52 04	4♓39 22	11♓25 56	22 28.5	0 01.8	23 26.3	28 31.7	3 10.4	2 13.9	25 07.0	15 48.5	25 05.3	28 28.5
24 Tu	16 06 18	2 49 45	18 07 20	24 43 46	22 28.8	29♉27.8	24 36.3	29 16.5	3 35.3	2 24.4	25 08.2	15 51.8	25 06.5	28 27.8
25 W	16 10 14	3 47 25	1♈15 30	7♈42 48	22 29.6	28 55.0	25 46.3	0♈01.3	4 00.3	2 34.8	25 09.3	15 55.2	25 07.6	28 27.2
26 Th	16 14 11	4 45 04	14 05 58	20 25 18	22 30.6	28 23.8	26 56.4	0 46.0	4 25.4	2 45.0	25 10.3	15 58.5	25 08.6	28 26.5
27 F	16 18 07	5 42 42	26 41 07	2♉53 43	22 31.7	27 54.8	28 06.5	1 30.7	4 50.5	2 55.2	25 11.3	16 01.8	25 09.7	28 25.7
28 Sa	16 22 04	6 40 19	9♉03 23	15 10 25	22 32.6	27 28.5	29 16.7	2 15.3	5 15.7	3 05.2	25 12.1	16 05.1	25 10.7	28 25.0
29 Su	16 26 00	7 37 56	21 15 05	27 17 38	22R 33.0	27 05.2	0♉27.0	2 59.9	5 40.9	3 15.2	25 12.8	16 08.4	25 11.7	28 24.2
30 M	16 29 57	8 35 31	3♊18 18	9♊17 22	22 32.7	26 45.4	1 37.3	3 44.5	6 06.2	3 25.0	25 13.5	16 11.7	25 12.6	28 23.4
31 Tu	16 33 54	9 33 05	15 15 03	21 11 36	22 31.5	26 29.3	2 47.6	4 29.0	6 31.5	3 34.7	25 14.0	16 14.9	25 13.6	28 22.6

LONGITUDE — June 2022

Day	Sid.Time	☉	0 hr ☽	Noon ☽	True ☊	☿	♀	♂	⚳	♃	♄	♅	♆	♇
1 W	16 37 50	10♊30 37	27♊07 17	3♋02 21	22♉29.5	26♉17.1	3♉58.0	5♈13.5	6♋56.9	3♈44.3	25♒14.4	16♉18.2	25♓14.5	28♑21.8
2 Th	16 41 47	11 28 09	8♋57 05	14 51 48	22R 26.8	26R 09.2	5 08.5	5 57.9	7 22.3	3 53.8	25 14.8	16 21.4	25 15.3	28R 21.0
3 F	16 45 43	12 25 40	20 46 48	26 42 27	22 23.7	26D 05.5	6 19.0	6 42.3	7 47.8	4 03.1	25 15.0	16 24.6	25 16.2	28 20.1
4 Sa	16 49 40	13 23 09	2♌39 07	8♌37 13	22 20.5	26 06.2	7 29.5	7 26.6	8 13.3	4 12.3	25R 15.1	16 27.8	25 17.0	28 19.2
5 Su	16 53 36	14 20 37	14 37 10	20 39 27	22 17.6	26 11.4	8 40.1	8 10.9	8 38.8	4 21.4	25 15.2	16 31.0	25 17.7	28 18.3
6 M	16 57 33	15 18 04	26 44 31	2♍52 53	22 15.4	26 21.1	9 50.8	8 55.1	9 04.4	4 30.4	25 15.1	16 34.1	25 18.5	28 17.3
7 Tu	17 01 29	16 15 30	9♍05 04	15 21 34	22D 14.3	26 35.3	11 01.4	9 39.2	9 30.0	4 39.2	25 15.0	16 37.3	25 19.2	28 16.4
8 W	17 05 26	17 12 55	21 42 54	28 09 32	22 14.1	26 53.9	12 12.1	10 23.3	9 55.7	4 47.9	25 14.7	16 40.4	25 19.8	28 15.4
9 Th	17 09 23	18 10 18	4♎41 55	11♎20 28	22 14.9	27 17.0	13 22.9	11 07.4	10 21.4	4 56.5	25 14.4	16 43.5	25 20.5	28 14.4
10 F	17 13 19	19 07 40	18 05 28	24 57 10	22 16.3	27 44.4	14 33.7	11 51.4	10 47.1	5 05.0	25 13.9	16 46.5	25 21.1	28 13.3
11 Sa	17 17 16	20 05 02	1♏55 39	9♏00 53	22 17.8	28 16.1	15 44.6	12 35.3	11 12.9	5 13.3	25 13.4	16 49.6	25 21.7	28 12.3
12 Su	17 21 12	21 02 22	16 12 40	23 30 36	22R 18.7	28 52.0	16 55.5	13 19.2	11 38.7	5 21.5	25 12.7	16 52.6	25 22.2	28 11.2
13 M	17 25 09	21 59 41	0♐54 08	8♐22 30	22 18.6	29 32.0	18 06.4	14 03.0	12 04.6	5 29.5	25 12.0	16 55.6	25 22.7	28 10.2
14 Tu	17 29 05	22 57 00	15 54 46	23 29 51	22 17.1	0♊16.1	19 17.4	14 46.8	12 30.4	5 37.4	25 11.1	16 58.5	25 23.2	28 09.1
15 W	17 33 02	23 54 18	1♑06 33	8♑43 36	22 14.2	1 04.2	20 28.4	15 30.5	12 56.4	5 45.2	25 10.2	17 01.5	25 23.7	28 08.0
16 Th	17 36 59	24 51 36	16 19 41	23 53 33	22 10.1	1 56.2	21 39.5	16 14.1	13 22.3	5 52.8	25 09.2	17 04.4	25 24.1	28 06.8
17 F	17 40 55	25 48 52	1♒24 02	8♒50 06	22 05.5	2 52.0	22 50.6	16 57.7	13 48.3	6 00.3	25 08.1	17 07.3	25 24.5	28 05.7
18 Sa	17 44 52	26 46 09	16 10 52	23 25 39	22 01.0	3 51.6	24 01.8	17 41.2	14 14.3	6 07.6	25 06.9	17 10.1	25 24.8	28 04.5
19 Su	17 48 48	27 43 25	0♓34 00	7♓35 35	21 57.3	4 54.8	25 13.0	18 24.7	14 40.4	6 14.8	25 05.6	17 13.0	25 25.1	28 03.3
20 M	17 52 45	28 40 41	14 30 20	21 18 17	21 54.9	6 01.7	26 24.2	19 08.1	15 06.4	6 21.8	25 04.2	17 15.8	25 25.4	28 02.2
21 Tu	17 56 41	29 37 56	27 59 38	4♈34 41	21D 54.0	7 12.1	27 35.5	19 51.4	15 32.5	6 28.7	25 02.7	17 18.6	25 25.7	28 00.9
22 W	18 00 38	0♋35 11	11♈03 49	17 27 31	21 54.4	8 26.1	28 46.9	20 34.6	15 58.7	6 35.4	25 01.1	17 21.3	25 25.9	27 59.7
23 Th	18 04 34	1 32 26	23 46 14	0♉00 31	21 55.7	9 43.5	29 58.2	21 17.8	16 24.9	6 42.0	24 59.4	17 24.0	25 26.1	27 58.5
24 F	18 08 31	2 29 42	6♉10 51	12 17 46	21 57.2	11 04.4	1♊09.7	22 00.9	16 51.1	6 48.4	24 57.6	17 26.7	25 26.3	27 57.2
25 Sa	18 12 28	3 26 56	18 21 45	24 23 15	21R 58.1	12 28.7	2 21.1	22 43.9	17 17.3	6 54.7	24 55.8	17 29.4	25 26.4	27 56.0
26 Su	18 16 24	4 24 11	0♊22 44	6♊20 36	21 57.8	13 56.4	3 32.6	23 26.9	17 43.5	7 00.8	24 53.8	17 32.0	25 26.5	27 54.7
27 M	18 20 21	5 21 26	12 17 12	18 12 53	21 55.7	15 27.4	4 44.2	24 09.7	18 09.8	7 06.7	24 51.8	17 34.6	25 26.5	27 53.4
28 Tu	18 24 17	6 18 41	24 07 57	0♋02 42	21 51.6	17 01.7	5 55.8	24 52.5	18 36.2	7 12.5	24 49.7	17 37.2	25R 26.6	27 52.1
29 W	18 28 14	7 15 55	5♋57 22	11 52 11	21 45.4	18 39.3	7 07.4	25 35.2	19 02.5	7 18.1	24 47.5	17 39.7	25 26.6	27 50.8
30 Th	18 32 10	8 13 09	17 47 23	23 43 11	21 37.7	20 20.0	8 19.1	26 17.8	19 28.9	7 23.5	24 45.2	17 42.2	25 26.5	27 49.4

Astro Data	Planet Ingress	Last Aspect	☽ Ingress	Last Aspect	☽ Ingress	☽ Phases & Eclipses	Astro Data
Dy Hr Mn	Dy Hr Mn	Dy Hr Mn	Dy Hr Mn	Dy Hr Mn	Dy Hr Mn	Dy Hr Mn	1 May 2022
☊D 1 19:54	♀ ♈ 2 16:12	2 10:14 ♀ ⚹	♊ 2 10:48	31 20:11 ♄ △	♋ 1 5:50	9 0:23 ☽ 18♌23	Julian Day # 44681
♃⚹♇ 3 22:35	♃ ♈ 10 23:23	4 20:38 ♃ □	♋ 4 23:06	3 15:16 ♇ ☍	♌ 3 18:39	16 4:15 ○ 25♏18	SVP 4♓57'07"
♀0N 5 17:44	⚳ ♋ 15 7:12	7 10:27 ♃ △	♌ 7 11:51	5 23:13 ☿ □	♍ 6 6:23	16 4:13 T 1.413	GC 27♐09.1 ⚴ 0♉16.5
☊R 9 0:30	☉ ♊ 21 1:24	9 12:40 ♄ ☍	♍ 9 22:54	8 12:10 ♇ △	♎ 8 15:24	22 18:44 ☾ 1♓39	Eris 24♈31.1 ⚵ 3♓36.1
☿R 10 11:49	☿ ♉R 23 1:16	12 4:01 ♇ △	♎ 12 6:36	10 17:38 ♇ □	♏ 10 20:42	30 11:31 ● 9♊03	⚷ 14♈00.1 ⚶ 22♒15.6
♃∠♅ 11 20:53	♂ ♈ 24 23:19	14 8:08 ♇ □	♏ 14 10:35	12 21:41 ☿ ☍	♐ 12 22:33		☽ Mean ☊ 23♉10.5
☽0S 12 21:43	♀ ♉ 28 14:47	16 9:29 ♇ ⚹	♐ 16 11:52	14 14:59 ♆ □	♑ 14 22:15	7 14:50 ☽ 16♍51	
☊D 13 7:05		18 4:01 ♄ ⚹	♑ 18 12:03	16 18:43 ♇ ☌	♒ 16 21:45	14 11:53 ○ 23♐25	1 June 2022
☊R 15 23:57	☿ ♊ 13 15:28	20 12:01 ☉ △	♒ 20 12:54	18 18:51 ☉ △	♓ 18 23:02	21 3:12 ☾ 29♓46	Julian Day # 44712
♄⚺♆ 17 15:40	☉ ♋ 21 9:15	22 7:20 ♄ ☌	♓ 22 15:51	21 3:12 ☉ □	♈ 21 3:38	29 2:53 ● 7♋23	SVP 4♓57'02"
☊D 22 18:51	♀ ♊ 23 0:36	24 21:35 ♂ ☌	♈ 24 21:41	23 8:04 ♇ □	♉ 23 11:59		GC 27♐09.1 ⚴ 14♉06.8
♃0N 25 8:20		27 3:21 ♇ □	♉ 27 6:24	25 19:04 ♇ △	♊ 25 23:14		Eris 24♈48.7 ⚵ 13♓10.1
☽0N 25 13:30		29 14:12 ♇ △	♊ 29 17:24	28 2:39 ♆ □	♋ 28 11:55		⚷ 15♈27.2 ⚶ 2♓00.9
☊R 29 2:36							☽ Mean ☊ 21♉32.0
♂0N 30 9:20							

*Giving the positions of planets daily at midnight, Greenwich Mean Time (0:00 UT)
Each planet's retrograde period is shaded gray.

July 2022

LONGITUDE

Day	Sid.Time	☉	0 hr ☽	Noon☽	True☊	☿	♀	♂	⚳	♃	♄	♅	♆	♇
1 F	18 36 07	9♋10 23	29♋39 48	5♌37 27	21♉28.9	22♊03.8	9♊30.8	27♈00.3	19♋55.2	7♈28.8	24♒42.8	17♉44.7	25♓26.4	27♑48.1
2 Sa	18 40 03	10 07 37	11♌36 23	17 36 51	21R 19.9	23 50.7	10 42.5	27 42.7	20 21.7	7 33.9	24R 40.3	17 47.1	25R 26.3	27R 46.8
3 Su	18 44 00	11 04 50	23 39 08	29 43 31	21 11.6	25 40.6	11 54.3	28 25.0	20 48.1	7 38.8	24 37.8	17 49.5	25 26.2	27 45.4
4 M	18 47 57	12 02 03	5♍50 22	12♍00 02	21 04.6	27 33.3	13 06.1	29 07.2	21 14.6	7 43.6	24 35.1	17 51.8	25 26.0	27 44.1
5 Tu	18 51 53	12 59 16	18 12 54	24 29 25	20 59.6	29 28.6	14 17.9	29 49.3	21 41.0	7 48.2	24 32.4	17 54.1	25 25.8	27 42.7
6 W	18 55 50	13 56 28	0♎50 00	7♎15 06	20 56.8	1♋26.5	15 29.8	0♉31.4	22 07.5	7 52.6	24 29.7	17 56.4	25 25.6	27 41.3
7 Th	18 59 46	14 53 41	13 45 09	20 20 37	20D 55.9	3 26.7	16 41.7	1 13.3	22 34.0	7 56.8	24 26.8	17 58.7	25 25.3	27 39.9
8 F	19 03 43	15 50 53	27 01 53	3♏49 17	20 56.3	5 29.0	17 53.7	1 55.1	23 00.6	8 00.9	24 23.8	18 00.9	25 25.0	27 38.5
9 Sa	19 07 39	16 48 05	10♏43 05	17 43 27	20R 57.2	7 33.1	19 05.7	2 36.8	23 27.1	8 04.8	24 20.8	18 03.0	25 24.7	27 37.1
10 Su	19 11 36	17 45 16	24 50 24	2♐03 48	20 57.4	9 38.9	20 17.7	3 18.4	23 53.7	8 08.5	24 17.8	18 05.2	25 24.3	27 35.7
11 M	19 15 32	18 42 28	9♐23 19	16 48 26	20 56.1	11 45.9	21 29.8	3 59.9	24 20.3	8 12.0	24 14.6	18 07.3	25 23.9	27 34.3
12 Tu	19 19 29	19 39 40	24 18 25	1♑52 19	20 52.6	13 53.9	22 41.9	4 41.4	24 46.9	8 15.3	24 11.4	18 09.3	25 23.5	27 32.9
13 W	19 23 26	20 36 52	9♑29 02	17 07 18	20 46.8	16 02.6	23 54.0	5 22.7	25 13.5	8 18.5	24 08.1	18 11.3	25 23.1	27 31.5
14 Th	19 27 22	21 34 04	24 45 46	2♒23 00	20 39.0	18 11.7	25 06.2	6 03.9	25 40.1	8 21.4	24 04.7	18 13.3	25 22.6	27 30.1
15 F	19 31 19	22 31 16	9♒57 40	17 28 29	20 30.1	20 20.9	26 18.4	6 44.9	26 06.8	8 24.2	24 01.3	18 15.2	25 22.1	27 28.6
16 Sa	19 35 15	23 28 28	24 54 19	2♓14 14	20 21.2	22 30.0	27 30.7	7 25.9	26 33.4	8 26.8	23 57.8	18 17.1	25 21.5	27 27.2
17 Su	19 39 12	24 25 41	9♓27 29	16 33 36	20 13.4	24 38.6	28 43.0	8 06.8	27 00.1	8 29.2	23 54.3	18 19.0	25 21.0	27 25.8
18 M	19 43 08	25 22 55	23 32 17	0♈23 28	20 07.5	26 46.6	29 55.3	8 47.5	27 26.8	8 31.5	23 50.7	18 20.8	25 20.4	27 24.3
19 Tu	19 47 05	26 20 09	7♈07 17	13 43 59	20 03.8	28 53.7	1♋07.7	9 28.2	27 53.5	8 33.5	23 47.0	18 22.6	25 19.7	27 22.9
20 W	19 51 01	27 17 24	20 13 59	26 37 45	20D 02.2	0♌59.7	2 20.1	10 08.7	28 20.2	8 35.3	23 43.2	18 24.3	25 19.1	27 21.5
21 Th	19 54 58	28 14 40	2♉55 52	9♉08 56	20 02.0	3 04.6	3 32.6	10 49.0	28 47.0	8 37.0	23 39.5	18 26.0	25 18.4	27 20.0
22 F	19 58 55	29 11 56	15 17 35	21 22 27	20R 02.4	5 08.2	4 45.1	11 29.3	29 13.7	8 38.4	23 35.6	18 27.6	25 17.6	27 18.6
23 Sa	20 02 51	0♌09 14	27 24 09	3♊23 19	20 02.3	7 10.4	5 57.7	12 09.4	29 40.5	8 39.7	23 31.7	18 29.2	25 16.9	27 17.2
24 Su	20 06 48	1 06 32	9♊20 30	15 16 15	20 00.6	9 11.0	7 10.3	12 49.4	0♌07.2	8 40.7	23 27.8	18 30.7	25 16.1	27 15.7
25 M	20 10 44	2 03 51	21 11 04	27 05 24	19 56.6	11 10.2	8 22.9	13 29.2	0 34.0	8 41.6	23 23.8	18 32.2	25 15.3	27 14.3
26 Tu	20 14 41	3 01 11	2♋59 40	8♋54 13	19 50.0	13 07.7	9 35.6	14 09.0	1 00.8	8 42.2	23 19.8	18 33.7	25 14.5	27 12.9
27 W	20 18 37	3 58 31	14 49 21	20 45 22	19 40.6	15 03.6	10 48.3	14 48.5	1 27.6	8 42.7	23 15.7	18 35.1	25 13.6	27 11.4
28 Th	20 22 34	4 55 52	26 42 29	2♌40 54	19 29.1	16 57.8	12 01.0	15 27.9	1 54.4	8R 43.0	23 11.6	18 36.5	25 12.7	27 10.0
29 F	20 26 30	5 53 14	8♌40 47	14 42 17	19 16.1	18 50.3	13 13.8	16 07.2	2 21.3	8 43.1	23 07.4	18 37.8	25 11.8	27 08.6
30 Sa	20 30 27	6 50 37	20 45 33	26 50 41	19 02.8	20 41.2	14 26.7	16 46.3	2 48.1	8 42.9	23 03.2	18 39.1	25 10.9	27 07.2
31 Su	20 34 24	7 48 01	2♍57 52	9♍07 13	18 50.2	22 30.4	15 39.5	17 25.3	3 14.9	8 42.6	22 59.0	18 40.3	25 09.9	27 05.8

August 2022

LONGITUDE

Day	Sid.Time	☉	0 hr ☽	Noon☽	True☊	☿	♀	♂	⚳	♃	♄	♅	♆	♇
1 M	20 38 20	8♌45 25	15♍18 55	21♍33 09	18♉39.5	24♌17.9	16♋52.4	18♉04.1	3♌41.7	8♈42.1	22♒54.7	18♉41.5	25♓08.9	27♑04.4
2 Tu	20 42 17	9 42 49	27 50 10	4♎10 11	18R 31.3	26 03.7	18 05.4	18 42.8	4 08.6	8R 41.4	22R 50.4	18 42.6	25R 07.9	27R 03.0
3 W	20 46 13	10 40 15	10♎33 32	17 00 29	18 26.0	27 47.9	19 18.3	19 21.2	4 35.4	8 40.4	22 46.1	18 43.7	25 06.8	27 01.6
4 Th	20 50 10	11 37 41	23 31 24	0♏06 38	18 23.2	29 30.5	20 31.3	19 59.6	5 02.3	8 39.3	22 41.7	18 44.7	25 05.8	27 00.2
5 F	20 54 06	12 35 08	6♏46 30	13 31 20	18 22.3	1♍11.4	21 44.4	20 37.7	5 29.1	8 38.0	22 37.3	18 45.7	25 04.7	26 58.8
6 Sa	20 58 03	13 32 35	20 21 26	27 17 01	18 22.3	2 50.6	22 57.5	21 15.7	5 55.9	8 36.5	22 32.9	18 46.7	25 03.5	26 57.5
7 Su	21 01 59	14 30 03	4♐18 13	11♐25 02	18 21.8	4 28.3	24 10.6	21 53.5	6 22.8	8 34.8	22 28.5	18 47.6	25 02.4	26 56.1
8 M	21 05 56	15 27 32	18 37 22	25 54 53	18 19.7	6 04.3	25 23.7	22 31.1	6 49.6	8 32.9	22 24.1	18 48.4	25 01.2	26 54.8
9 Tu	21 09 53	16 25 02	3♑17 08	10♑43 27	18 15.3	7 38.7	26 36.9	23 08.6	7 16.5	8 30.8	22 19.6	18 49.2	25 00.1	26 53.4
10 W	21 13 49	17 22 32	18 12 59	25 44 41	18 08.1	9 11.4	27 50.2	23 45.9	7 43.3	8 28.5	22 15.2	18 50.0	24 58.9	26 52.1
11 Th	21 17 46	18 20 04	3♒17 25	10♒49 56	17 58.7	10 42.6	29 03.4	24 23.0	8 10.2	8 26.0	22 10.7	18 50.7	24 57.6	26 50.8
12 F	21 21 42	19 17 36	18 20 58	25 49 14	17 47.8	12 12.1	0♌16.7	24 59.9	8 37.0	8 23.4	22 06.2	18 51.3	24 56.4	26 49.5
13 Sa	21 25 39	20 15 10	3♓13 34	10♓32 57	17 36.8	13 39.9	1 30.1	25 36.7	9 03.9	8 20.5	22 01.7	18 51.9	24 55.1	26 48.2
14 Su	21 29 35	21 12 45	17 46 31	24 53 35	17 26.9	15 06.1	2 43.5	26 13.2	9 30.7	8 17.5	21 57.2	18 52.5	24 53.8	26 46.9
15 M	21 33 32	22 10 21	1♈53 43	8♈46 40	17 19.1	16 30.6	3 56.9	26 49.6	9 57.5	8 14.2	21 52.7	18 53.0	24 52.5	26 45.7
16 Tu	21 37 28	23 07 58	15 32 23	22 10 59	17 13.8	17 53.5	5 10.3	27 25.7	10 24.4	8 10.8	21 48.2	18 53.4	24 51.2	26 44.4
17 W	21 41 25	24 05 37	28 42 45	5♉08 06	17 10.9	19 14.5	6 23.8	28 01.7	10 51.2	8 07.2	21 43.7	18 53.8	24 49.8	26 43.2
18 Th	21 45 22	25 03 17	11♉27 32	17 41 37	17D 10.0	20 33.8	7 37.4	28 37.5	11 18.0	8 03.4	21 39.2	18 54.2	24 48.4	26 41.9
19 F	21 49 18	26 01 00	23 50 59	29 56 18	17R 10.0	21 51.3	8 51.0	29 13.0	11 44.8	7 59.5	21 34.8	18 54.5	24 47.1	26 40.7
20 Sa	21 53 15	26 58 43	5♊58 13	11♊57 25	17 09.7	23 06.9	10 04.6	29 48.3	12 11.7	7 55.3	21 30.3	18 54.7	24 45.6	26 39.5
21 Su	21 57 11	27 56 29	17 54 33	23 50 15	17 08.2	24 20.6	11 18.2	0♊23.4	12 38.5	7 51.0	21 25.8	18 54.9	24 44.2	26 38.3
22 M	22 01 08	28 54 16	29 45 07	5♋39 43	17 04.6	25 32.2	12 31.9	0 58.3	13 05.3	7 46.5	21 21.4	18 55.1	24 42.8	26 37.2
23 Tu	22 05 04	29 52 05	11♋34 33	17 30 06	16 58.4	26 41.8	13 45.7	1 33.0	13 32.1	7 41.8	21 16.9	18 55.2	24 41.3	26 36.0
24 W	22 09 01	0♍49 55	23 26 46	29 24 55	16 49.6	27 49.3	14 59.4	2 07.4	13 58.9	7 37.0	21 12.5	18R 55.2	24 39.9	26 34.9
25 Th	22 12 57	1 47 47	5♌24 52	11♌26 50	16 38.5	28 54.5	16 13.3	2 41.6	14 25.6	7 32.0	21 08.1	18 55.2	24 38.4	26 33.8
26 F	22 16 54	2 45 40	17 31 02	23 37 38	16 25.9	29 57.3	17 27.1	3 15.5	14 52.4	7 26.8	21 03.8	18 55.2	24 36.9	26 32.7
27 Sa	22 20 51	3 43 35	29 46 42	5♍58 21	16 13.0	0♎57.6	18 41.0	3 49.2	15 19.2	7 21.5	20 59.4	18 55.1	24 35.4	26 31.6
28 Su	22 24 47	4 41 32	12♍12 37	18 29 32	16 00.8	1 55.3	19 54.9	4 22.6	15 45.9	7 16.0	20 55.1	18 55.0	24 33.9	26 30.5
29 M	22 28 44	5 39 30	24 49 06	1♎11 22	15 50.3	2 50.2	21 08.8	4 55.7	16 12.6	7 10.3	20 50.8	18 54.8	24 32.3	26 29.5
30 Tu	22 32 40	6 37 29	7♎36 22	14 04 08	15 42.4	3 42.2	22 22.8	5 28.6	16 39.4	7 04.6	20 46.6	18 54.5	24 30.8	26 28.4
31 W	22 36 37	7 35 30	20 34 45	27 08 20	15 37.3	4 31.0	23 36.8	6 01.2	17 06.1	6 58.6	20 42.4	18 54.2	24 29.2	26 27.4

Astro Data	Dy Hr Mn
☽0S	6 13:32
☊D	7 2:07
☊R	9 17:30
☽0N	19 1:24
☊D	20 14:28
♃∠♄	21 11:18
☊R	22 9:23
♃R	28 20:39
☽0S	2 18:30
☽0N	15 9:42
☊D	18 11:00
☊R	19 4:46
☿0S	22 22:28
♅R	24 13:55
☽0S	29 23:22

Planet Ingress		Dy Hr Mn
♂	♉	5 6:05
☿	♋	5 6:26
♀	♋	18 1:33
☿	♌	19 12:36
☉	♌	22 20:08
⚳	♌	23 17:30
☿	♍	4 6:59
♀	♌	11 18:31
♂	♊	20 7:57
☉	♍	23 3:17
☿	♎	26 1:04

Last Aspect Dy Hr Mn			☽ Ingress	Dy Hr Mn
30 20:15	♇	☍	♌	1 0:41
3 10:00	♂	△	♍	3 12:32
5 18:05	♇	△	♎	5 22:26
8 1:05	♇	□	♏	8 5:16
10 4:35	♇	⚹	♐	10 8:35
12 1:44	♆	□	♑	12 9:02
14 4:18	♇	☌	♒	14 8:14
16 4:38	♀	△	♓	16 8:19
18 6:44	♇	⚹	♈	18 11:19
20 14:20	☉	□	♉	20 18:24
22 23:46	♇	△	♊	23 5:12
25 8:16	♆	□	♋	25 17:55
28 0:55	♇	☍	♌	28 6:37
30 4:30	♄	☍	♍	30 18:12

Last Aspect Dy Hr Mn			☽ Ingress	Dy Hr Mn
1 22:30	♇	△	♎	2 4:07
4 6:21	♇	□	♏	4 11:48
6 11:25	♇	⚹	♐	6 16:40
8 10:31	♆	□	♑	8 18:40
10 16:41	♀	☍	♒	10 18:46
12 11:08	♂	□	♓	12 18:45
14 15:12	♇	⚹	♈	14 20:44
16 20:19	♇	□	♉	17 2:23
19 11:07	♂	☌	♊	19 12:07
21 22:08	☉	⚹	♋	22 0:30
24 9:41	☿	⚹	♌	24 13:10
26 6:56	♄	☍	♍	27 0:26
29 3:09	♇	△	♎	29 9:46
31 10:45	♇	□	♏	31 17:12

☽ Phases & Eclipses Dy Hr Mn	
7 2:15	☽ 14♎59
13 18:39	○ 21♑21
20 14:20	☾ 27♈52
28 17:56	● 5♌39
5 11:08	☽ 13♏02
12 1:37	○ 19♒21
19 4:37	☾ 26♉12
27 8:18	● 4♍04

Astro Data

1 July 2022
Julian Day # 44742
SVP 4♓56'56"
GC 27♐09.2 ⚴ 28♉02.7
Eris 24♈59.3 ⚵ 19♓37.1
⚷ 16♈17.0 ⚶ 6♓42.7
☽ Mean ☊ 19♉56.7

1 August 2022
Julian Day # 44773
SVP 4♓56'51"
GC 27♐09.3 ⚴ 12♊48.9
Eris 25♈00.9R ⚵ 21♓21.8R
⚷ 16♈22.1R ⚶ 4♓37.9R
☽ Mean ☊ 18♉18.2

*Giving the positions of planets daily at midnight, Greenwich Mean Time (0:00 UT)
Each planet's retrograde period is shaded gray.

2022 Planetary Ephemeris

LONGITUDE — September 2022

Day	Sid.Time	☉	0 hr ☽	Noon ☽	True☊	☿	♀	♂	⚳	♃	♄	♅	♆	♇
1 Th	22 40 33	8♍33 32	3♏44 59	10♏24 52	15♉34.8	5♎16.5	24♌50.9	6♊33.6	17♌32.7	6♈52.5	20♒38.2	18♉53.9	24♓27.6	26♑26.5
2 F	22 44 30	9 31 36	17 08 08	23 54 56	15D 34.2	5 58.5	26 04.9	7 05.6	17 59.4	6R 46.3	20R 34.0	18R 53.5	24R 26.0	26R 25.5
3 Sa	22 48 26	10 29 41	0♐45 28	7♐39 49	15R 34.6	6 36.7	27 19.0	7 37.4	18 26.1	6 40.0	20 29.9	18 53.0	24 24.5	26 24.5
4 Su	22 52 23	11 27 48	14 38 06	21 40 19	15 34.8	7 10.9	28 33.2	8 08.9	18 52.7	6 33.5	20 25.9	18 52.5	24 22.9	26 23.6
5 M	22 56 20	12 25 56	28 46 24	5♑56 12	15 33.7	7 40.8	29 47.3	8 40.1	19 19.3	6 26.9	20 21.9	18 52.0	24 21.3	26 22.7
6 Tu	23 00 16	13 24 06	13♑09 24	20 25 34	15 30.5	8 06.1	1♍01.5	9 10.9	19 45.9	6 20.2	20 17.9	18 51.4	24 19.6	26 21.9
7 W	23 04 13	14 22 16	27 44 09	5♒04 27	15 25.0	8 26.5	2 15.7	9 41.5	20 12.5	6 13.3	20 14.0	18 50.8	24 18.0	26 21.0
8 Th	23 08 09	15 20 29	12♒25 40	19 46 53	15 17.4	8 41.7	3 30.0	10 11.8	20 39.0	6 06.4	20 10.2	18 50.1	24 16.4	26 20.2
9 F	23 12 06	16 18 43	27 07 10	4♓25 32	15 08.5	8 51.5	4 44.2	10 41.8	21 05.5	5 59.3	20 06.4	18 49.3	24 14.8	26 19.4
10 Sa	23 16 02	17 16 58	11♓41 02	18 52 48	14 59.4	8R 55.4	5 58.5	11 11.4	21 32.0	5 52.2	20 02.6	18 48.6	24 13.1	26 18.6
11 Su	23 19 59	18 15 15	26 00 02	3♈02 05	14 51.1	8 53.2	7 12.9	11 40.7	21 58.5	5 44.9	19 58.9	18 47.7	24 11.5	26 17.8
12 M	23 23 55	19 13 34	9♈58 27	16 48 47	14 44.6	8 44.7	8 27.2	12 09.7	22 25.0	5 37.6	19 55.3	18 46.9	24 09.8	26 17.1
13 Tu	23 27 52	20 11 55	23 32 54	0♉10 46	14 40.3	8 29.6	9 41.6	12 38.3	22 51.4	5 30.2	19 51.7	18 45.9	24 08.2	26 16.3
14 W	23 31 49	21 10 18	6♉42 29	13 08 17	14D 38.3	8 07.8	10 56.0	13 06.6	23 17.8	5 22.6	19 48.2	18 45.0	24 06.5	26 15.6
15 Th	23 35 45	22 08 43	19 28 32	25 43 40	14 38.1	7 39.3	12 10.5	13 34.5	23 44.2	5 15.1	19 44.8	18 43.9	24 04.9	26 15.0
16 F	23 39 42	23 07 10	1♊54 11	8♊00 39	14 39.0	7 04.1	13 25.0	14 02.1	24 10.6	5 07.4	19 41.4	18 42.9	24 03.2	26 14.3
17 Sa	23 43 38	24 05 40	14 03 41	20 03 55	14R 40.1	6 22.3	14 39.5	14 29.2	24 36.9	4 59.7	19 38.1	18 41.8	24 01.6	26 13.7
18 Su	23 47 35	25 04 11	26 01 59	1♋58 33	14 40.6	5 34.5	15 54.0	14 56.0	25 03.2	4 51.9	19 34.8	18 40.6	23 59.9	26 13.1
19 M	23 51 31	26 02 45	7♋54 14	13 49 40	14 39.7	4 41.2	17 08.6	15 22.4	25 29.5	4 44.1	19 31.7	18 39.4	23 58.3	26 12.6
20 Tu	23 55 28	27 01 21	19 45 27	25 42 08	14 36.9	3 43.3	18 23.2	15 48.4	25 55.7	4 36.2	19 28.6	18 38.2	23 56.6	26 12.0
21 W	23 59 24	27 59 59	1♌40 15	7♌40 16	14 32.2	2 41.7	19 37.8	16 14.0	26 21.9	4 28.3	19 25.5	18 36.9	23 54.9	26 11.5
22 Th	0 03 21	28 58 39	13 42 36	19 47 39	14 25.8	1 37.6	20 52.4	16 39.2	26 48.1	4 20.3	19 22.6	18 35.6	23 53.3	26 11.0
23 F	0 07 18	29 57 21	25 55 41	2♍06 57	14 18.1	0 32.6	22 07.1	17 03.9	27 14.2	4 12.3	19 19.7	18 34.2	23 51.7	26 10.6
24 Sa	0 11 14	0♎56 06	8♍21 38	14 39 51	14 10.0	29♍28.2	23 21.8	17 28.2	27 40.4	4 04.3	19 16.9	18 32.8	23 50.0	26 10.1
25 Su	0 15 11	1 54 52	21 01 40	27 27 03	14 02.4	28 26.0	24 36.5	17 52.0	28 06.4	3 56.3	19 14.2	18 31.4	23 48.4	26 09.7
26 M	0 19 07	2 53 41	3♎55 59	10♎28 21	13 55.9	27 27.6	25 51.2	18 15.3	28 32.5	3 48.2	19 11.6	18 29.9	23 46.7	26 09.3
27 Tu	0 23 04	3 52 31	17 04 02	23 42 54	13 51.2	26 34.6	27 06.0	18 38.2	28 58.4	3 40.2	19 09.0	18 28.3	23 45.1	26 09.0
28 W	0 27 00	4 51 23	0♏24 48	7♏09 32	13D 48.5	25 48.5	28 20.8	19 00.6	29 24.4	3 32.1	19 06.6	18 26.8	23 43.5	26 08.7
29 Th	0 30 57	5 50 18	13 56 59	20 46 59	13 47.7	25 10.4	29 35.6	19 22.5	29 50.3	3 24.1	19 04.2	18 25.2	23 41.9	26 08.4
30 F	0 34 53	6 49 14	27 39 25	4♐34 07	13 48.4	24 41.2	0♎50.4	19 43.9	0♍16.2	3 16.1	19 01.9	18 23.5	23 40.3	26 08.1

LONGITUDE — October 2022

Day	Sid.Time	☉	0 hr ☽	Noon ☽	True☊	☿	♀	♂	⚳	♃	♄	♅	♆	♇
1 Sa	0 38 50	7♎48 12	11♐31 00	18♐29 57	13♉49.8	24♍21.9	2♎05.2	20♊04.8	0♍42.0	3♈08.1	18♒59.7	18♉21.8	23♓38.7	26♑07.9
2 Su	0 42 47	8 47 11	25 30 50	2♑33 32	13 51.1	24D 12.7	3 20.1	20 25.2	1 07.8	3R 00.1	18R 57.6	18R 20.1	23R 37.1	26R 07.6
3 M	0 46 43	9 46 13	9♑37 52	16 43 39	13R 51.7	24 14.0	4 34.9	20 45.0	1 33.5	2 52.2	18 55.6	18 18.4	23 35.5	26 07.5
4 Tu	0 50 40	10 45 16	23 50 38	0♒58 32	13 51.0	24 25.6	5 49.8	21 04.3	1 59.2	2 44.3	18 53.7	18 16.6	23 33.9	26 07.3
5 W	0 54 36	11 44 21	8♒07 01	15 15 38	13 48.9	24 47.3	7 04.7	21 23.1	2 24.8	2 36.4	18 51.8	18 14.7	23 32.4	26 07.2
6 Th	0 58 33	12 43 28	22 23 57	29 31 28	13 45.4	25 18.8	8 19.6	21 41.3	2 50.4	2 28.6	18 50.1	18 12.9	23 30.8	26 07.1
7 F	1 02 29	13 42 36	6♓37 37	13♓41 52	13 41.1	25 59.5	9 34.5	21 58.9	3 15.9	2 20.9	18 48.4	18 11.0	23 29.3	26 07.0
8 Sa	1 06 26	14 41 46	20 43 39	27 42 26	13 36.6	26 48.7	10 49.5	22 15.9	3 41.4	2 13.2	18 46.9	18 09.0	23 27.8	26D 07.0
9 Su	1 10 22	15 40 58	4♈37 44	11♈29 06	13 32.5	27 45.8	12 04.4	22 32.4	4 06.8	2 05.6	18 45.4	18 07.1	23 26.2	26 07.0
10 M	1 14 19	16 40 12	18 16 10	24 58 38	13 29.4	28 49.9	13 19.4	22 48.2	4 32.2	1 58.1	18 44.0	18 05.1	23 24.8	26 07.0
11 Tu	1 18 15	17 39 28	1♉36 20	8♉09 10	13D 27.6	0♎00.4	14 34.4	23 03.4	4 57.5	1 50.6	18 42.8	18 03.1	23 23.3	26 07.0
12 W	1 22 12	18 38 46	14 37 08	21 00 18	13 27.1	1 16.5	15 49.4	23 18.0	5 22.7	1 43.3	18 41.6	18 01.0	23 21.8	26 07.1
13 Th	1 26 09	19 38 07	27 18 52	3♊33 06	13 27.7	2 37.4	17 04.4	23 32.0	5 47.9	1 36.0	18 40.5	17 58.9	23 20.4	26 07.2
14 F	1 30 05	20 37 29	9♊43 20	15 49 57	13 29.1	4 02.5	18 19.4	23 45.3	6 13.1	1 28.8	18 39.6	17 56.8	23 18.9	26 07.4
15 Sa	1 34 02	21 36 54	21 53 26	27 54 15	13 30.8	5 31.2	19 34.5	23 57.9	6 38.1	1 21.7	18 38.7	17 54.7	23 17.5	26 07.5
16 Su	1 37 58	22 36 21	3♋52 59	9♋50 10	13 32.3	7 02.8	20 49.5	24 09.8	7 03.2	1 14.8	18 37.9	17 52.6	23 16.1	26 07.7
17 M	1 41 55	23 35 51	15 46 25	21 42 18	13R 33.3	8 36.9	22 04.6	24 21.0	7 28.1	1 07.9	18 37.2	17 50.4	23 14.7	26 07.9
18 Tu	1 45 51	24 35 23	27 38 28	3♌35 29	13 33.5	10 12.9	23 19.7	24 31.5	7 53.0	1 01.1	18 36.7	17 48.2	23 13.4	26 08.2
19 W	1 49 48	25 34 57	9♌33 57	15 34 26	13 32.8	11 50.6	24 34.8	24 41.3	8 17.8	0 54.5	18 36.2	17 45.9	23 12.0	26 08.5
20 Th	1 53 45	26 34 33	21 37 28	27 43 35	13 31.4	13 29.5	25 49.9	24 50.3	8 42.6	0 48.0	18 35.8	17 43.7	23 10.7	26 08.8
21 F	1 57 41	27 34 11	3♍53 12	10♍06 45	13 29.3	15 09.4	27 05.0	24 58.5	9 07.3	0 41.7	18 35.5	17 41.4	23 09.4	26 09.1
22 Sa	2 01 38	28 33 52	16 24 33	22 46 52	13 27.1	16 50.0	28 20.2	25 06.0	9 31.9	0 35.4	18 35.4	17 39.1	23 08.1	26 09.5
23 Su	2 05 34	29 33 35	29 13 54	5♎45 45	13 25.0	18 31.0	29 35.3	25 12.7	9 56.4	0 29.3	18D 35.3	17 36.8	23 06.8	26 09.9
24 M	2 09 31	0♏33 20	12♎22 25	19 03 51	13 23.2	20 12.3	0♏50.5	25 18.6	10 20.8	0 23.4	18 35.3	17 34.5	23 05.6	26 10.3
25 Tu	2 13 27	1 33 07	25 49 53	2♏40 16	13 22.1	21 53.8	2 05.6	25 23.7	10 45.2	0 17.6	18 35.5	17 32.1	23 04.4	26 10.8
26 W	2 17 24	2 32 56	9♏34 40	16 32 44	13D 21.6	23 35.2	3 20.8	25 28.0	11 09.5	0 11.9	18 35.7	17 29.7	23 03.2	26 11.3
27 Th	2 21 20	3 32 47	23 33 59	0♐37 57	13 21.7	25 16.6	4 36.0	25 31.4	11 33.7	0 06.5	18 36.1	17 27.4	23 02.0	26 11.8
28 F	2 25 17	4 32 40	7♐44 07	14 51 59	13 22.3	26 57.7	5 51.2	25 34.0	11 57.9	0 01.1	18 36.5	17 25.0	23 00.9	26 12.3
29 Sa	2 29 13	5 32 35	22 01 01	29 10 44	13 23.0	28 38.7	7 06.4	25 35.8	12 21.9	29♓56.0	18 37.1	17 22.5	22 59.7	26 12.9
30 Su	2 33 10	6 32 31	6♑20 37	13♑30 16	13 23.7	0♏19.3	8 21.6	25R 36.7	12 45.9	29 51.0	18 37.7	17 20.1	22 58.7	26 13.5
31 M	2 37 07	7 32 29	20 39 14	27 47 12	13 24.1	1 59.6	9 36.8	25 36.8	13 09.7	29 46.2	18 38.5	17 17.7	22 57.6	26 14.1

Astro Data	Planet Ingress	Last Aspect	☽ Ingress	Last Aspect	☽ Ingress	☽ Phases & Eclipses	Astro Data
Dy Hr Mn	Dy Hr Mn	Dy Hr Mn	Dy Hr Mn	Dy Hr Mn	Dy Hr Mn	Dy Hr Mn	1 September 2022
☊D 1 21:14	♀ ♍ 5 4:06	2 17:23 ♀ □	♐ 2 22:41	1 21:47 ☿ □	♑ 2 7:39	3 18:09 ☽ 11♐14	Julian Day # 44804
☊R 3 18:02	☉ ♎ 23 1:05	5 1:52 ♀ △	♑ 5 2:04	4 3:50 ♇ ☌	♒ 4 10:22	10 10:00 ○ 17♓41	SVP 4♓56'47"
☿R 10 3:39	☿ ♍R 23 12:06	6 21:44 ♇ ☌	♒ 7 3:42	5 22:47 ♂ △	♓ 6 12:48	17 21:53 ☾ 24♊59	GC 27♐09.4 ⚴ 27♊34.4
☽0N 11 19:11	♀ ♎ 29 7:50	8 12:35 ♄ ☌	♓ 9 4:43	8 11:12 ☿ ☍	♈ 8 15:58	25 21:56 ● 2♎49	Eris 24♈52.9R ⚵ 16♓40.2R
☊D 14 14:50	⚳ ♍ 29 9:00	11 0:30 ♇ ⚹	♈ 11 6:48	10 14:03 ♇ □	♉ 10 21:05		⚷ 15♈39.6R ⚶ 27♒25.0R
☊R 17 22:05		13 4:54 ♇ □	♉ 13 11:40	12 21:43 ♇ △	♊ 13 5:09	3 0:15 ☽ 9♑47	☽ Mean ☊ 16♉39.7
♃∠♄ 21 13:09	☿ ♎ 10 23:52	15 13:00 ♇ △	♊ 15 20:17	15 4:12 ♂ ☌	♋ 15 16:12	9 20:56 ○ 16♈33	
☉0S 23 1:06	♀ ♏ 23 7:53	17 21:53 ☉ □	♋ 18 8:00	17 20:58 ♇ ☍	♌ 18 4:46	17 17:16 ☾ 24♋19	1 October 2022
☽0S 26 5:55	☉ ♏ 23 10:37	20 15:58 ☉ ⚹	♌ 20 20:39	20 10:36 ☉ ⚹	♍ 20 16:27	25 10:50 ● 2♏00	Julian Day # 44834
♃0S 26 10:58	♃ ♓R 28 5:11	22 11:08 ♄ ☍	♍ 23 7:55	22 18:19 ♇ △	♎ 23 1:25	25 11:01:21 ✔ P 0.862	SVP 4♓56'44"
☿0N 27 7:37	☿ ♏ 29 19:23	25 12:50 ☿ ☌	♎ 25 16:44	25 0:37 ♇ □	♏ 25 7:20		GC 27♐09.4 ⚴ 11♋00.3
♃∠♅ 28 19:59		27 16:22 ♇ □	♏ 27 23:16	27 4:29 ♇ ⚹	♐ 27 10:56		Eris 24♈38.0R ⚵ 9♓46.4R
☊D 28 23:45		29 21:21 ♇ ⚹	♐ 30 4:05	29 13:11 ♃ □	♑ 29 13:23		⚷ 14♈26.8R ⚶ 23♒03.5R
♀0S 1 22:34				31 15:16 ♃ ⚹	♒ 31 15:44		☽ Mean ☊ 15♉04.4
☿D 2 9:09							

*Giving the positions of planets daily at midnight, Greenwich Mean Time (0:00 UT)
Each planet's retrograde period is shaded gray.

2022 Planetary Ephemeris

November 2022 — LONGITUDE

Day	Sid.Time	☉	0 hr ☽	Noon ☽	True ☊	☿	♀	♂	⚳	♃	♄	♅	♆	♇
1 Tu	2 41 03	8♏32 29	4♒53 48	11♒58 45	13♉24.4	3♏39.5	10♏52.0	25♊35.9	13♍33.5	29♓41.5	18♒39.4	17♉15.3	22♓56.5	26♑14.8
2 W	2 45 00	9 32 30	19 01 49	26 02 46	13R 24.3	5 19.1	12 07.3	25R 34.3	13 57.2	29R 37.1	18 40.3	17R 12.8	22R 55.5	26 15.5
3 Th	2 48 56	10 32 33	3♓01 23	9♓57 30	13 24.1	6 58.2	13 22.5	25 31.7	14 20.8	29 32.8	18 41.4	17 10.3	22 54.5	26 16.2
4 F	2 52 53	11 32 37	16 50 57	23 41 35	13 23.9	8 36.9	14 37.7	25 28.3	14 44.3	29 28.7	18 42.5	17 07.9	22 53.6	26 17.0
5 Sa	2 56 49	12 32 42	0♈29 16	7♈13 51	13D 23.7	10 15.2	15 52.9	25 24.0	15 07.6	29 24.8	18 43.8	17 05.4	22 52.6	26 17.7
6 Su	3 00 46	13 32 50	13 55 14	20 33 18	13 23.7	11 53.1	17 08.1	25 18.8	15 30.9	29 21.1	18 45.2	17 02.9	22 51.7	26 18.5
7 M	3 04 42	14 32 59	27 07 58	3♉39 10	13 23.7	13 30.6	18 23.4	25 12.7	15 54.1	29 17.5	18 46.7	17 00.4	22 50.8	26 19.3
8 Tu	3 08 39	15 33 10	10♉06 51	16 31 01	13R 23.8	15 07.7	19 38.6	25 05.8	16 17.2	29 14.2	18 48.2	16 58.0	22 50.0	26 20.2
9 W	3 12 36	16 33 22	22 51 40	29 08 52	13 23.8	16 44.4	20 53.9	24 58.0	16 40.2	29 11.0	18 49.9	16 55.5	22 49.1	26 21.1
10 Th	3 16 32	17 33 37	5♊22 44	11♊33 23	13 23.5	18 20.7	22 09.1	24 49.3	17 03.0	29 08.1	18 51.7	16 53.0	22 48.3	26 22.0
11 F	3 20 29	18 33 53	17 41 02	23 45 54	13 23.0	19 56.7	23 24.3	24 39.7	17 25.8	29 05.3	18 53.5	16 50.5	22 47.6	26 22.9
12 Sa	3 24 25	19 34 11	29 48 16	5♋48 29	13 22.2	21 32.3	24 39.6	24 29.3	17 48.4	29 02.8	18 55.5	16 48.0	22 46.8	26 23.9
13 Su	3 28 22	20 34 31	11♋46 55	17 43 58	13 21.3	23 07.6	25 54.9	24 18.1	18 11.0	29 00.4	18 57.6	16 45.5	22 46.1	26 24.9
14 M	3 32 18	21 34 53	23 40 07	29 35 51	13 20.3	24 42.6	27 10.1	24 05.9	18 33.4	28 58.2	18 59.7	16 43.1	22 45.4	26 25.9
15 Tu	3 36 15	22 35 16	5♌31 42	11♌28 11	13 19.4	26 17.3	28 25.4	23 53.0	18 55.7	28 56.3	19 02.0	16 40.6	22 44.8	26 26.9
16 W	3 40 12	23 35 42	17 25 54	23 25 25	13D 18.9	27 51.7	29 40.7	23 39.2	19 17.8	28 54.5	19 04.4	16 38.1	22 44.2	26 28.0
17 Th	3 44 08	24 36 09	29 27 21	5♍32 15	13 18.9	29 25.9	0♐56.0	23 24.6	19 39.9	28 53.0	19 06.8	16 35.7	22 43.6	26 29.1
18 F	3 48 05	25 36 38	11♍40 42	17 53 16	13 19.4	0♐59.8	2 11.2	23 09.3	20 01.8	28 51.6	19 09.4	16 33.2	22 43.0	26 30.2
19 Sa	3 52 01	26 37 09	24 10 27	0♎32 44	13 20.3	2 33.4	3 26.5	22 53.2	20 23.6	28 50.5	19 12.0	16 30.8	22 42.5	26 31.4
20 Su	3 55 58	27 37 42	7♎00 30	13 34 04	13 21.6	4 06.9	4 41.8	22 36.3	20 45.2	28 49.6	19 14.8	16 28.3	22 42.0	26 32.5
21 M	3 59 54	28 38 17	20 13 40	26 59 25	13 22.8	5 40.1	5 57.1	22 18.8	21 06.7	28 48.8	19 17.6	16 25.9	22 41.6	26 33.7
22 Tu	4 03 51	29 38 53	3♏51 17	10♏49 08	13R 23.7	7 13.2	7 12.4	22 00.5	21 28.1	28 48.3	19 20.5	16 23.5	22 41.1	26 34.9
23 W	4 07 47	0♐39 31	17 52 40	25 01 25	13 23.8	8 46.1	8 27.7	21 41.7	21 49.3	28D 48.0	19 23.6	16 21.1	22 40.8	26 36.2
24 Th	4 11 44	1 40 10	2♐14 50	9♐32 10	13 23.0	10 18.8	9 43.0	21 22.2	22 10.4	28 47.9	19 26.7	16 18.7	22 40.4	26 37.4
25 F	4 15 40	2 40 51	16 52 36	24 15 15	13 21.3	11 51.3	10 58.3	21 02.1	22 31.3	28 48.0	19 29.9	16 16.4	22 40.1	26 38.7
26 Sa	4 19 37	3 41 33	1♑39 07	9♑03 15	13 18.7	13 23.7	12 13.6	20 41.6	22 52.1	28 48.3	19 33.2	16 14.0	22 39.8	26 40.0
27 Su	4 23 34	4 42 17	16 26 42	23 48 35	13 15.8	14 55.9	13 28.9	20 20.5	23 12.7	28 48.9	19 36.6	16 11.7	22 39.5	26 41.4
28 M	4 27 30	5 43 01	1♒08 06	8♒24 32	13 12.9	16 27.9	14 44.3	19 59.1	23 33.1	28 49.6	19 40.1	16 09.4	22 39.3	26 42.7
29 Tu	4 31 27	6 43 47	15 37 21	22 46 05	13 10.7	17 59.8	15 59.6	19 37.2	23 53.4	28 50.6	19 43.7	16 07.1	22 39.1	26 44.1
30 W	4 35 23	7 44 33	29 50 27	6♓50 16	13D 09.4	19 31.5	17 14.9	19 15.0	24 13.6	28 51.7	19 47.3	16 04.9	22 39.0	26 45.5

December 2022 — LONGITUDE

Day	Sid.Time	☉	0 hr ☽	Noon ☽	True ☊	☿	♀	♂	⚳	♃	♄	♅	♆	♇
1 Th	4 39 20	8♐45 21	13♓45 27	20♓36 02	13♉09.3	21♐03.1	18♐30.2	18♊52.5	24♍33.5	28♓53.1	19♒51.1	16♉02.6	22♓38.9	26♑46.9
2 F	4 43 16	9 46 09	27 22 06	4♈03 48	13 10.2	22 34.4	19 45.5	18R 29.8	24 53.3	28 54.7	19 54.9	16R 00.4	22R 38.8	26 48.4
3 Sa	4 47 13	10 46 58	10♈41 21	17 14 56	13 11.7	24 05.5	21 00.7	18 06.9	25 12.9	28 56.4	19 58.8	15 58.2	22 38.7	26 49.8
4 Su	4 51 10	11 47 48	23 44 48	0♉11 11	13 13.4	25 36.3	22 16.0	17 43.9	25 32.3	28 58.4	20 02.8	15 56.0	22D 38.7	26 51.3
5 M	4 55 06	12 48 39	6♉34 18	12 54 21	13R 14.5	27 06.9	23 31.3	17 20.7	25 51.6	29 00.6	20 06.9	15 53.9	22 38.7	26 52.8
6 Tu	4 59 03	13 49 30	19 11 33	25 26 04	13 14.5	28 37.1	24 46.6	16 57.5	26 10.7	29 03.0	20 11.1	15 51.7	22 38.8	26 54.3
7 W	5 02 59	14 50 23	1♊38 04	7♊47 41	13 13.0	0♑06.9	26 01.9	16 34.4	26 29.5	29 05.5	20 15.3	15 49.7	22 38.9	26 55.9
8 Th	5 06 56	15 51 17	13 55 05	20 00 25	13 09.8	1 36.3	27 17.2	16 11.3	26 48.2	29 08.3	20 19.7	15 47.6	22 39.0	26 57.4
9 F	5 10 52	16 52 12	26 03 48	2♋05 24	13 04.9	3 05.1	28 32.4	15 48.3	27 06.7	29 11.3	20 24.1	15 45.6	22 39.1	26 59.0
10 Sa	5 14 49	17 53 07	8♋05 24	14 03 59	12 58.7	4 33.3	29 47.7	15 25.4	27 25.1	29 14.5	20 28.5	15 43.6	22 39.3	27 00.6
11 Su	5 18 45	18 54 04	20 01 23	25 57 51	12 51.7	6 00.7	1♑03.0	15 02.8	27 43.2	29 17.9	20 33.1	15 41.6	22 39.6	27 02.2
12 M	5 22 42	19 55 02	1♌53 42	7♌49 14	12 44.7	7 27.2	2 18.2	14 40.4	28 01.1	29 21.4	20 37.8	15 39.7	22 39.8	27 03.8
13 Tu	5 26 39	20 56 01	13 44 51	19 40 57	12 38.4	8 52.7	3 33.5	14 18.3	28 18.8	29 25.2	20 42.5	15 37.8	22 40.1	27 05.5
14 W	5 30 35	21 57 00	25 38 00	1♍36 31	12 33.3	10 16.9	4 48.8	13 56.5	28 36.2	29 29.2	20 47.3	15 35.9	22 40.4	27 07.2
15 Th	5 34 32	22 58 01	7♍37 00	13 40 02	12 30.0	11 39.7	6 04.0	13 35.1	28 53.5	29 33.3	20 52.1	15 34.0	22 40.8	27 08.8
16 F	5 38 28	23 59 03	19 46 12	25 56 06	12D 28.6	13 00.7	7 19.3	13 14.2	29 10.5	29 37.6	20 57.1	15 32.2	22 41.2	27 10.5
17 Sa	5 42 25	25 00 06	2♎10 19	8♎29 28	12 28.7	14 19.7	8 34.5	12 53.7	29 27.4	29 42.1	21 02.1	15 30.5	22 41.6	27 12.2
18 Su	5 46 21	26 01 09	14 54 07	21 24 47	12 29.9	15 36.4	9 49.8	12 33.7	29 43.9	29 46.9	21 07.1	15 28.7	22 42.1	27 14.0
19 M	5 50 18	27 02 14	28 01 54	4♏45 52	12 31.3	16 50.2	11 05.1	12 14.3	0♎00.3	29 51.8	21 12.3	15 27.0	22 42.6	27 15.7
20 Tu	5 54 14	28 03 19	11♏36 55	18 35 08	12R 32.1	18 00.8	12 20.3	11 55.4	0 16.4	29 56.8	21 17.5	15 25.4	22 43.1	27 17.5
21 W	5 58 11	29 04 26	25 40 27	2♐52 38	12 31.3	19 07.6	13 35.6	11 37.1	0 32.3	0♈02.1	21 22.8	15 23.8	22 43.7	27 19.2
22 Th	6 02 08	0♑05 33	10♐11 11	17 35 25	12 28.4	20 10.1	14 50.8	11 19.5	0 47.9	0 07.5	21 28.2	15 22.2	22 44.3	27 21.0
23 F	6 06 04	1 06 41	25 04 27	2♑37 13	12 23.3	21 07.5	16 06.1	11 02.6	1 03.2	0 13.2	21 33.6	15 20.7	22 45.0	27 22.8
24 Sa	6 10 01	2 07 49	10♑12 28	17 48 54	12 16.2	21 59.1	17 21.3	10 46.3	1 18.3	0 19.0	21 39.1	15 19.2	22 45.6	27 24.6
25 Su	6 13 57	3 08 58	25 25 08	2♒59 49	12 08.0	22 44.1	18 36.5	10 30.8	1 33.2	0 25.0	21 44.6	15 17.8	22 46.3	27 26.4
26 M	6 17 54	4 10 06	10♒31 44	17 59 43	11 59.8	23 21.7	19 51.8	10 16.1	1 47.8	0 31.1	21 50.2	15 16.4	22 47.1	27 28.3
27 Tu	6 21 50	5 11 15	25 22 51	2♓40 23	11 52.7	23 50.9	21 07.0	10 02.0	2 02.1	0 37.4	21 55.9	15 15.0	22 47.9	27 30.1
28 W	6 25 47	6 12 24	9♓51 47	16 56 45	11 47.5	24 10.8	22 22.2	9 48.8	2 16.1	0 43.9	22 01.6	15 13.7	22 48.7	27 32.0
29 Th	6 29 44	7 13 33	23 55 09	0♈47 01	11 44.6	24R 20.5	23 37.4	9 36.4	2 29.8	0 50.6	22 07.4	15 12.4	22 49.5	27 33.8
30 F	6 33 40	8 14 42	7♈32 32	14 12 01	11D 43.7	24 19.3	24 52.6	9 24.8	2 43.3	0 57.4	22 13.3	15 11.2	22 50.4	27 35.7
31 Sa	6 37 37	9 15 51	20 45 50	27 14 26	11 44.1	24 06.7	26 07.7	9 13.9	2 56.4	1 04.4	22 19.2	15 10.0	22 51.3	27 37.6

Astro Data Dy Hr Mn	Planet Ingress Dy Hr Mn	Last Aspect Dy Hr Mn	☽ Ingress Dy Hr Mn	Last Aspect Dy Hr Mn	☽ Ingress Dy Hr Mn	☽ Phases & Eclipses Dy Hr Mn
☊R 1 6:57	♀ ♐ 16 6:10	2 11:09 ♂ △	♓ 2 18:48	2 2:46 ♃ ☌	♈ 2 4:42	1 6:38 ☽ 8♒49
☽0N 5 12:00	☿ ♐ 17 8:43	4 22:06 ♃ ☌	♈ 4 23:08	4 5:47 ♇ □	♉ 4 11:39	8 11:03 ○ 16♉01
☊D 5 20:32	☉ ♐ 22 8:22	6 22:31 ♇ □	♉ 7 5:16	6 19:03 ♃ ⚹	♊ 6 20:50	8 11:00 ☍ T 1.359
☊R 8 6:07		9 12:01 ♃ ⚹	♊ 9 13:38	9 6:15 ♃ □	♋ 9 7:50	16 13:28 ☾ 24♌10
☊D 16 13:36	☿ ♑ 6 22:09	11 22:30 ♃ □	♋ 12 0:23	11 18:50 ♃ △	♌ 11 20:10	23 22:58 ● 1♐38
☽0S 20 0:23	♀ ♑ 10 3:55	14 10:42 ♃ △	♌ 14 12:49	13 15:53 ☉ △	♍ 14 8:47	30 14:38 ☽ 8♓22
☊R 22 16:25	⚳ ♎ 18 23:35	16 23:57 ☿ □	♍ 17 1:05	16 19:14 ♃ ☍	♎ 16 19:50	
♃D 23 23:03	♃ ♈ 20 14:33	19 8:48 ♃ ☍	♎ 19 10:59	18 22:37 ♇ □	♏ 19 3:32	8 4:09 ○ 16♊02
☊D 30 14:31	☉ ♑ 21 21:49	21 11:16 ♇ □	♏ 21 17:17	21 2:46 ♇ ⚹	♐ 21 7:14	16 8:57 ☾ 24♍22
☽0N 2 17:34		23 18:17 ♃ △	♐ 23 20:17	22 20:17 ♆ □	♑ 23 7:51	23 10:18 ● 1♑33
♆D 4 0:16		25 19:23 ♃ □	♑ 25 21:19	25 3:12 ♇ ☌	♒ 25 7:15	30 1:22 ☽ 8♈18
☊R 5 12:40	♃∠∠24 0:44	27 20:12 ♃ ⚹	♒ 27 22:08	26 18:21 ♄ ☌	♓ 27 7:35	
☊D 16 9:09	☿ R29 9:33	29 6:55 ♄ ☌	♓ 30 0:16	29 6:22 ♇ ⚹	♈ 29 10:37	
☽0S 17 9:06	☽ 0N29 22:39			31 12:45 ♇ □	♉ 31 17:10	
☊R 20 1:37	☊ D30 1:14					

Astro Data

1 November 2022
Julian Day # 44865
SVP 4♓56'40"
GC 27♐09.5 ⚵ 22♋05.7
Eris 24♈19.7R ⚶ 7♓59.7
⚷ 13♈05.3R ⚴ 25♒25.7
☽ Mean ☊ 13♉25.9

1 December 2022
Julian Day # 44895
SVP 4♓56'35"
GC 27♐09.6 ⚵ 26♋32.8R
Eris 24♈04.3R ⚶ 13♓28.7
⚷ 12♈09.8R ⚴ 2♓58.8
☽ Mean ☊ 11♉50.6

*Giving the positions of planets daily at midnight, Greenwich Mean Time (0:00 UT)
Each planet's retrograde period is shaded gray.

2022 ASTEROID EPHEMERIS

Ceres ⚳ / Pallas ⚴ / Juno ⚵ / Vesta ⚶

2022	Ceres	Pallas	Juno	Vesta
JAN 1	28R38.0	16♓27.5	17♍22.9	24♐31.5
JAN 11	28♉01.0	19 05.9	21 17.5	29 52.8
JAN 21	28D05.4	22 00.8	25 14.5	5♑11.4
JAN 31	28 49.1	25 09.8	29 13.0	10 26.8
FEB 10	0♉08.6	28 31.1	3♎32.3	15 37.8
FEB 20	1 59.5	2♈03.1	7 11.2	20 43.6
MAR 2	4 17.3	5 44.5	11 09.2	25 43.3
MAR 12	6 58.1	9 34.0	15 05.0	0♒35.6
MAR 22	9 58.2	13 30.7	18 57.9	5 19.2
APR 1	13 14.5	17 34.0	22 46.7	9 53.0
APR 11	16 44.4	21 43.0	26 30.3	14 14.9
APR 21	20 25.6	25 57.3	0♏07.2	18 23.2
MAY 1	24 16.4	0♉16.4	3 36.1	22 15.6
MAY 11	28 15.2	4 40.1	6 54.9	25 49.0
MAY 21	2♊20.5	9 07.2	10 01.7	29 00.4
MAY 31	6 31.5	13 39.4	12 53.8	1♓46.0
JUN 10	10 47.1	18 14.5	15 28.0	4 00.8
JUN 20	15 06.4	22 53.0	17 40.9	5 40.4
JUN 30	19 28.8	27 34.4	19 28.2	6 39.3
JUL 10	23 53.6	2♊18.0	20 44.5	6R52.9
JUL 20	28 20.2	7 04.1	21 25.7	6 19.1
JUL 30	2♋48.0	11 51.3	21R26.8	4 59.1
AUG 9	7 16.4	16 38.8	20 45.0	3 00.2
AUG 19	11 44.8	21 25.9	19 22.9	0 36.8
AUG 29	16 12.6	26 09.8	17 21.5	28♒07.8
SEP 8	20 39.0	0♏49.6	14 58.9	25 53.9
SEP 18	25 03.1	5 22.2	12 31.8	24 12.0
SEP 28	29 24.3	9 44.4	10 20.2	23 12.4
OCT 8	3♌41.3	13 51.3	8 42.2	22D59.5
OCT 18	7 52.9	17 37.7	7 44.4	23 31.1
OCT 28	11 57.8	20 56.2	7D46.6	24 45.6
NOV 7	15 54.1	23 37.8	8 34.1	26 36.1
NOV 17	19 39.8	25 32.7	10 08.1	28 57.6
NOV 27	23 12.7	26R29.1	12 23.3	1♓40.0
DEC 7	26 29.5	26R17.3	15 16.1	4 55.0
DEC 17	29 27.3	24 53.1	18 39.6	8 22.6
DEC 27	2♍02.1	22 22.8	22 30.1	12 05.1
JAN 6	4♍09.2	19♈10.0	26♎43.4	15♓59.9

(continuation — 2023)

2022	Ceres	Pallas	Juno	Vesta
JAN 1	17♍47.7	11♉54.2	13♎49.2	21♓04.0
JAN 21	18 54.0	10 51.5	13 01.0	21 32.8
FEB 10	20 21.5	9 22.6	11 43.2	23 14.5
MAR 2	22 00.2	7 38.9	9 59.9	26 16.4
MAR 22	23 38.0	5 59.3	7 57.7	0♈41.2
APR 11	25 03.7	4 40.6	6 05.5	5 03.7
MAY 1	26 07.8	3 50.2	4 40.4	10 05.3
MAY 21	26 43.3	3D31.6	4 00.1	15 27.5
JUN 10	26 45.7	3 47.4	4D09.9	21 06.9
JUN 30	26 13.5	4 35.0	5 08.4	27 03.3
JUL 20	25 07.5	5 48.2	6 53.5	3♈02.8
AUG 9	23 31.4	7 23.6	9 23.0	9 07.5
AUG 29	21 30.9	9 16.2	12 32.8	15 12.7
SEP 18	19 13.5	11 26.1	16 14.8	21 21.7
OCT 8	16 48.4	13 51.0	20 24.7	27 05.8
OCT 28	14 26.2	16 42.1	24 57.2	3♉18.3
NOV 17	12 19.1	19 50.4	29 49.9	9 07.9
DEC 7	10 40.6	23 14.4	4♏55.8	15 02.5
DEC 27	9♍N44.4	32♉12.4	9♏06.4	21♈01.2

Psyche ⚳ / Eros / Lilith ⚸ / Toro

2022	Psyche	Eros	Lilith	Toro
JAN 1	19♏37.0	19♏12.3	16♈16.0	9♑59.8
JAN 11	19R49.3	25 11.1	19 27.4	17 15.5
JAN 21	19 27.1	1♐18.6	23 03.9	24 55.5
JAN 31	18 30.6	7 35.0	27 01.1	2♒03.3
FEB 10	17 03.0	14 00.5	1♉05.1	11 43.0
FEB 20	15 11.4	20 35.2	5 43.5	20 58.0
MAR 2	13 06.0	27 19.5	10 22.7	0♓52.3
MAR 12	10 59.3	4♑13.7	15 11.0	11 28.4
MAR 22	9 04.1	11 18.0	20 06.1	22 47.1
APR 1	7 30.4	18 33.1	25 06.7	4♈46.2
APR 11	6 25.5	25 59.2	0♊11.5	17 19.4
APR 21	5 52.8	3♒36.5	5 19.1	0♉15.4
MAY 1	5D52.6	11 25.5	10 28.6	13 20.0
MAY 11	6 23.4	19 26.1	15 39.3	26 16.9
MAY 21	7 22.3	27 38.0	20 50.2	8♊51.5
MAY 31	8 46.2	6♓10.1	26 00.9	20 54.0
JUN 10	10 32.0	14 35.1	1♋10.7	2♋19.7
JUN 20	12 36.3	23 18.7	6 19.0	13 00.5
JUN 30	14 57.2	2♈11.1	11 25.4	23 03.9
JUL 10	17 30.7	11 10.8	16 29.4	2♌27.7
JUL 20	20 16.0	20 16.3	21 30.4	11 16.2
AUG 9	26 14.3	8♉37.8	1♍22.1	27 24.2
AUG 19	29 24.1	17 49.6	6 11.4	4♍59.7
AUG 29	2♐39.4	27 00.6	10 55.1	11 54.2
SEP 8	5 59.2	6♊07.3	15 34.1	18 40.0
SEP 18	9 22.2	15 08.7	20 05.8	25 09.5
SEP 28	12 47.7	24 03.2	24 29.8	1♎25.0
OCT 8	16 14.6	2♊49.1	28 44.9	7 27.7
OCT 18	19 41.9	11 25.0	2♊48.6	13 19.2
OCT 28	23 08.8	19 50.3	6 42.2	19 00.7
NOV 7	26 34.0	28 03.8	10 20.7	24 32.7
NOV 17	29 56.6	6♋05.1	13 42.6	29 55.9
NOV 27	3♑15.3	13 54.1	16 45.7	5♏10.3
DEC 7	6 28.7	21 30.1	19 24.5	10 17.2
DEC 17	9 35.3	28 53.4	21 37.3	15 15.4
DEC 27	12 33.5	6♋04.0	23 19.1	20 05.0
JAN 6	15♑21.2	13♋01.9	24♋25.3	24♏45.2

(continuation — 2023)

2022	Psyche	Eros	Lilith	Toro
JAN 1	04♑15.2	10♋38.6	10♋07.9	22♏33.8
JAN 21	04 32.8	06 08.4	11 46.0	29 40.8
FEB 10	05 44.4	01 03.3	13 56.2	14 50.1
MAR 2	07 31.0	04D28.3	16 18.0	07 51.7
MAR 22	09 15.0	11 03.8	18 33.7	01N00.1
APR 11	10 22.1	15 55.0	20 28.8	10 37.6
MAY 1	10 38.8	21 05.1	21 49.1	18 43.3
MAY 21	10 07.9	25 07.9	22 28.8	22 51.5
JUN 10	08 58.0	27 19.5	22 27.2	22 26.5
JUN 30	07 17.7	27 00.6	21 30.4	18 43.8
JUL 20	05 14.5	23 56.6	19 30.4	13 36.4
AUG 9	02 54.6	18 23.5	17 41.8	07 53.3
AUG 29	00 44.0	11 06.0	14 58.0	02 09.2
SEP 18	02S12.0	02 56.8	11 54.6	03S16.7
OCT 8	07 18.2	12 55.8	05 19.1	13 08.8
NOV 17	09 37.9	19 29.7	02 07.9	17 18.1
DEC 27	13♑25.3	28♋07.7	03♊02.3	24♏09.2

Saffo ⚳ / Amor ⚳ / Pandora / Icarus

2022	Saffo	Amor	Pandora	Icarus
JAN 1	21♓37.8	29♉51.1	23♎26.5	6♎35.1
JAN 11	27 01.8	0♊32.1	26 36.4	10♏32.8
JAN 21	2♈32.3	1 55.7	29 36.1	0♐17.3
JAN 31	8 07.5	3 56.2	2♏23.6	20♑31.8
FEB 10	13 46.1	6 29.1	4 56.1	23♒31.8
FEB 20	19 26.5	9 29.7	7 11.2	27 54.4
MAR 2	25 07.6	12 54.4	9 05.4	2♓13.6
MAR 12	0♉48.8	16 40.5	10 35.9	6 12.8
MAR 22	6 28.9	20 45.6	11 38.5	9 53.9
APR 1	12 07.5	25 08.8	12 10.2	12 59.9
APR 11	17 44.1	29 47.0	12R07.9	15 42.7
APR 21	23 17.9	4♋41.2	11 30.1	17 53.2
MAY 1	28 48.8	9 50.5	10 19.2	19 27.5
MAY 11	4♊11.6	15 14.8	8 36.1	20 25.1
MAY 21	9 40.2	20 54.1	6 36.0	20R57.9
MAY 31	15 00.3	26 49.0	4 24.3	18 50.5
JUN 10	20 16.1	3♋00.3	2 16.7	16 07.6
JUN 20	25 27.5	9 28.5	0 26.3	11 46.9
JUN 30	0♌53.4	16 14.8	29♎08.2	5 46.8
JUL 10	5 36.1	23 20.1	28 32.5	28♒30.3
JUL 20	10 32.6	0♌45.5	27D58.4	20 49.1
JUL 30	15 23.4	8 32.1	28 19.4	13 45.1
AUG 9	20 08.0	16 40.5	29 14.9	8 04.7
AUG 19	24 45.6	25 10.7	0♏40.4	4 09.9
AUG 29	29 16.2	4♍00.3	2 33.3	1 40.5
SEP 8	3♍38.1	13 16.5	4 50.1	0 37.9
SEP 18	7 50.5	22 48.7	7 27.7	0♓41.2
SEP 28	11 52.0	2♎37.5	10 23.3	1 37.3
OCT 8	15 41.0	12 37.5	13 34.9	3 16.1
OCT 18	19 15.4	22 44.0	17 00.0	5 29.4
OCT 28	22 32.7	2♏53.4	20 37.1	8 04.0
NOV 7	25 30.8	13 00.2	24 24.4	10 59.7
NOV 17	28 03.2	23 03.4	28 24.0	14 10.5
DEC 7	1♐41.3	11 47.8	2♐34.4	17 22.5
DEC 17	2 36.4	20 44.8	6 50.4	20 42.7
DEC 27	2R49.1	29 18.3	11 07.7	23♓32.2
JAN 6	2♍58.1	2♍49.1	19♍33.4	8♎01.0

(continuation — 2023)

2022	Saffo	Amor	Pandora	Icarus
JAN 1	01S00.9	01S00.0	21S30.8	28S56.6
JAN 21	02N07.0	00N47.7	23 29.0	17 00.3
FEB 10	05 32.6	03 14.4	25 11.3	16 41.6
MAR 2	08 58.8	05 59.7	26 40.0	17 55.0
MAR 22	12 10.9	08 48.2	27 57.7	19 29.5
APR 11	14 44.1	11 27.0	00D41.5	21 07.2
MAY 1	17 04.9	13 44.1	22 14.9	22 45.8
MAY 21	18 30.2	15 26.2	29 29.1	23 46.0
JUN 10	19 08.6	16 22.1	29 29.4	24 42.4
JUN 30	18 59.6	16 55.7	28 34.0	25 49.6
JUL 20	18 03.4	14 32.5	27 34.3	27 49.8
AUG 9	16 32.5	11 57.4	27 42.8	43 00.0
SEP 18	14 05.6	02 46.2	27 52.0	40 44.8
OCT 8	06 15.5	08 48.0	28 59.2	37 38.0
NOV 17	01 10.6	15 49.1	28 40.1	35 47.6
DEC 27	00S25.0	16S36.0	27S46.5	31S14.1

Diana / Hidalgo / Urania / Chiron ⚷

2022	Diana	Hidalgo	Urania	Chiron
JAN 1	3♈46.7	17♍33.6	5♈17.8	8♈30.4
JAN 11	7 17.8	18 29.0	10 17.2	8 39.8
JAN 21	10 51.7	19 13.8	15 21.4	8 54.5
JAN 31	14 27.4	19 46.7	20 29.7	9 13.9
FEB 10	18 03.8	20 06.5	25 41.4	9 37.3
FEB 20	21 39.8	20R12.3	0♉56.0	10 04.9
MAR 2	25 14.6	20 03.4	6 12.3	10 35.3
MAR 12	28 46.9	19 39.9	11 30.4	11 08.0
MAR 22	2♉16.0	19 02.9	16 49.4	11 42.2
APR 1	5 40.6	18 11.8	22 08.4	12 17.3
APR 11	8 59.7	17 10.6	27 28.2	12 52.4
APR 21	12 11.8	16 00.3	2♊46.7	13 26.9
MAY 1	15 15.8	14 47.3	8 04.1	14 00.1
MAY 11	18 09.9	13 32.0	13 18.7	14 31.6
MAY 21	20 52.0	12 20.1	18 30.0	14 59.7
MAY 31	23 20.0	11 13.6	23 41.6	15 24.9
JUN 10	25 31.0	10 16.8	28 48.8	15 46.3
JUN 20	27 24.8	9 30.0	3♋47.5	16 03.8
JUN 30	28 56.2	8 56.0	8 43.0	16 16.8
JUL 10	0♊33.1	8 36.3	13 29.5	16R26.0
JUL 20	0R34.5	8 30.5	18 07.7	16 30.5
AUG 9	0 00.6	8 54.7	26 40.7	16 27.6
AUG 19	29♉01.8	9 26.1	0♌41.1	16 21.1
AUG 29	27 32.6	10 07.2	4 27.7	16 10.7
SEP 8	25 04.4	10 57.0	7 17.3	15 57.4
SEP 18	22 45.1	11 56.0	11 55.5	15 41.0
SEP 28	20 06.4	13 01.5	15 14.0	15 22.9
OCT 8	16 46.9	14 13.4	18 22.3	15 04.8
OCT 18	15 45.6	15 30.6	21 19.0	14 48.0
NOV 7	15 00.3	18 09.5	26 12.5	14 22.5
NOV 17	15D00.1	19 34.5	28 08.1	14 15.3
DEC 7	15 51.6	22 26.0	0♍02.9	14 10.1
DEC 17	16 33.6	23 48.5	1 29.9	14 11.7
DEC 27	22 20.4	24 46.0	2 59.3	11 57.3
JAN 6	25♈05.8	25♍26.0	0♍50.3	12♈01.2

(continuation — 2023)

2022	Diana	Hidalgo	Urania	Chiron
JAN 1	21S33.5	32S15.1	18S44.4	05N21.5
JAN 21	19 41.2	33 42.7	17 55.2	06 06.0
FEB 10	14 35.4	33 46.1	18 13.3	06 42.0
MAR 2	11 49.7	30 54.6	19 29.0	06 51.2
APR 11	09 01.9	27 36.4	21 15.1	07 41.5
MAY 1	06 17.7	25 04.9	04N12.3	07 46.1
JUN 10	03 43.0	23 08.8	08 26.1	07 21.5
JUL 10	01 50.1	21 41.4	10 20.4	06 55.5
AUG 9	00 12.7	21 29.9	11 18.1	06 29.6
SEP 18	01 05.2	21 45.9	11 20.1	06 10.7
OCT 8	15D04.0	25 48.3	08 36.1	06 15.1
NOV 17	00N19.3	35 14.2	24 25.3	06 27.3
DEC 27	01N57.4	39S34.1	23N13.1	06N21.5

Giving the positions of asteroids every ten days in LONGITUDE at 00:00 GMT

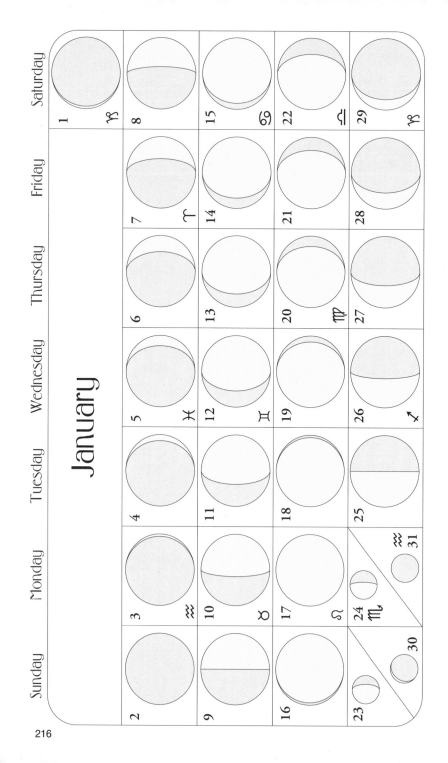

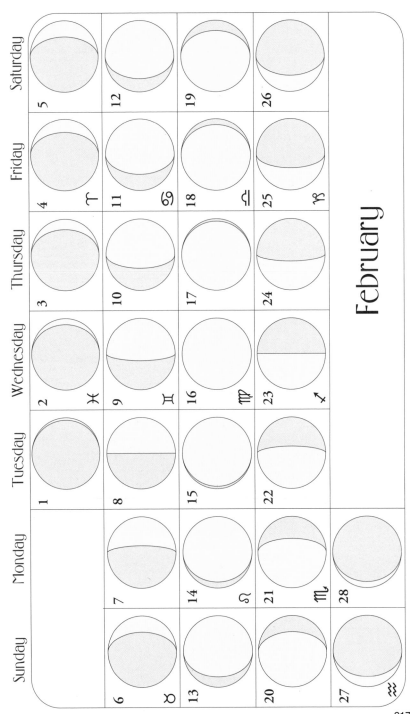

February

217

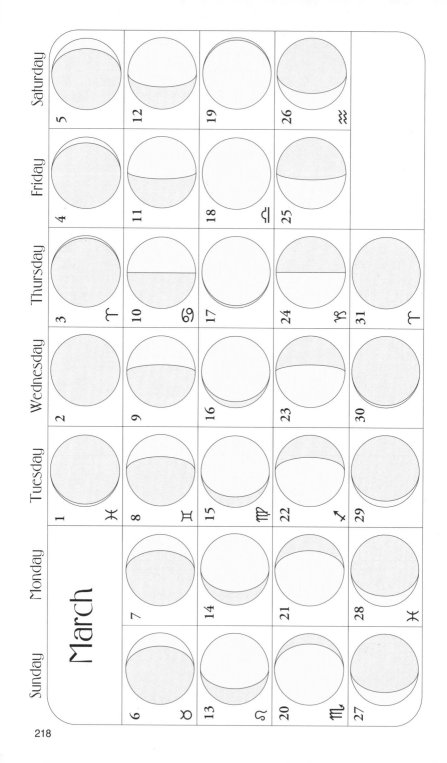

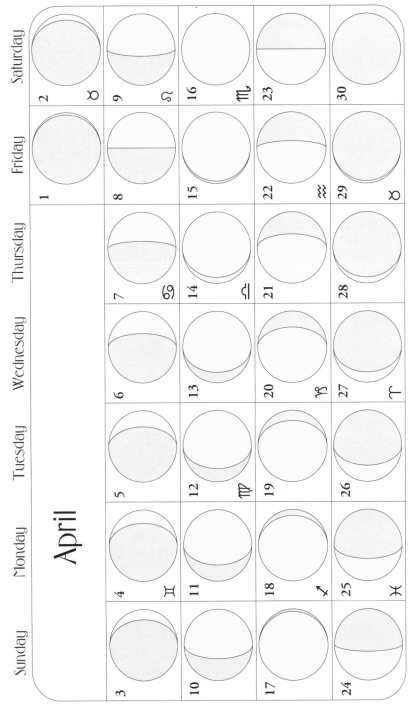

April

Sunday	Monday	Tuesday	Wednesday	Thursday	Friday	Saturday
					1	2 ♉
3	4 ♊	5	6	7 ♋	8	9 ♌
10	11	12 ♍	13	14 ♎	15	16 ♏
17	18 ♐	19	20 ♑	21	22 ♒	23
24	25 ♓	26	27 ♈	28	29 ♉	30

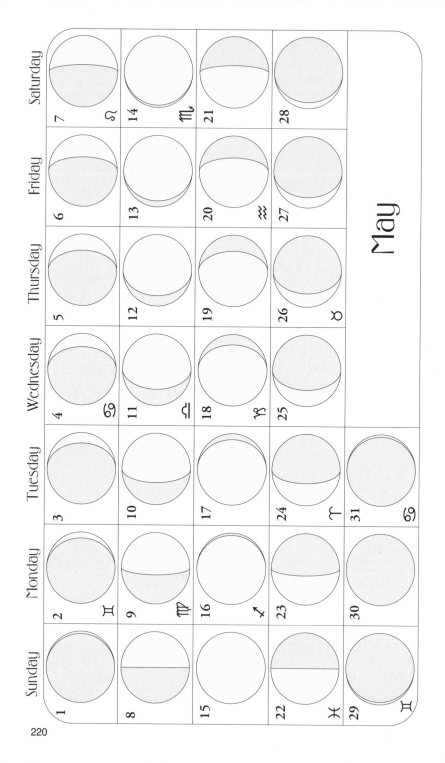

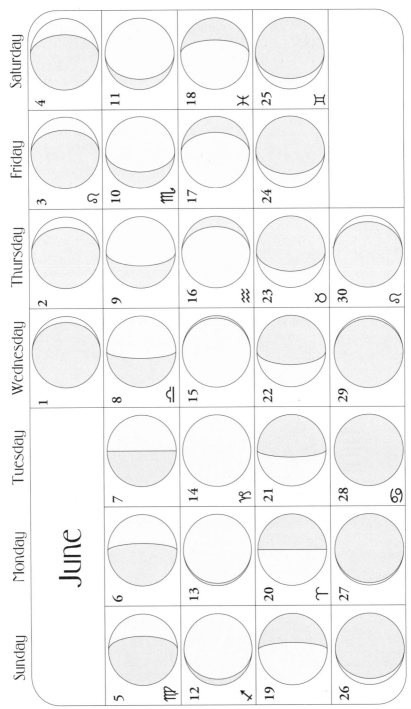

June

Sunday	Monday	Tuesday	Wednesday	Thursday	Friday	Saturday
			1	2	3 ♌	4
5 ♍	6	7	8 ♎	9	10 ♏	11
12 ♐	13	14 ♑	15	16 ♒	17	18 ♓
19	20 ♈	21	22	23 ♉	24	25 ♊
26	27	28 ♋	29	30 ♌		

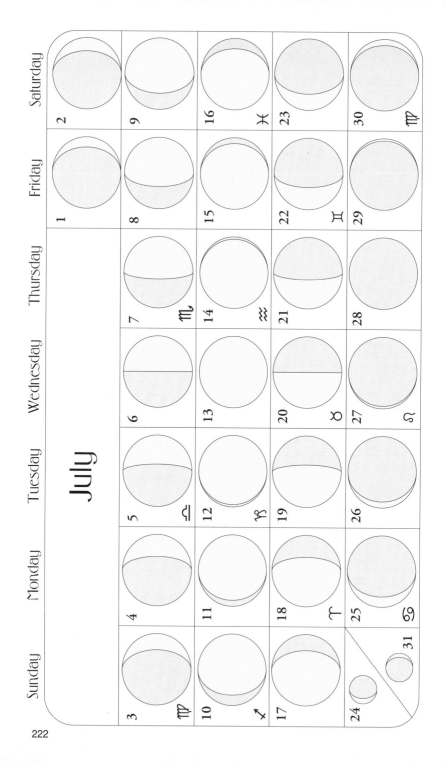

July

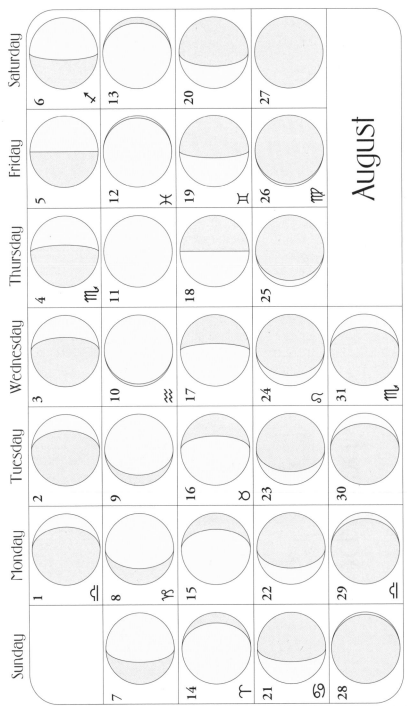

August

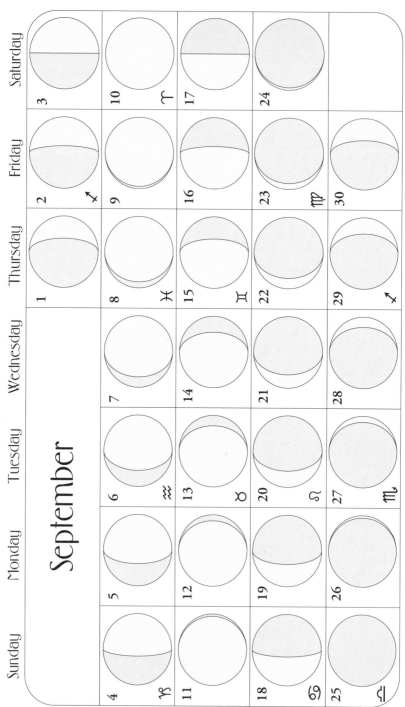

September

Sunday	Monday	Tuesday	Wednesday	Thursday	Friday	Saturday
				1	2 ♐	3
4 ♑	5	6 ♒	7	8 ♓	9	10 ♈
11	12	13 ♉	14	15 ♊	16	17
18 ♋	19	20	21	22	23 ♍	24
25 ♎	26	27 ♏	28	29 ♐	30	

224

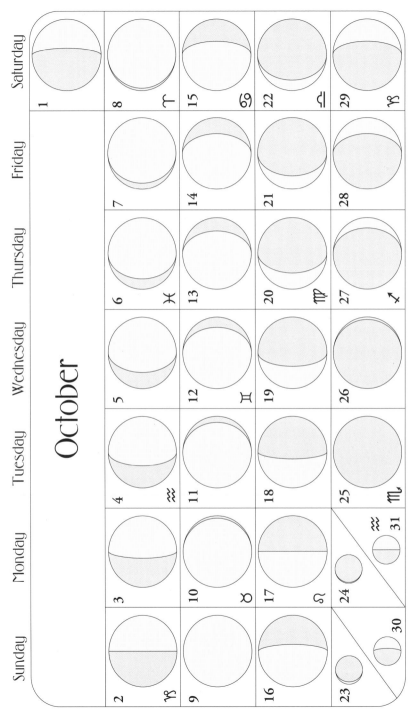

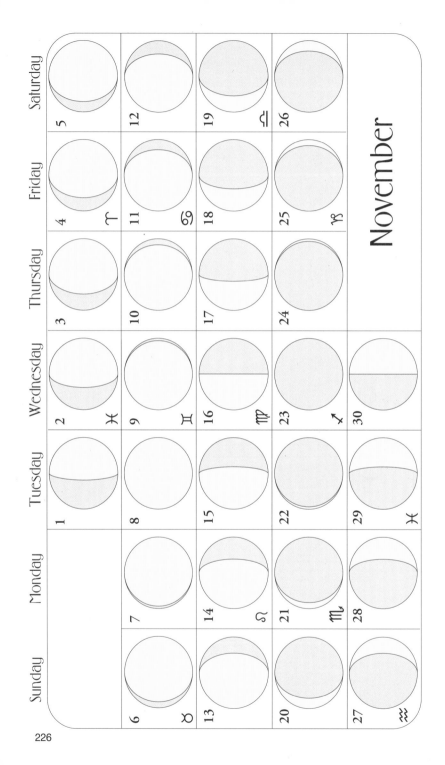

226

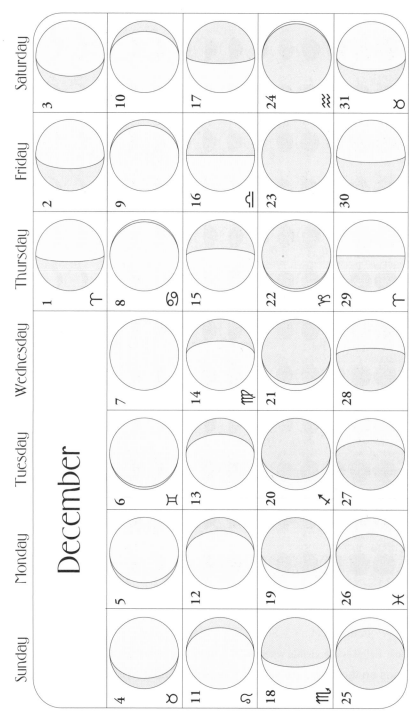

Eclipse Key: ☾ = Solar ☾ = Lunar T = Total P = Partial

Lunar Eclipses are visible wherever it is night and cloud free during full moon time.

Times on this page are in EST (Eastern Standard Time -5 from GMT)
or EDT, Eastern Daylight Time (Mar 13 - Nov 6, 2021)

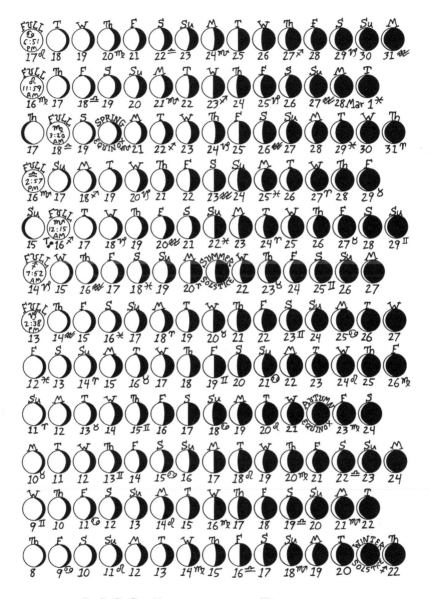

2022 Lunar Phases

This format available on cards from: **http://snakeandsnake.com**

Snake and Snake Productions 3037 Dixon Rd Durham, NC 27707

Conventional Holidays 2022

January 1	New Years Day*
January 17	Martin Luther King Jr. Day
February 1	Chinese/Lunar New Year
February 14	Valentine's Day*
February 21	President's Day
March 2	Ash Wednesday
March 8	International Women's Day*
March 12	Mexika (Aztec) New Year
March 13	Daylight Saving Time Begins
March 17	St. Patrick's Day*
April 3–May 1	Ramadan
April 10	Palm Sunday
April 16–April 22	Passover
April 15	Good Friday
April 17	Easter
April 22	Earth Day*
May 5	Cinco de Mayo*
May 8	Mother's Day
May 30	Memorial Day
June 19	Juneteenth
June 19	Father's Day
July 4	Independence Day*
September 5	Labor Day
September 26–27	Rosh Hashanah
October 5	Yom Kippur
October 10	Indigenous Peoples' Day
October 31	Halloween*
November 1	All Saints' Day*
November 2	Day of the Dead*
November 6	Daylight Saving Time Ends
November 11	Veteran's Day*
November 24	Thanksgiving Day
December 19–26	Chanukah/Hanukkah
December 25	Christmas Day*
December 26	Boxing Day*
Dec. 26–Jan. 1	Kwanzaa*
December 31	New Years Eve*
	* Same date every year

WORLD TIME ZONES

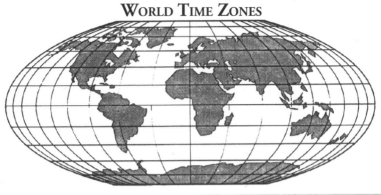

| ID | | NT | CA | YST | PST | MST | CST | EST | AST | BST | AT | WAT | GMT | CET | EET | BT | USSR | USSR | USSR | SST | CCT | JST | GST | USSR | ID |
LW		BT	HT														Z3	Z4	Z5					Z10	LE
-12		-11	-10	-9	-8	-7	-6	-5	-4	-3	-2	-1	0	+1	+2	+3	+4	+5	+6	+7	+8	+9	+10	+11	+12
-4		-3	-2	-1	0	+1	+2	+3	+4	+5	+6	+7	+8	+9	+10	+11	+12	+13	+14	+15	+16	+17	+18	+19	+20

STANDARD TIME ZONES FROM WEST TO EAST CALCULATED FROM PST AS ZERO POINT:

IDLW:	International Date Line West	-4	**BT:**	Bagdhad Time	+11
NT/BT:	Nome Time/Bering Time	-3	**IT:**	Iran Time	+11 1/2
CA/HT:	Central Alaska & Hawaiian Time	-2	**USSR**	Zone 3	+12
YST:	Yukon Standard Time	-1	**USSR**	Zone 4	+13
PST:	Pacific Standard Time	0	**IST:**	Indian Standard Time	+13 1/2
MST:	Mountain Standard Time	+1	**USSR**	Zone 5	+14
CST:	Central Standard Time	+2	**NST:**	North Sumatra Time	+14 1/2
EST:	Eastern Standard Time	+3	**SST:**	South Sumatra Time & USSR Zone 6	+15
AST:	Atlantic Standard Time	+4	**JT:**	Java Time	+15 1/2
NFT:	Newfoundland Time	+4 1/2	**CCT:**	China Coast Time	+16
BST:	Brazil Standard Time	+5	**MT:**	Moluccas Time	+16 1/2
AT:	Azores Time	+6	**JST:**	Japanese Standard Time	+17
WAT:	West African Time	+7	**SAST:**	South Australian Standard Time	+17 1/2
GMT:	Greenwich Mean Time	+8	**GST:**	Guam Standard Time	+18
WET:	Western European Time (England)	+8	**USSR**	Zone 10	+19
CET:	Central European Time	+9	**IDLE:**	International Date Line East	+20
EET:	Eastern European Time	+10			

HOW TO CALCULATE TIME ZONE CORRECTIONS IN YOUR AREA:

ADD if you are **east** of PST (Pacific Standard Time); **SUBTRACT** if you are **west** of PST on this map (see right-hand column of chart above).

All times in this calendar are calculated from the West Coast of North America where We'Moon is made. Pacific Standard Time (PST Zone 8) is zero point for this calendar, except during Daylight Saving Time (March 13–November 6, 2022, during which times are given for PDT Zone 7). If your time zone does not use Daylight Saving Time, add one hour to the standard correction during this time. At the bottom of each page, EST/EDT (Eastern Standard or Daylight Time) and GMT (Greenwich Mean Time) times are also given. For all other time zones, calculate your time zone correction(s) from this map and write it on the inside cover for easy reference.

2023

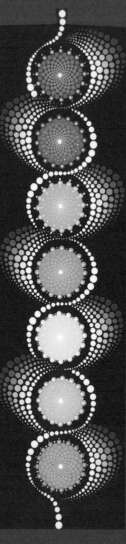

JANUARY

S	M	T	W	T	F	S
1	2	3	4	5	⑥	7
8	9	10	11	12	13	14
15	16	17	18	19	20	㉑
22	23	24	25	26	27	28
29	30	31				

FEBRUARY

S	M	T	W	T	F	S
			1	2	3	4
⑤	6	7	8	9	10	11
12	13	14	15	16	17	18
⑲	20	21	22	23	24	25
26	27	28				

MARCH

S	M	T	W	T	F	S
			1	2	3	4
5	6	⑦	8	9	10	11
12	13	14	15	16	17	18
19	20	㉑	22	23	24	25
26	27	28	29	30	31	

APRIL

S	M	T	W	T	F	S
						1
2	3	4	⑤	6	7	8
9	10	11	12	13	14	15
16	17	18	⑲	20	21	22
23	24	25	26	27	28	29
30						

MAY

S	M	T	W	T	F	S
	1	2	3	4	⑤	6
7	8	9	10	11	12	13
14	15	16	17	18	⑲	20
21	22	23	24	25	26	27
28	29	30	31			

JUNE

S	M	T	W	T	F	S
				1	2	③
4	5	6	7	8	9	10
11	12	13	14	15	16	⑰
18	19	20	21	22	23	24
25	26	27	28	29	30	

JULY

S	M	T	W	T	F	S
						1
2	③	4	5	6	7	8
9	10	11	12	13	14	15
16	⑰	18	19	20	21	22
23	24	25	26	27	28	29
30	31					

AUGUST

S	M	T	W	T	F	S
		①	2	3	4	5
6	7	8	9	10	11	12
13	14	15	⑯	17	18	19
20	21	22	23	24	25	26
27	28	29	㉚	31		

SEPTEMBER

S	M	T	W	T	F	S
					1	2
3	4	5	6	7	8	9
10	11	12	13	⑭	15	16
17	18	19	20	21	22	23
24	25	26	27	28	㉙	30

OCTOBER

S	M	T	W	T	F	S
1	2	3	4	5	6	7
8	9	10	11	12	13	⑭
15	16	17	18	19	20	21
22	23	24	25	26	27	㉘
29	30	31				

NOVEMBER

S	M	T	W	T	F	S
			1	2	3	4
5	6	7	8	9	10	11
12	⑬	14	15	16	17	18
19	20	21	22	23	24	25
26	㉗	28	29	30		

DECEMBER

S	M	T	W	T	F	S
					1	2
3	4	5	6	7	8	9
10	11	⑫	13	14	15	16
17	18	19	20	21	22	23
24	25	㉖	27	28	29	30
31						

Chakra Flow
© Mandalamy Arts 2020

◯ = NEW MOON, PST/PDT

⬤ = FULL MOON, PST/PDT

We'Moon 2022: The Magical Dark

• **Datebook** The best-selling astrological moon calendar, earth-spirited handbook in natural rhythms, and visionary collection of women's creative work. Week-at-a-glance format. Choice of 3 bindings: Spiral, Sturdy Paperback Binding or Unbound. We proudly offer a full translation of the classic datebook, in Spanish, too! 8x5¼, 240 pages, $21.95

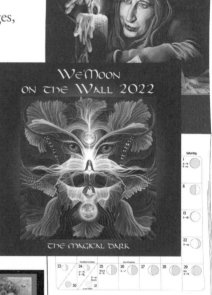

• **Cover Poster** featuring art by Marnie Recker: "*Venus Rising*," celebrating the beauty and the power that dwells within the magical dark. 11x17, $10

• **We'Moon on the Wall**
A beautiful full color wall calendar featuring inspired art and writing from *We'Moon 2022,* with key astrological information, interpretive articles, lunar phases and signs. 12x12, $16.95

• **We'Moon Totes** made with organic cotton, proudly displaying the cover of We'Moon. Perfect for stowing all of your goodies in style. Sm: 13x14x3", $13 & Lg: 18x13x6", $15

• **Greeting Cards** An assortment of six gorgeous note cards featuring art from *We'Moon 2022*, with writings from each artist on the back. Wonderful to send for any occasion: Holy Day, Birthday, Anniversary, Sympathy, or just to say hello. Each pack is wrapped in biodegradable cellophane. Blank inside. 5x7, $11.95

Check out page 233 for details on these offerings:

• *The Last Wild Witch* by Starhawk, illustrated by Lindy Kehoe.

• *In the Spirit of We'Moon ~ Celebrating 30 Years: An Anthology of We'Moon Art and Writing*

• *Preacher Woman for the Goddess: Poems, Invocations, Plays and Other Holy Writ* by We'Moon Special Editor Bethroot Gwynn.

• *We'Moon Tarot:* New release this Fall!

All products printed in full color on recycled paper with low VOC soy-based ink.

Become a We'Moon Contributor!

Send submissions for

We'Moon 2024
The 43rd Edition!

Call for Contributions: Available in the spring of 2022
Postmark-by Date for all art and writing: August 1, 2022
Note: It is too late to contribute to
We'Moon 2023

We'Moon is made up by writers and artists like you! We welcome creative work by women from around the world, and aim to amplify diverse perspectives. We especially encourage those of us who are women of color or who are marginalized by the mainstream, to participate in helping We'Moon reflect our unique visions and experiences. We are eager to publish more words and images depicting people of color created by WOC. By nurturing space for all women to share their gifts, we unleash insight and wisdom upon the world—a blessing to us all.

> ## We invite you to send in your art and writing for the next edition of We'Moon!

Here's how:

Step 1: Visit wemoon.ws to download a Call for Contributions or send your request for one with a SASE (legal size) to **We'Moon Submissions, PO Box 187, Wolf Creek, OR 97497.** (If you are not within the US, you do not need to include postage.) The Call contains current information about the theme, specifications about how to submit your art and writing, and terms of compensation. There are no jury fees. The Call comes out in the early Spring every year.

Step 2: Fill in the accompanying Contributor's License, giving all the requested information, and return it with your art/writing by the due date. *No work will be accepted without a signed license!* We now accept email submissions, too. See our website for details.

Step 3: Plan ahead! To assure your work is considered for *We'Moon 2024*, get your submissions postmarked by August 1, 2022.

Fierce Love
© Autumn Skye
2019

Throwing Shadows
© Helen Seay Art 2016

Fros and Frappes
© *Destiney Powell 2017*

Darkest Night:
Winter Solstice
© *Toni Truesdale 2006*

*Las Tres Princesas
de la Noche*
© Molly Brown 2020

**Nocturnal
Journey**
© *Jenny Hahn 2017*